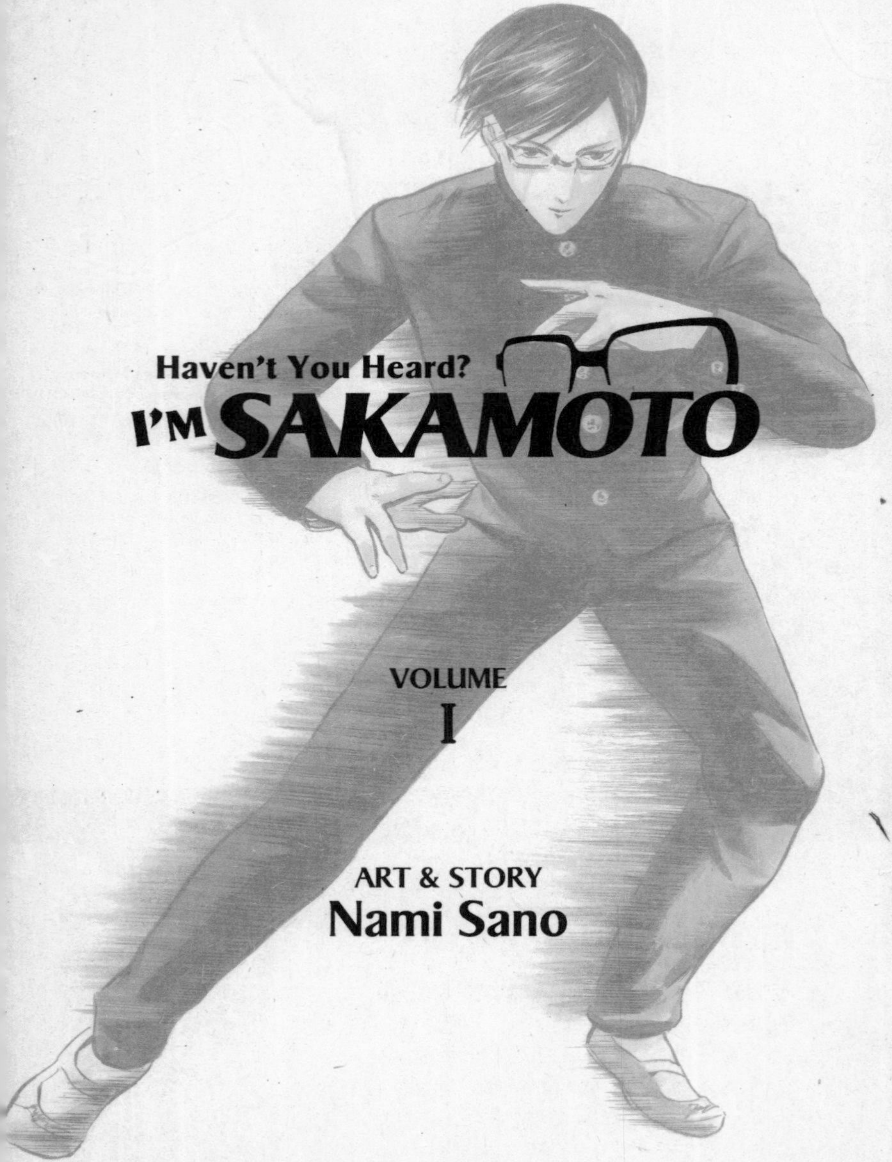

Haven't You Heard?

I'M SAKAMOTO

VOLUME

I

ART & STORY

Nami Sano

SEVEN SEAS ENTERTAINMENT PRESENTS

Haven't You Heard?
I'M SAKAMOTO

story and art by NAMI SANO   VOLUME 1

TRANSLATION
Adrienne Beck

ADAPTATION
Janet Gilbert

LETTERING AND LAYOUT
Lys Blakeslee

COVER DESIGN
Nicky Lim

PROOFREADER
Shanti Whitesides

ASSISTANT EDITOR
Lissa Pattillo

MANAGING EDITOR
Adam Arnold

PUBLISHER
Jason DeAngelis

Sakamoto Desuga? Vol.1
©2013 Nami Sano
All Rights reserved.
First published in Japan in 2013 by KADOKAWA CORPORATION ENTERBRAIN.
English translation rights arranged with KADOKAWA CORPORATION
ENTERBRAIN through TOHAN CORPORATION., Tokyo.

Seven Seas books may be purchased in bulk for educational, business, or
promotional use. For information on bulk purchases, please contact Macmillan
Corporate & Premium Sales Department at 1-800-221-7945 (ext 5442)
or write specialmarkets@macmillan.com.

Seven Seas and the Seven Seas logo are trademarks of
Seven Seas Entertainment, LLC.

ISBN: 978-1-626921-96-2

Printed in Canada

First Printing: August 2015

10 9 8 7 6 5 4 3 2 1

FOLLOW US ONLINE: *www.gomanga.com*

READING DIRECTIONS
The manga prelude and epilogue sections that
bookend this light novel read from right to left,
Japanese style. If this is your first time reading
manga, you start reading from the top right panel on
each page and take it from there. If you get lost, just
follow the numbered diagram here. Enjoy!!

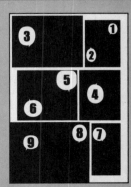

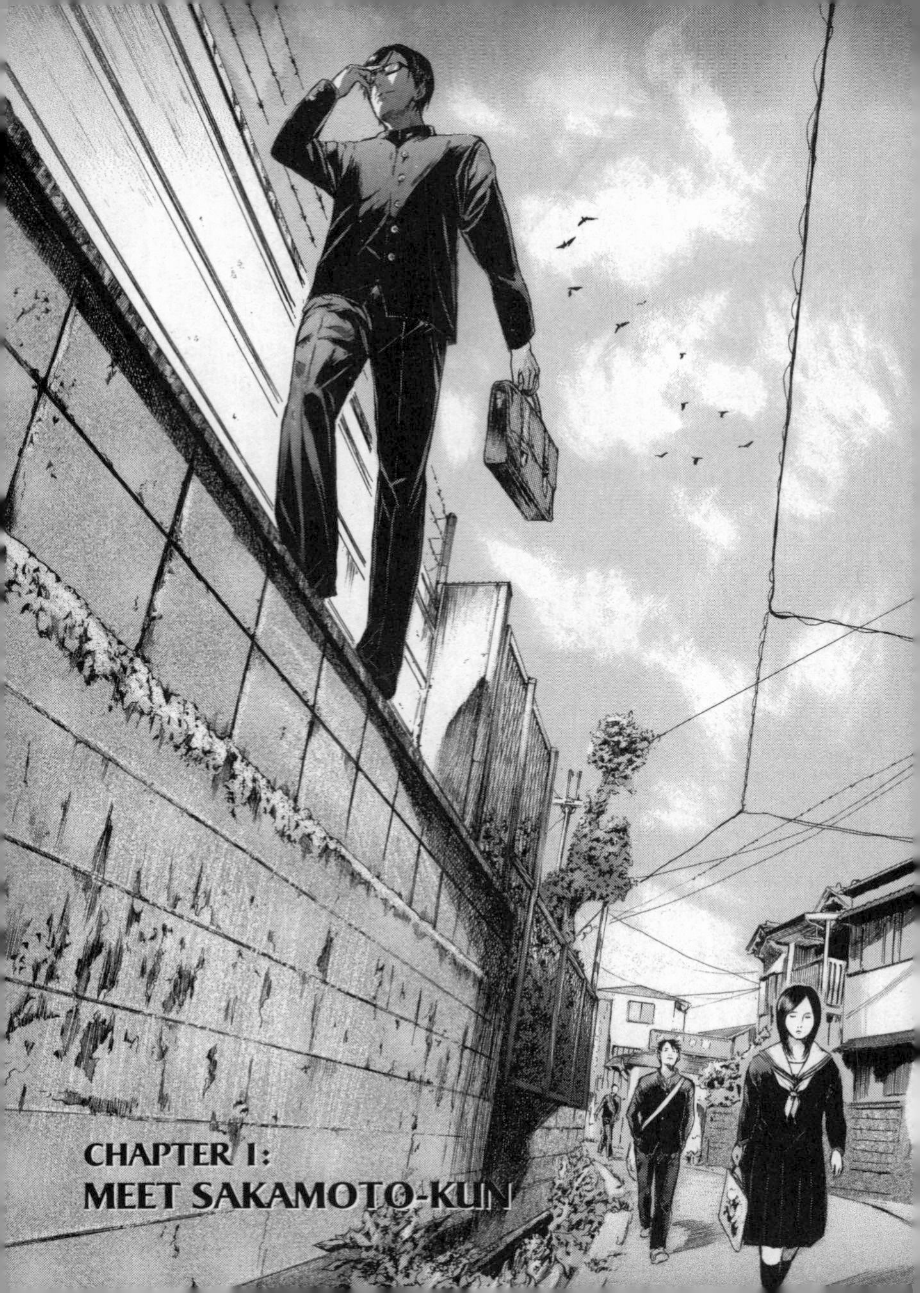
CHAPTER 1:
MEET SAKAMOTO-KUN

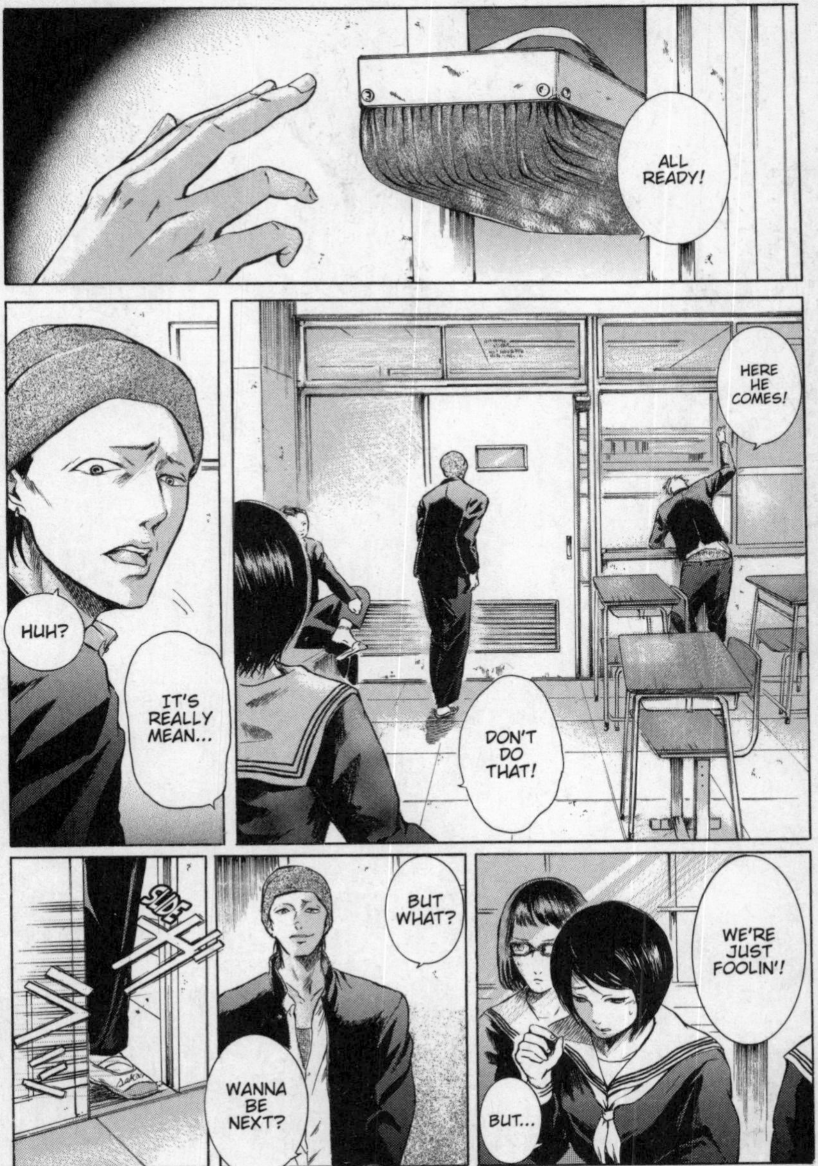
ALL READY!
HERE HE COMES!
DON'T DO THAT!
HUH?
IT'S REALLY MEAN...
WE'RE JUST FOOLIN'!
BUT...
BUT WHAT?
WANNA BE NEXT?
SLIDE

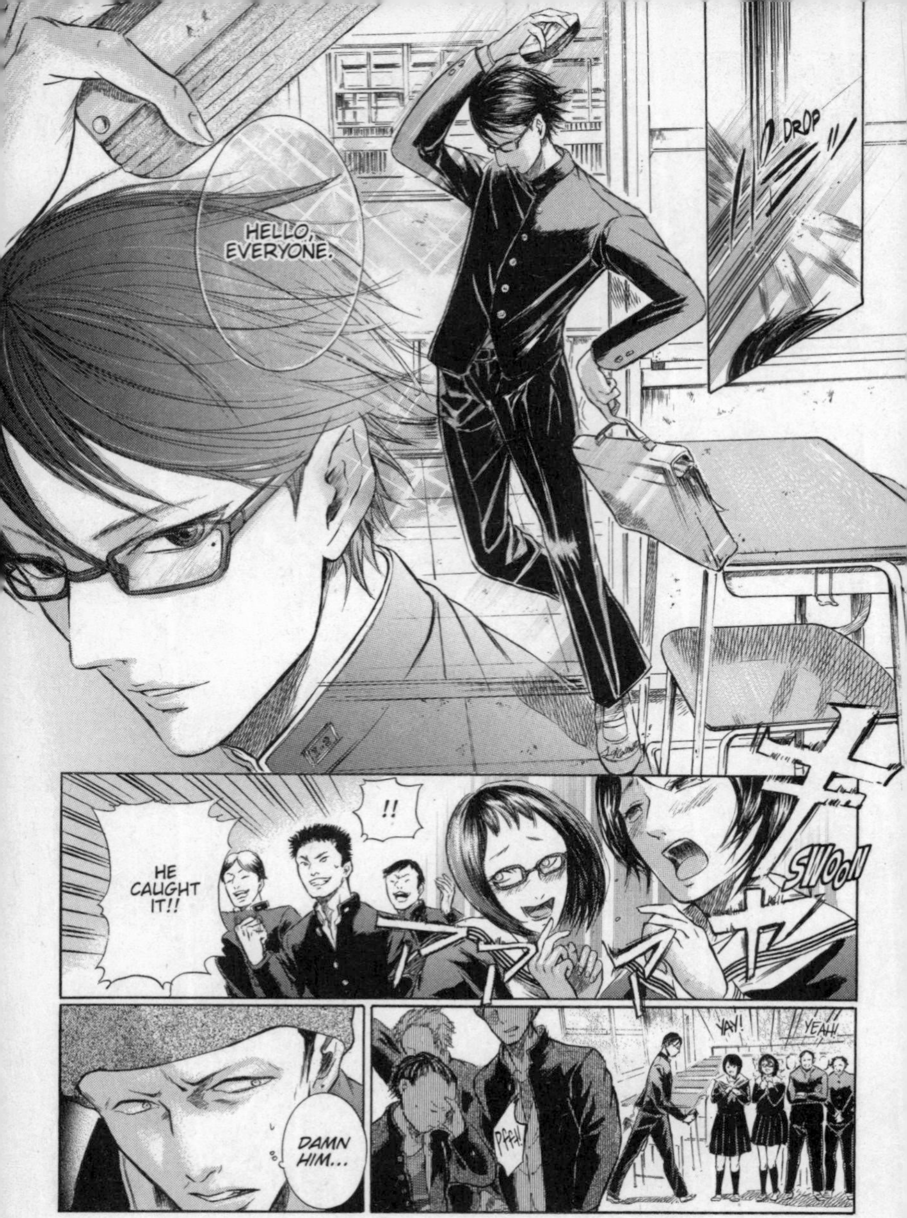
DROP
HELLO, EVERYONE.
SWOON
!!
HE CAUGHT IT!!
YEAH!
YAY!
PFFT!
DAMN HIM...

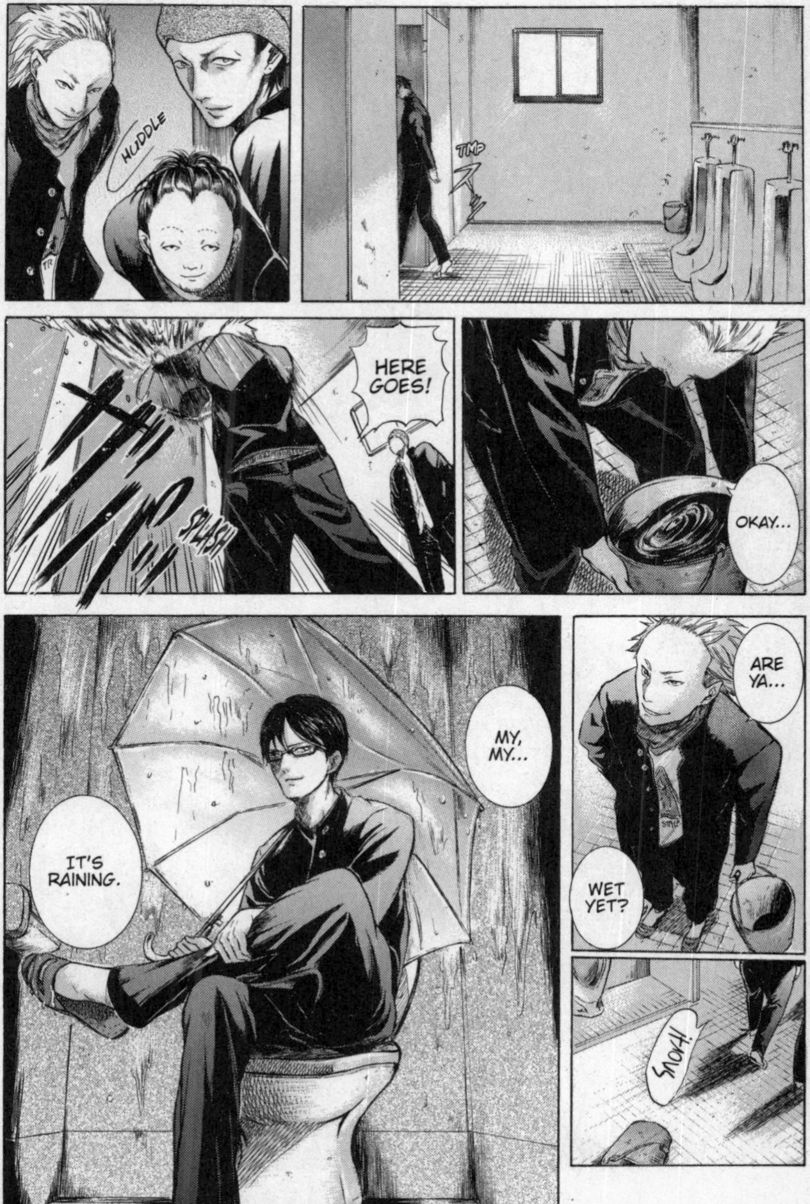
TMP
HUDDLE
OKAY...
HERE GOES!
SPLASH
ARE YA...
WET YET?
SHOVE!
MY, MY...
IT'S RAINING.

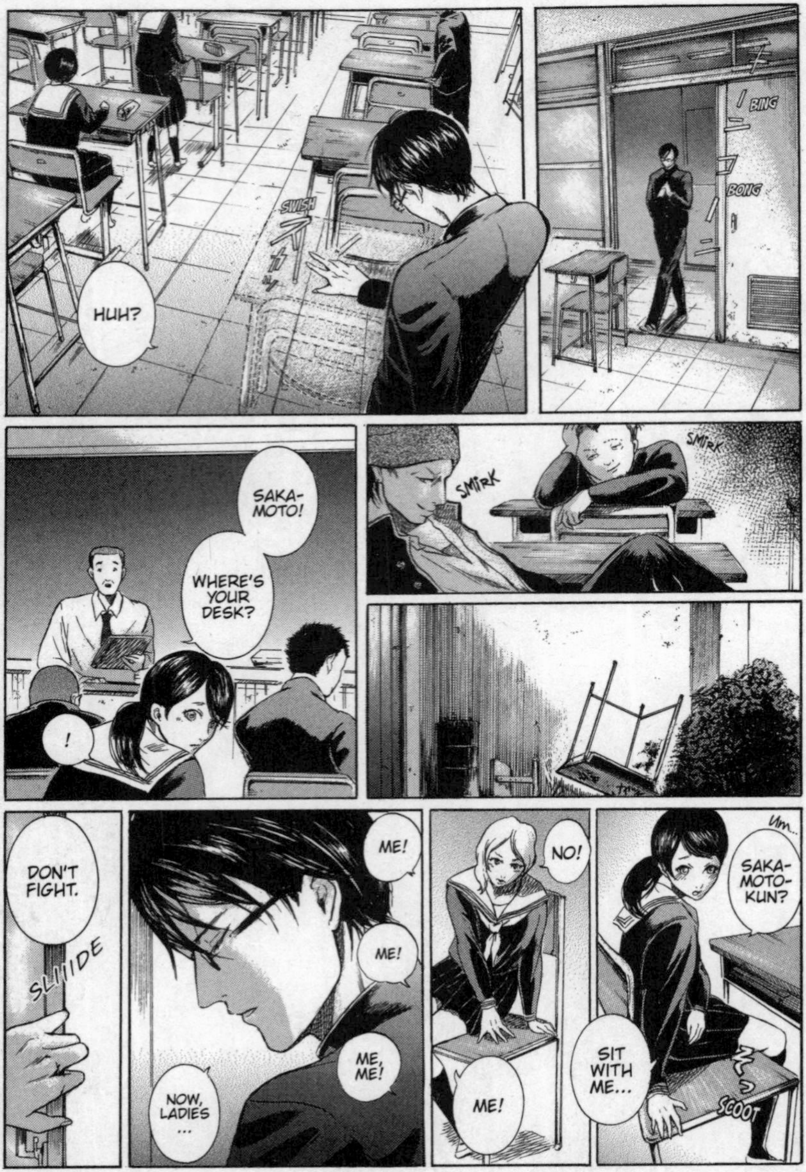
BING
BONG
SWISH
HUH?
SMIRK
SMIRK
SAKA-MOTO!
WHERE'S YOUR DESK?
!
Um...
SAKA-MOTO-KUN?
SIT WITH ME...
SCOOT
NO!
ME!
ME!
ME!
ME, ME!
NOW, LADIES ...
DON'T FIGHT.
SLIIIDE

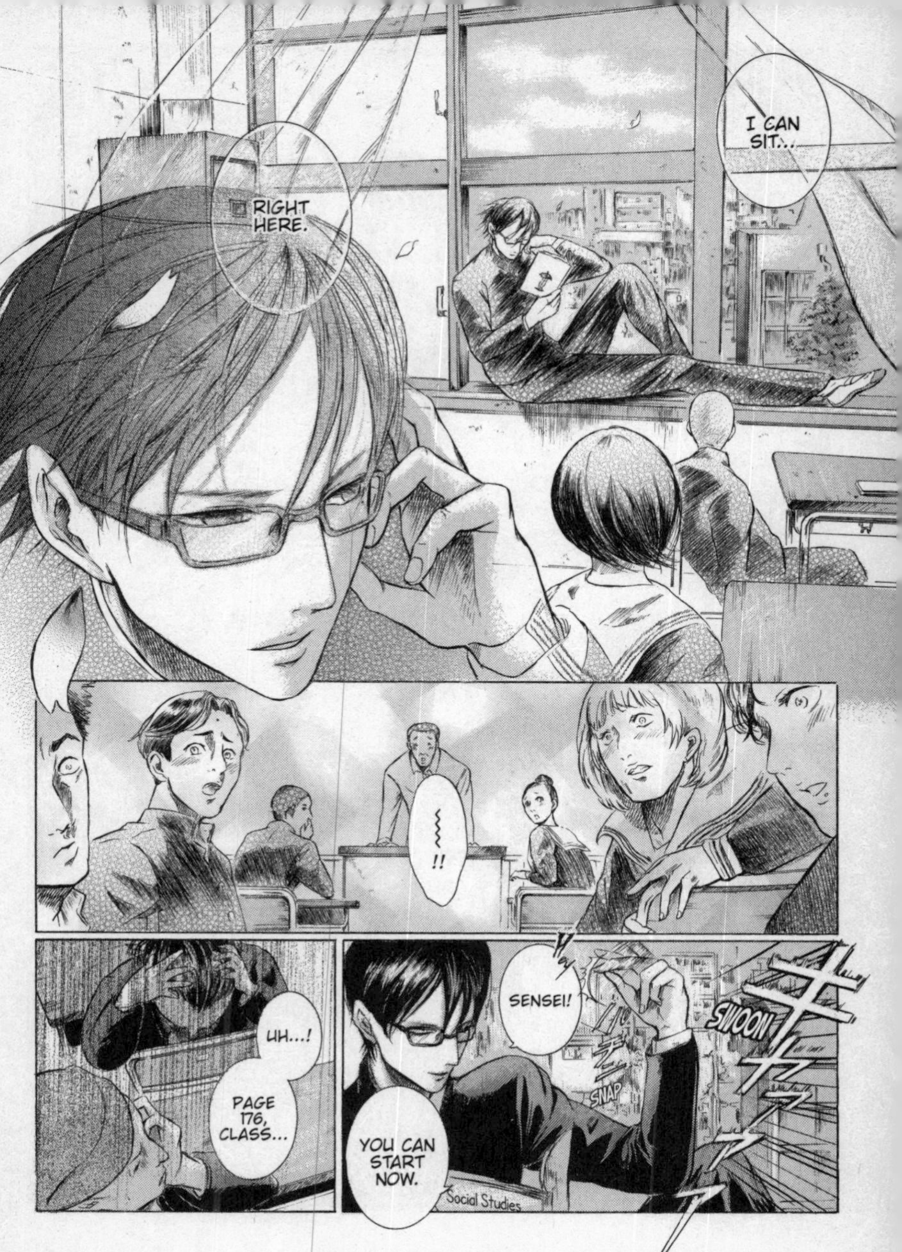
I CAN SIT...
RIGHT HERE.
!!
SWOON
SENSEI!
SNAP
YOU CAN START NOW.
Social Studies
UH...!
PAGE 176, CLASS...

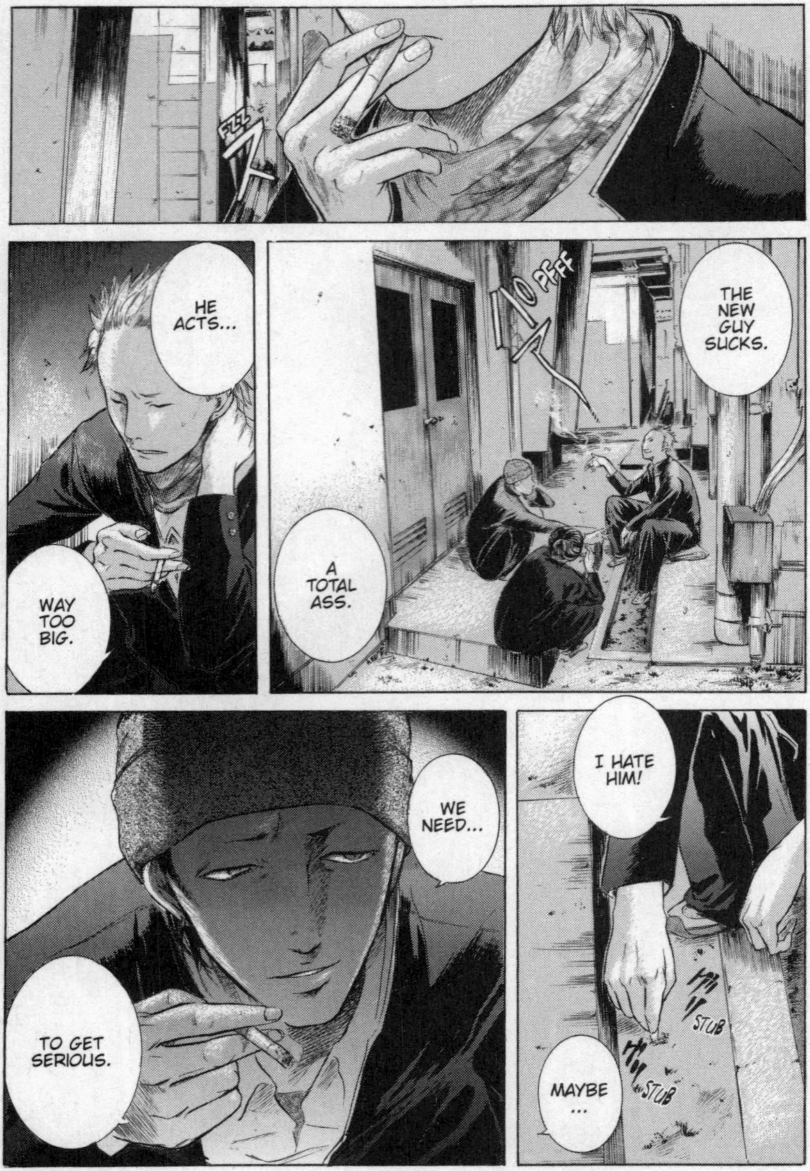
FZZ
THE NEW GUY SUCKS.
PFFF
A TOTAL ASS.
HE ACTS...
WAY TOO BIG.
I HATE HIM!
STUB
STUB
MAYBE ...
WE NEED...
TO GET SERIOUS.

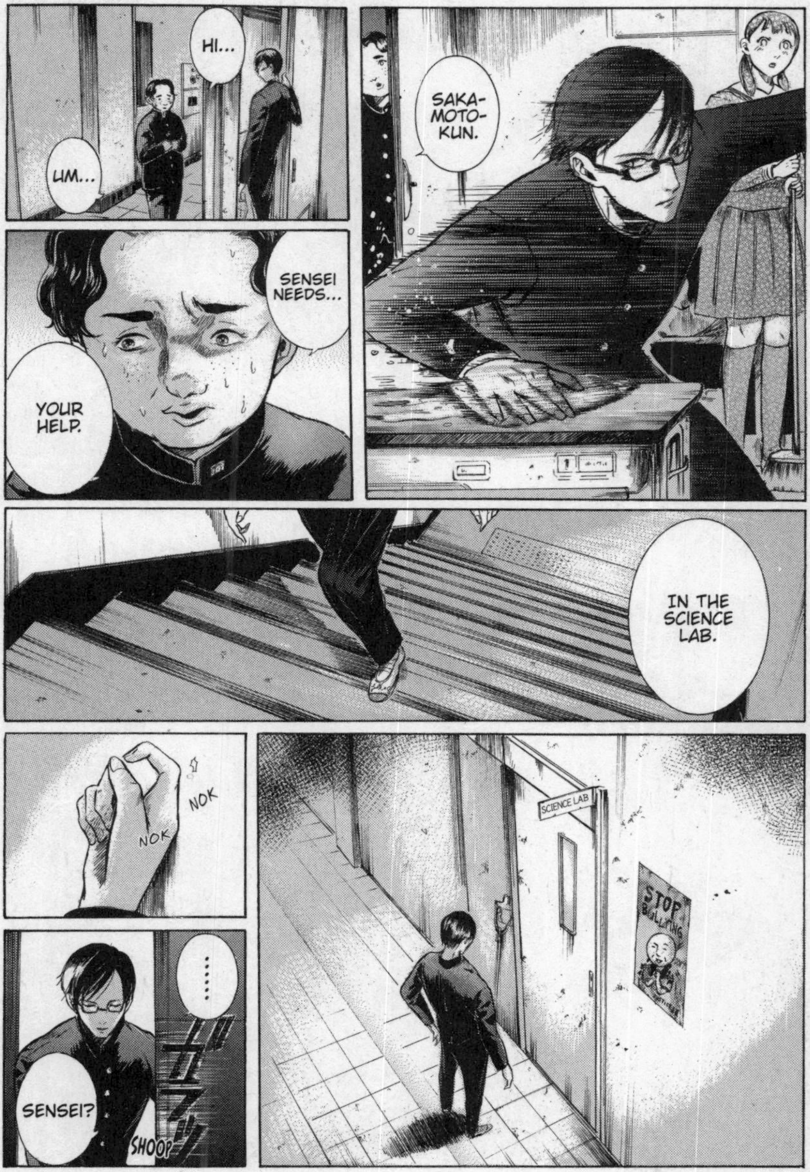
SAKA-MOTO-KUN.
HI...
UM...
SENSEI NEEDS...
YOUR HELP.
IN THE SCIENCE LAB.
SCIENCE LAB
STOP BULLYING
NOK
NOK
......
SENSEI?
SHOOP

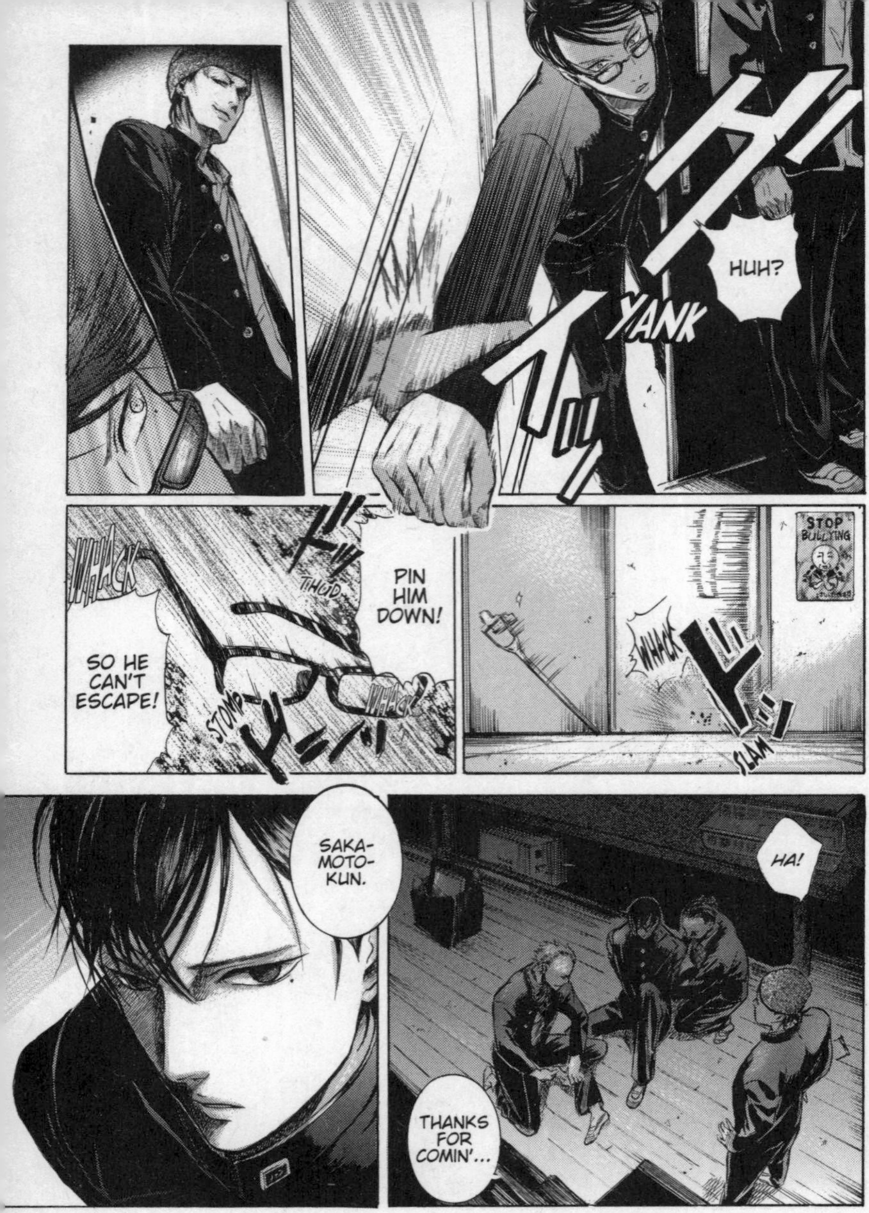
HUH?
YANK
STOP BULLYING
WHACK
SLAM
PIN HIM DOWN!
THUD
WHACK
SO HE CAN'T ESCAPE!
STOMP
WHACK
HA!
THANKS FOR COMIN'...
SAKA-MOTO-KUN.

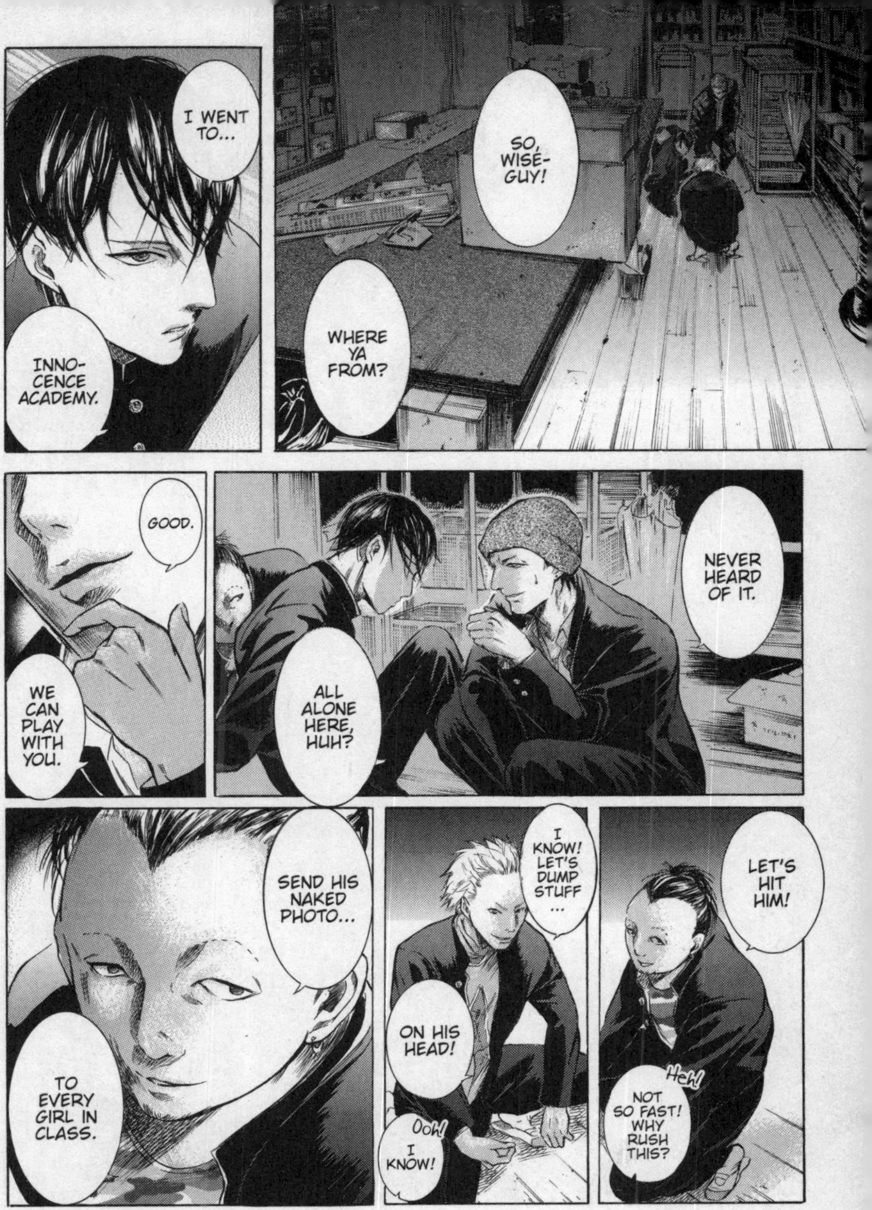
SO, WISE-GUY!
WHERE YA FROM?
I WENT TO...
INNO-CENCE ACADEMY.
NEVER HEARD OF IT.
ALL ALONE HERE, HUH?
GOOD.
WE CAN PLAY WITH YOU.
LET'S HIT HIM!
Heh!
NOT SO FAST! WHY RUSH THIS?
I KNOW! LET'S DUMP STUFF...
ON HIS HEAD!
Ooh!
I KNOW!
SEND HIS NAKED PHOTO...
TO EVERY GIRL IN CLASS.

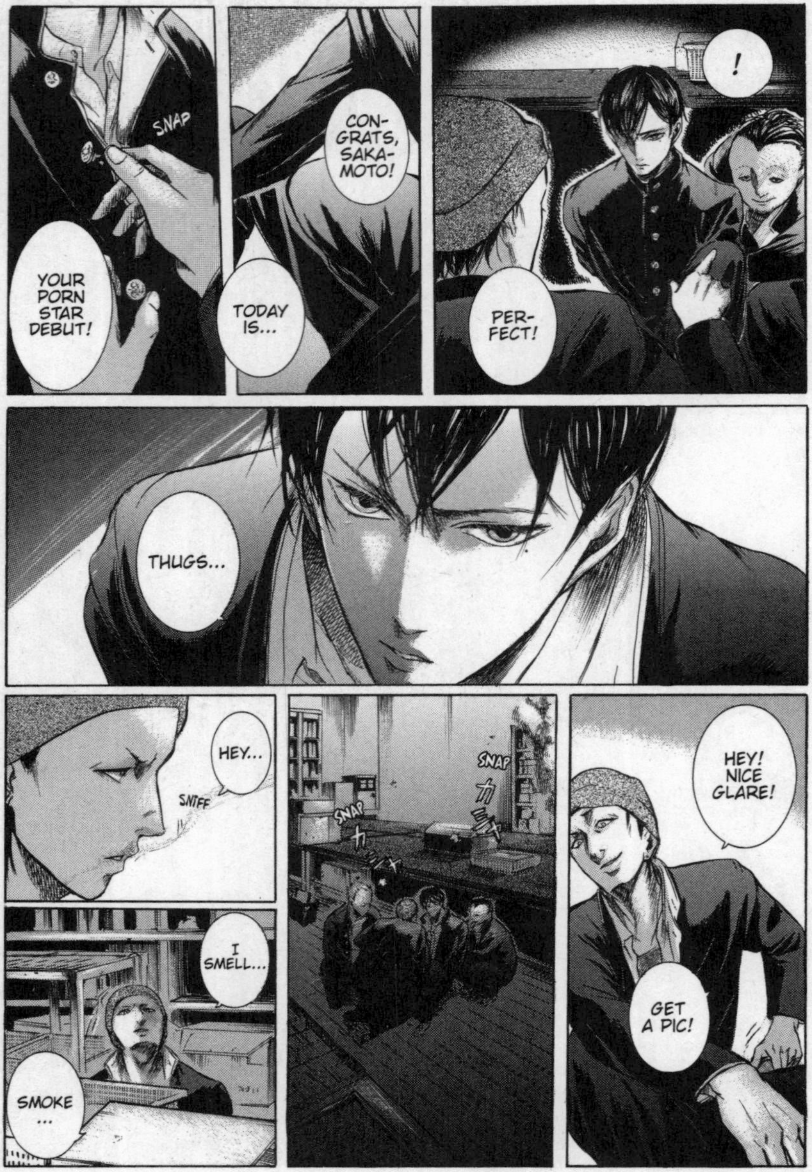
!
PER-FECT!
CON-GRATS, SAKA-MOTO!
TODAY IS...
SNAP
YOUR PORN STAR DEBUT!
THUGS...
HEY! NICE GLARE!
GET A PIC!
SNAP
SNAP
HEY...
SNIFF
I SMELL...
SMOKE ...

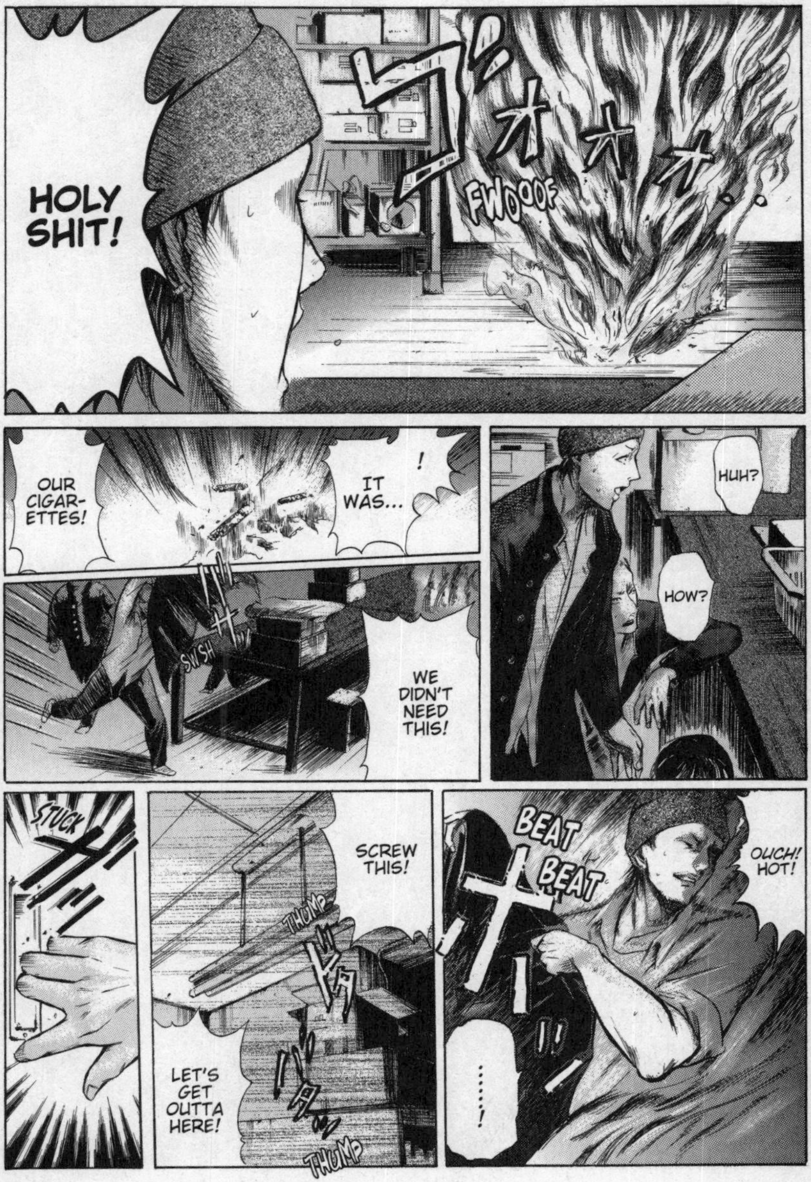
FWOOOF
HOLY SHIT!
HUH?
HOW?
!
IT WAS...
OUR CIGARETTES!
SWISH
WE DIDN'T NEED THIS!
BEAT
BEAT
OUCH! HOT!
......!
SCREW THIS!
THUMP
LET'S GET OUTTA HERE!
THUMP
STUCK

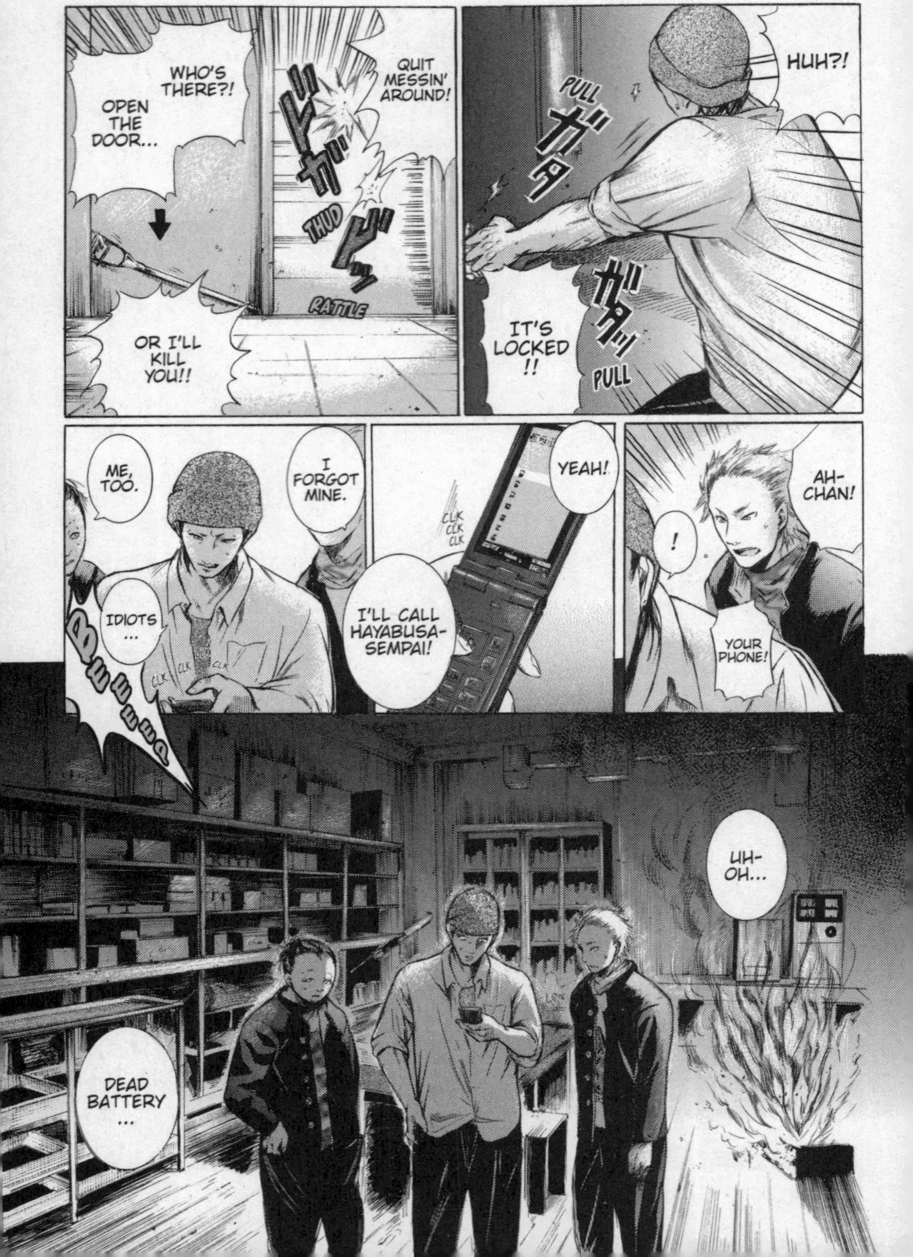
HUH?!
PULL
IT'S LOCKED!!
PULL
QUIT MESSIN' AROUND!
WHO'S THERE?!
OPEN THE DOOR...
THUD
RATTLE
OR I'LL KILL YOU!!
AH-CHAN!
!
YOUR PHONE!
YEAH!
CLK CLK CLK
I'LL CALL HAYABUSA-SEMPAI!
I FORGOT MINE.
ME, TOO.
IDIOTS...
CLK CLK CLK CLK
UH-OH...
DEAD BATTERY...

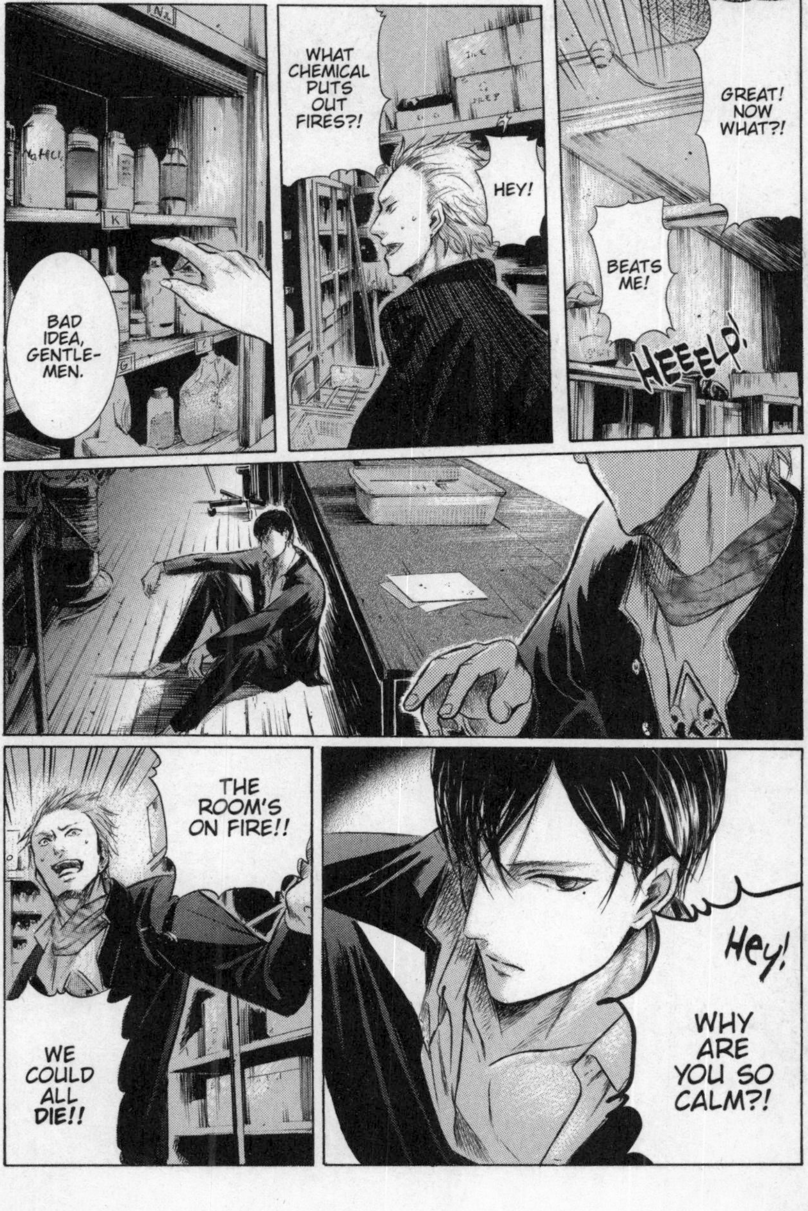
GREAT! NOW WHAT?!
BEATS ME!
HEEELP!
WHAT CHEMICAL PUTS OUT FIRES?!
HEY!
BAD IDEA, GENTLEMEN.
Hey!
WHY ARE YOU SO CALM?!
THE ROOM'S ON FIRE!!
WE COULD ALL DIE!!

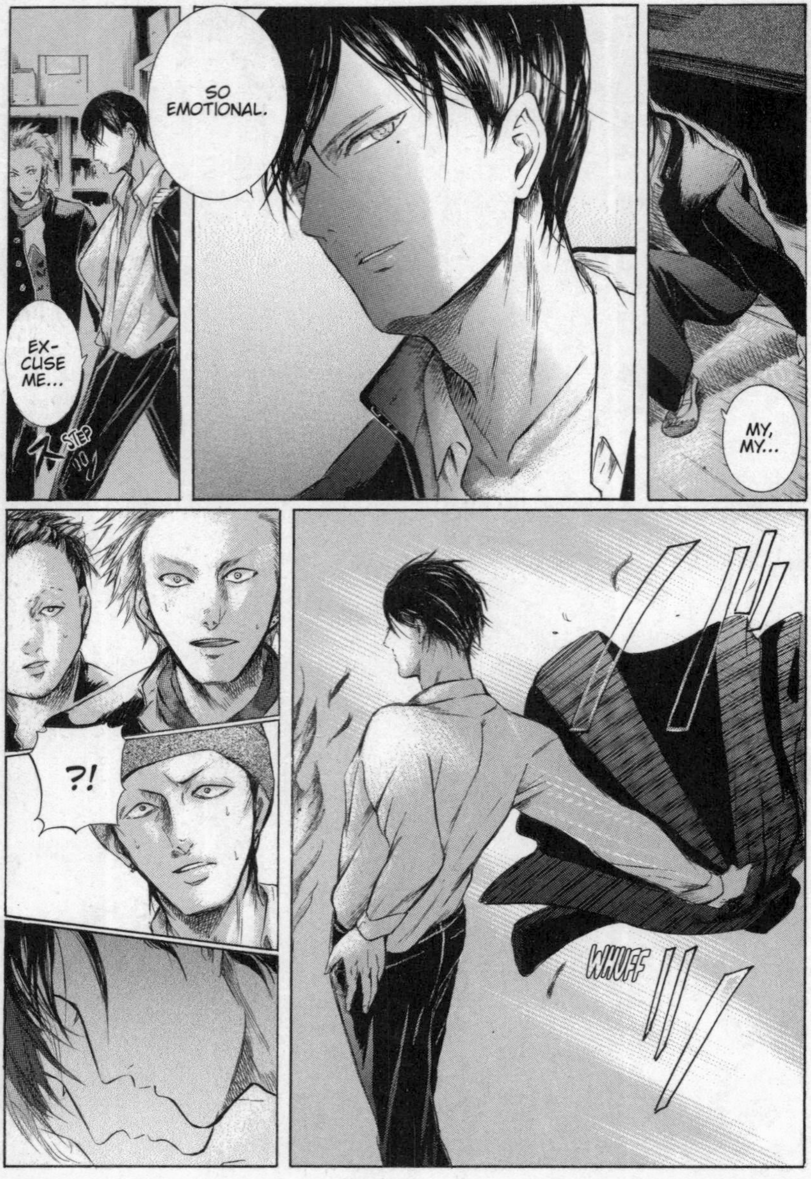
MY, MY...
SO EMOTIONAL.
EX-CUSE ME...
STEP
WHUFF
?!

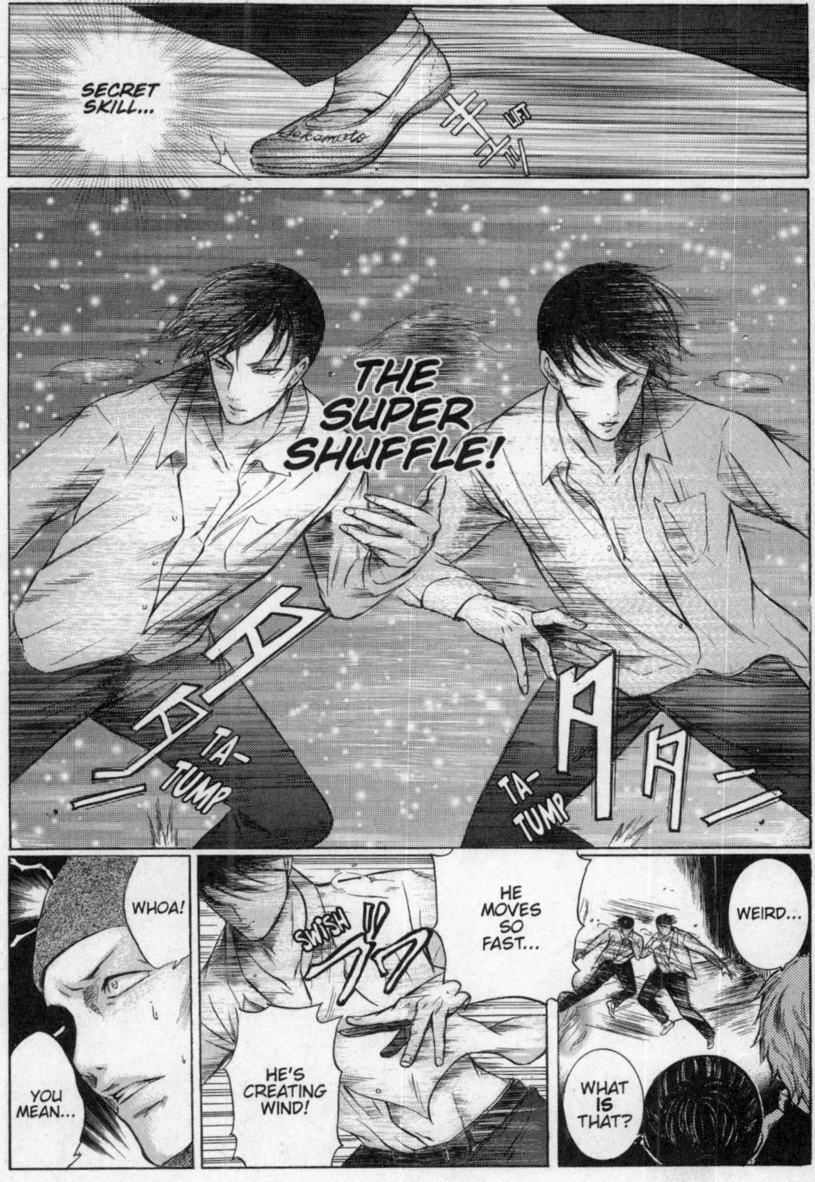
SECRET SKILL...
LIFT
THE SUPER SHUFFLE!
TA-TUMP
TA-TUMP
WEIRD...
WHAT IS THAT?
HE MOVES SO FAST...
SWISH
HE'S CREATING WIND!
WHOA!
YOU MEAN...

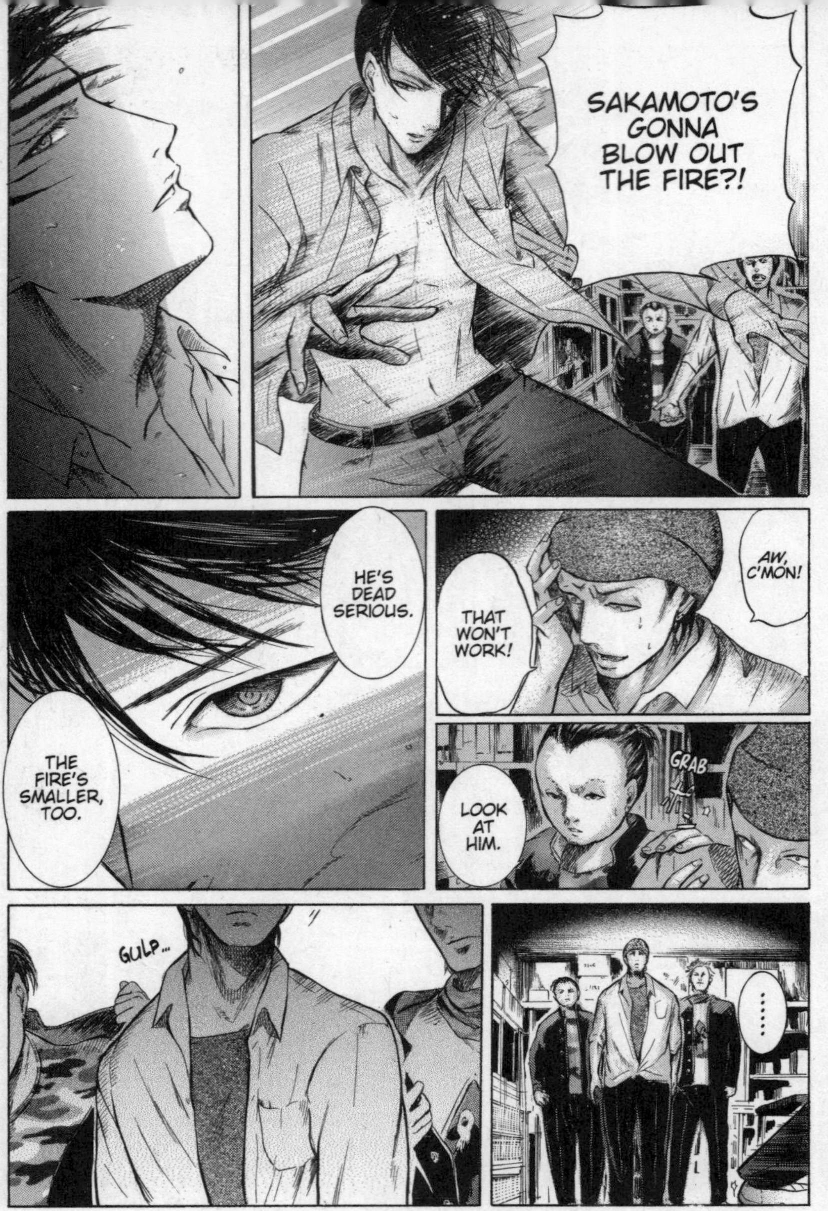
SAKAMOTO'S GONNA BLOW OUT THE FIRE?!
AW, C'MON!
THAT WON'T WORK!
GRAB
LOOK AT HIM.
HE'S DEAD SERIOUS.
THE FIRE'S SMALLER, TOO.
......
GULP...

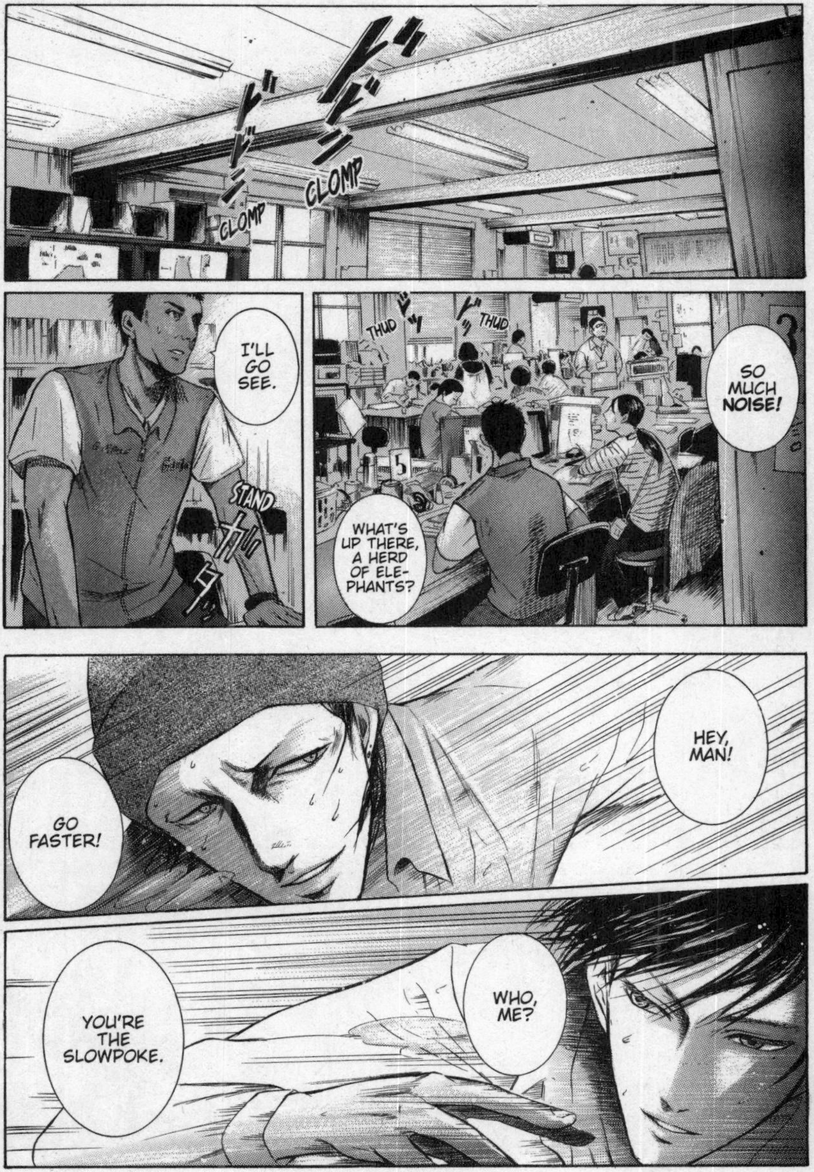
CLOMP
CLOMP
THUD
THUD
SO MUCH NOISE!
WHAT'S UP THERE, A HERD OF ELEPHANTS?
I'LL GO SEE.
STAND
HEY, MAN!
GO FASTER!
WHO, ME?
YOU'RE THE SLOWPOKE.

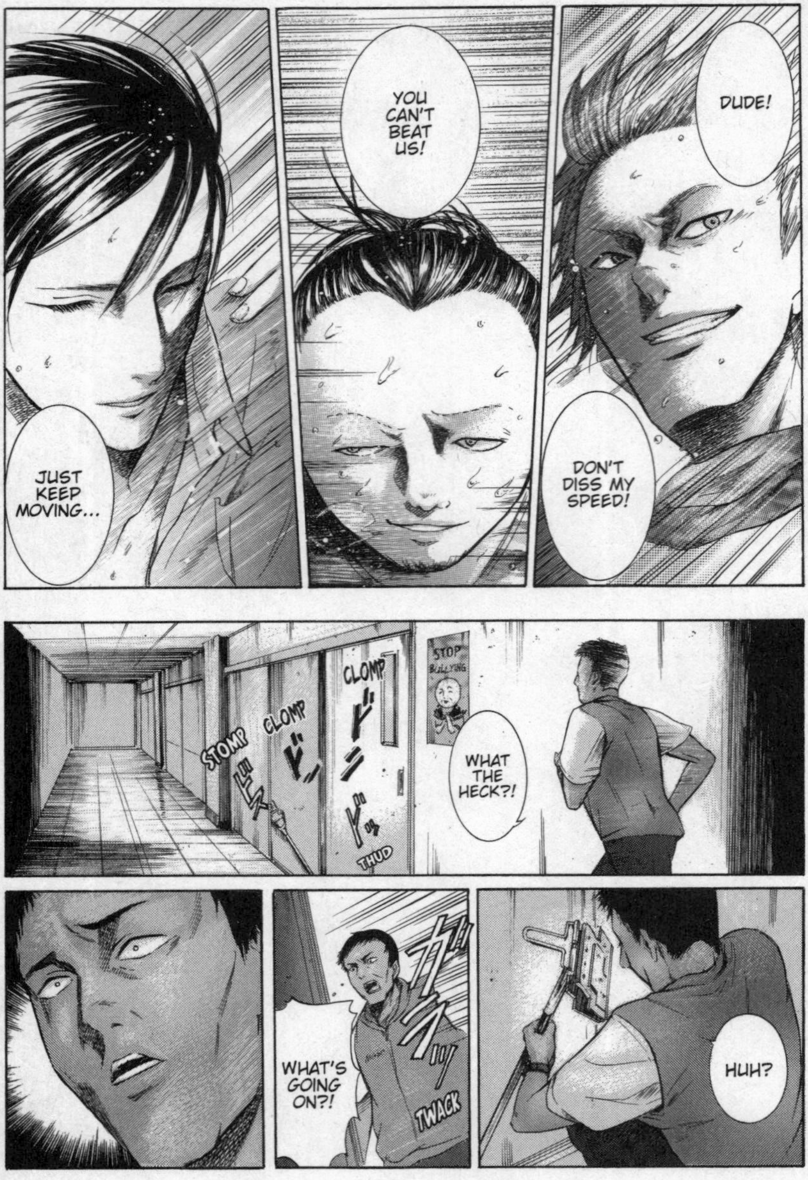
DUDE!
DON'T DISS MY SPEED!
YOU CAN'T BEAT US!
JUST KEEP MOVING...
WHAT THE HECK?!
STOP BULLYING
CLOMP
CLOMP
STOMP
THUD
HUH?
TWACK
WHAT'S GOING ON?!

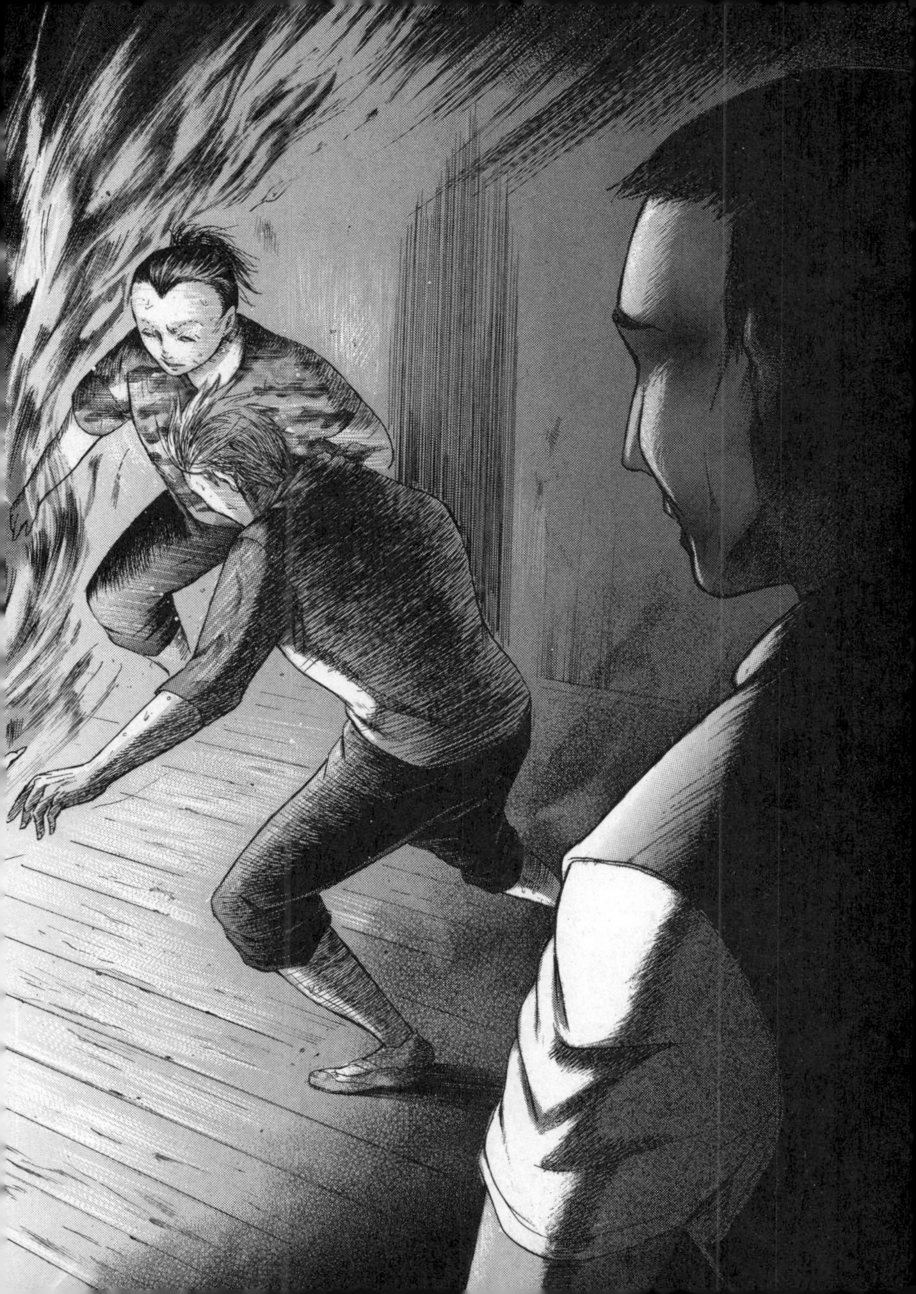

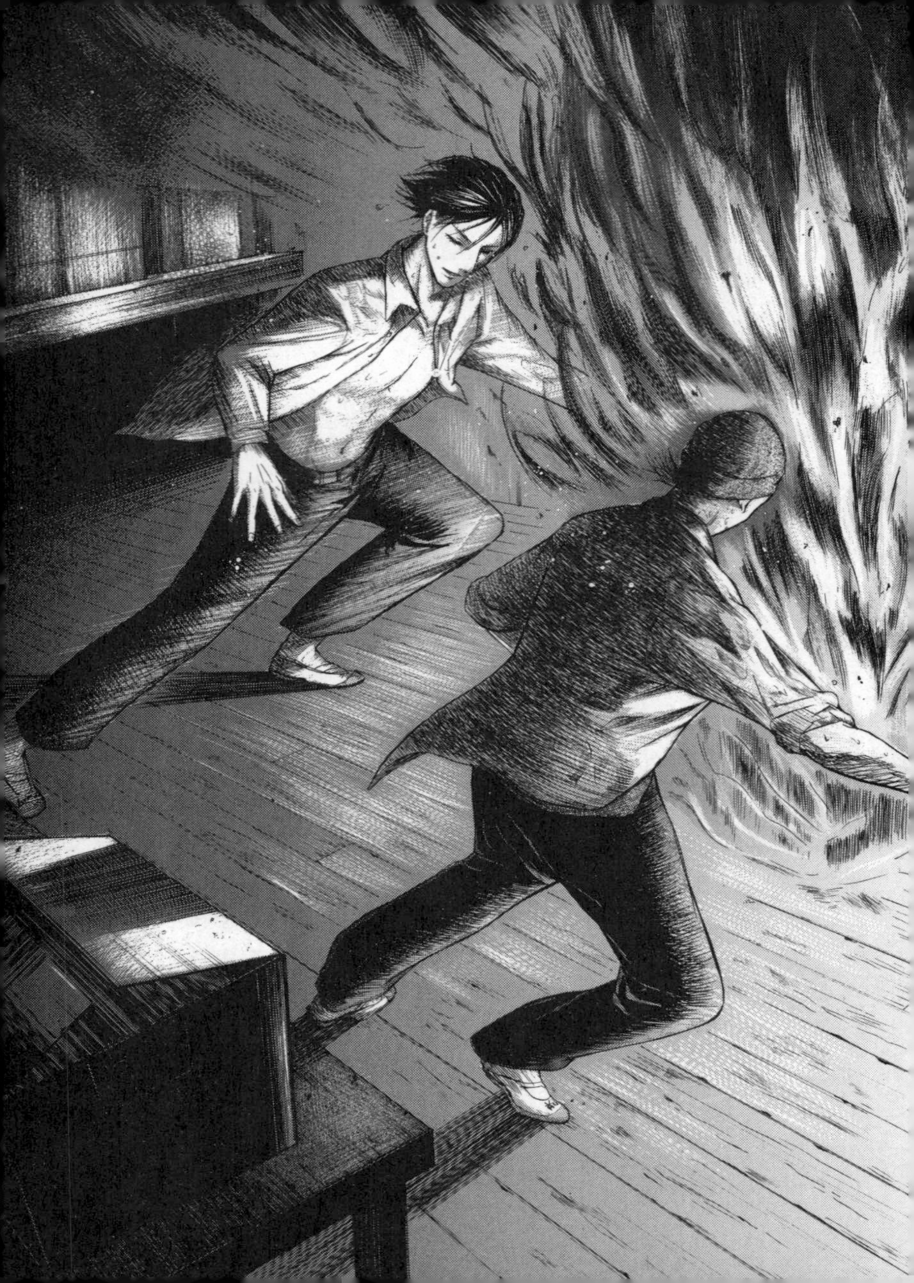

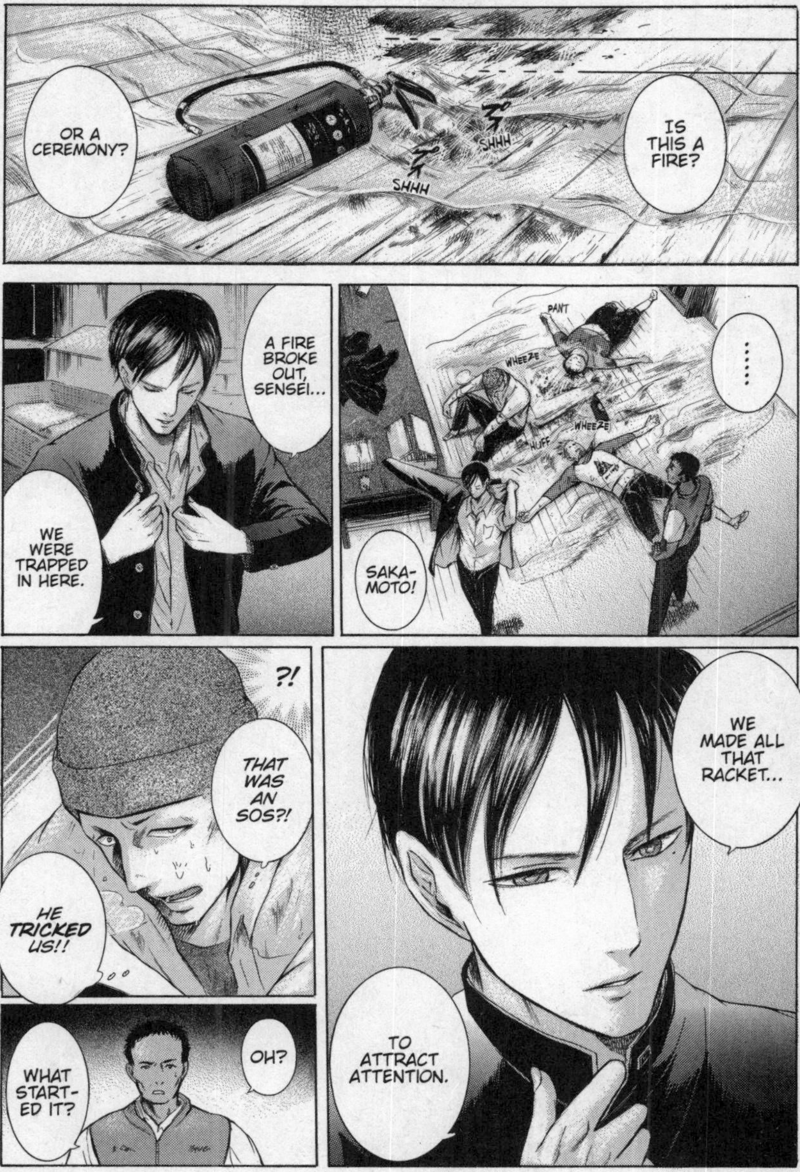
IS THIS A FIRE?
SHHH
SHHH
OR A CEREMONY?
......
PANT
WHEEZE
WHEEZE
HUFF
SAKA-MOTO!
A FIRE BROKE OUT, SENSEI...
WE WERE TRAPPED IN HERE.
WE MADE ALL THAT RACKET...
TO ATTRACT ATTENTION.
?!
THAT WAS AN SOS?!
HE TRICKED US!!
OH?
WHAT START-ED IT?

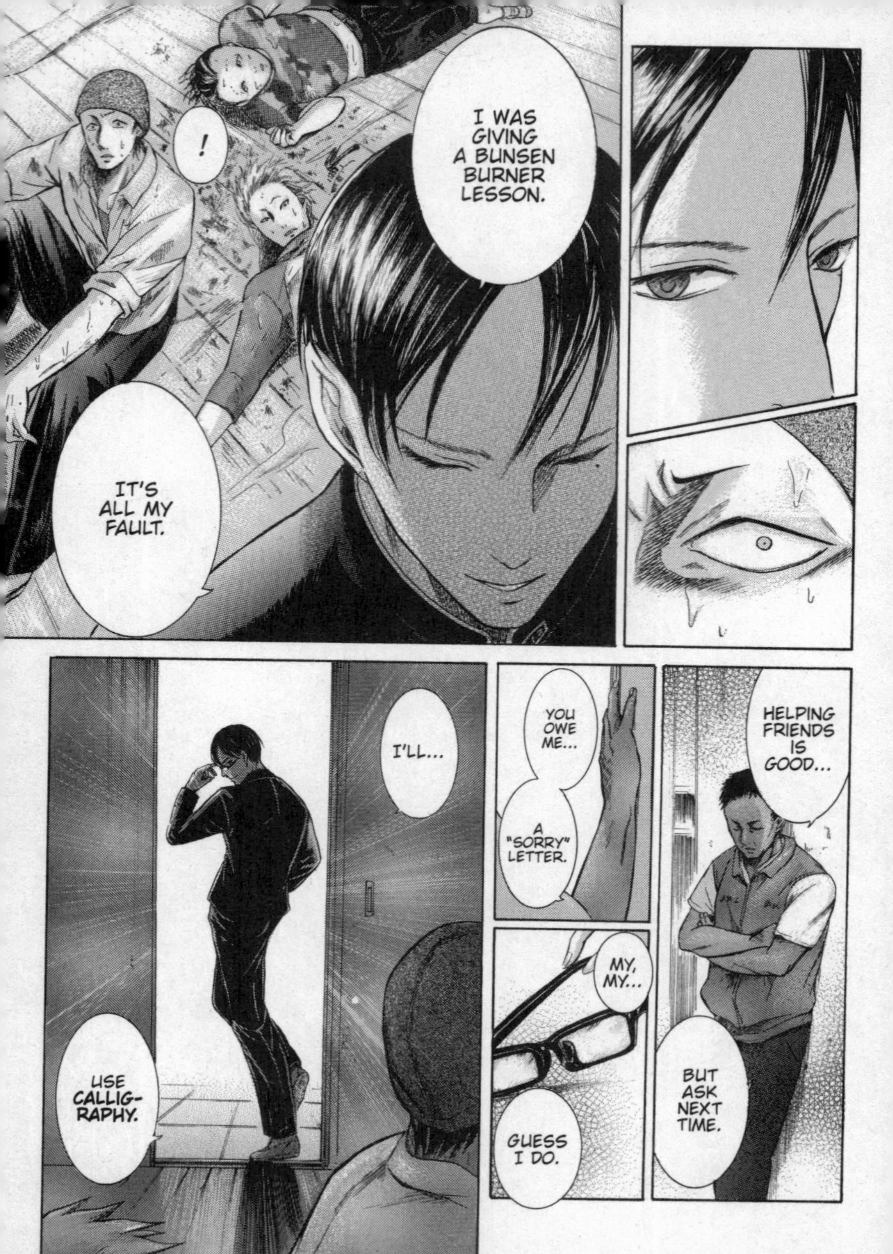
I WAS GIVING A BUNSEN BURNER LESSON.
!
IT'S ALL MY FAULT.
HELPING FRIENDS IS GOOD...
BUT ASK NEXT TIME.
YOU OWE ME...
A "SORRY" LETTER.
MY, MY...
GUESS I DO.
I'LL...
USE CALLIG-RAPHY.

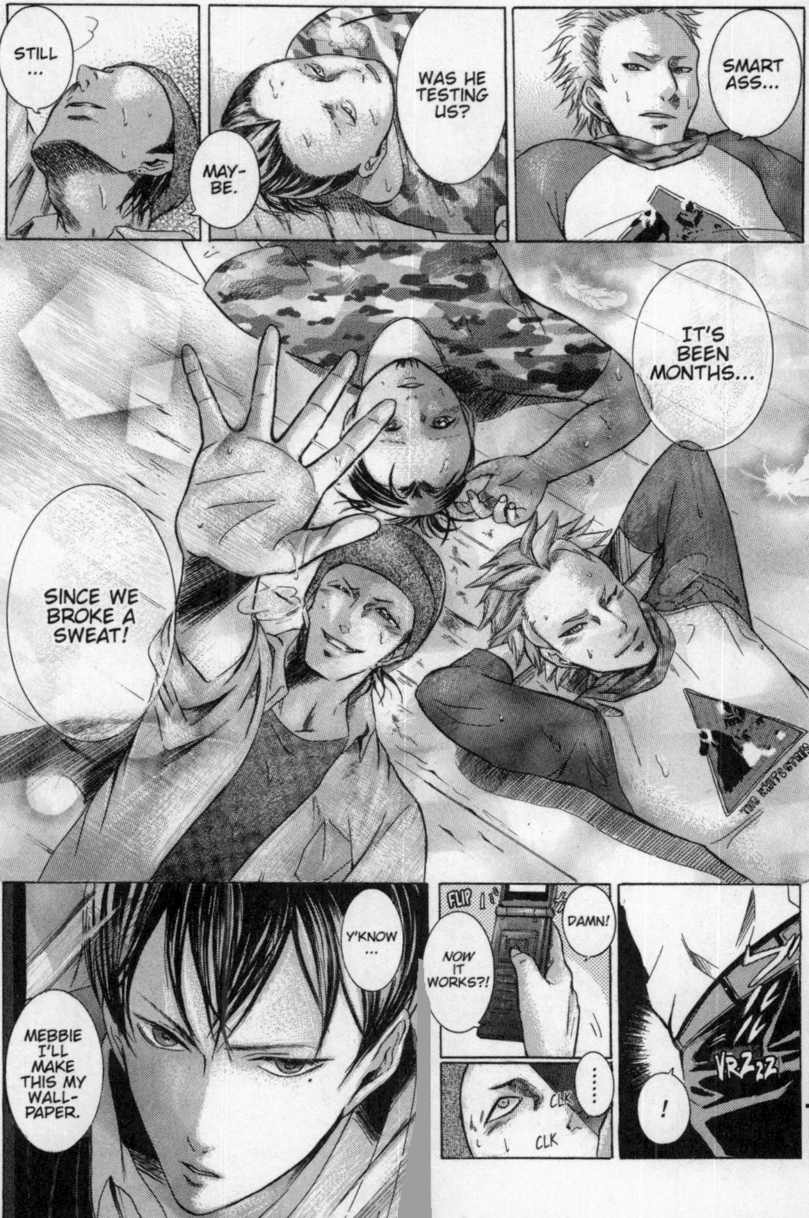
SMART ASS...
WAS HE TESTING US?
MAY-BE.
STILL ...
IT'S BEEN MONTHS...
SINCE WE BROKE A SWEAT!
VRZZZ
!
FLIP
DAMN!
NOW IT WORKS?!
......
CLK
CLK
Y'KNOW ...
MEBBIE I'LL MAKE THIS MY WALL-PAPER.

End of Chapter 1

P.E. Test #1:
50 Meter Dash

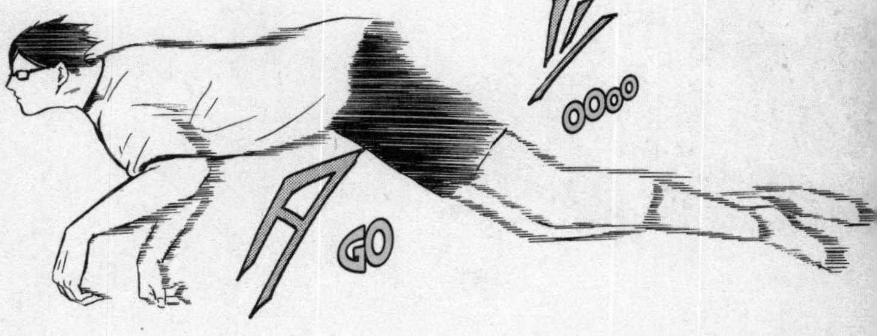
A GOoooo

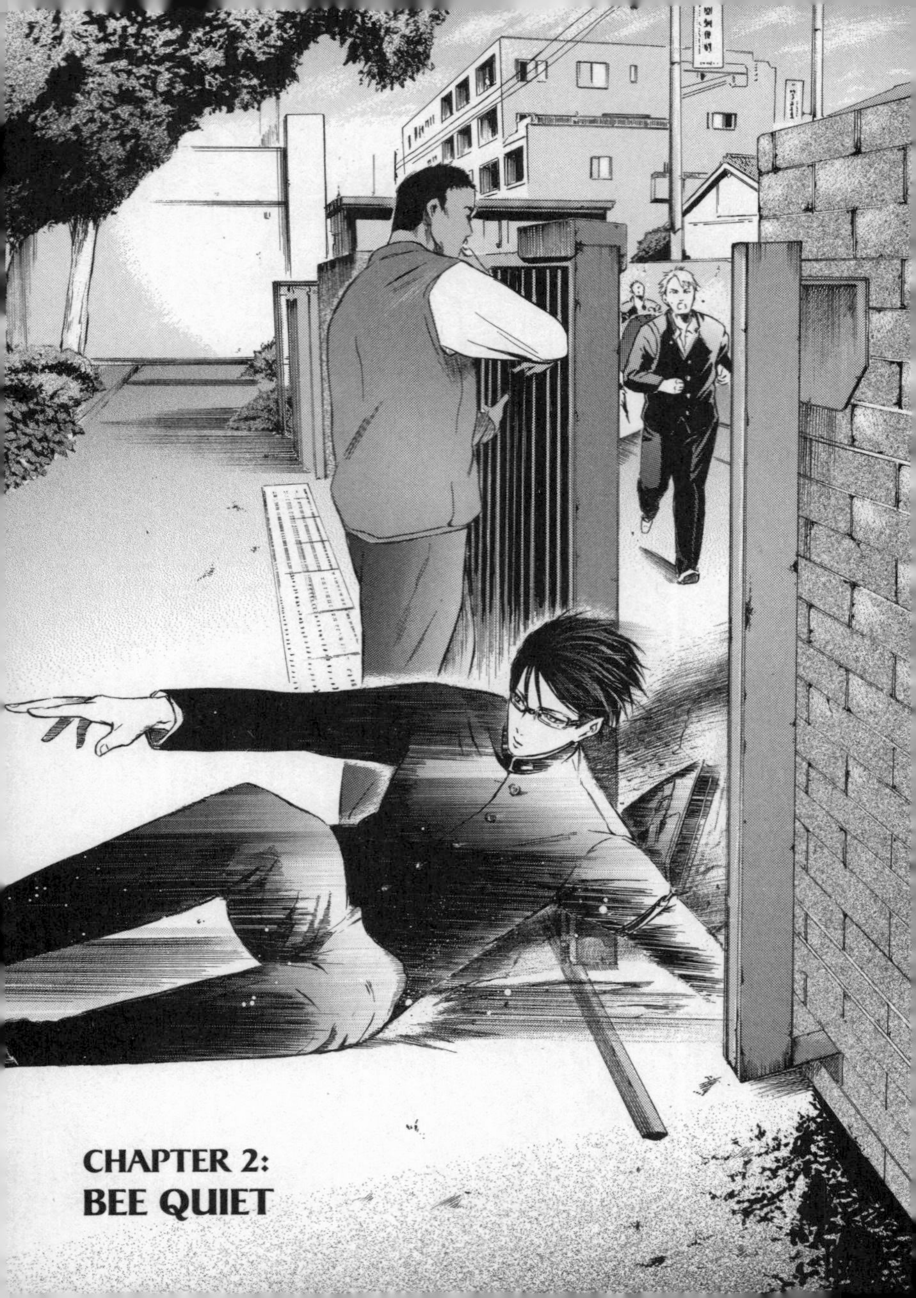

CHAPTER 2:
BEE QUIET

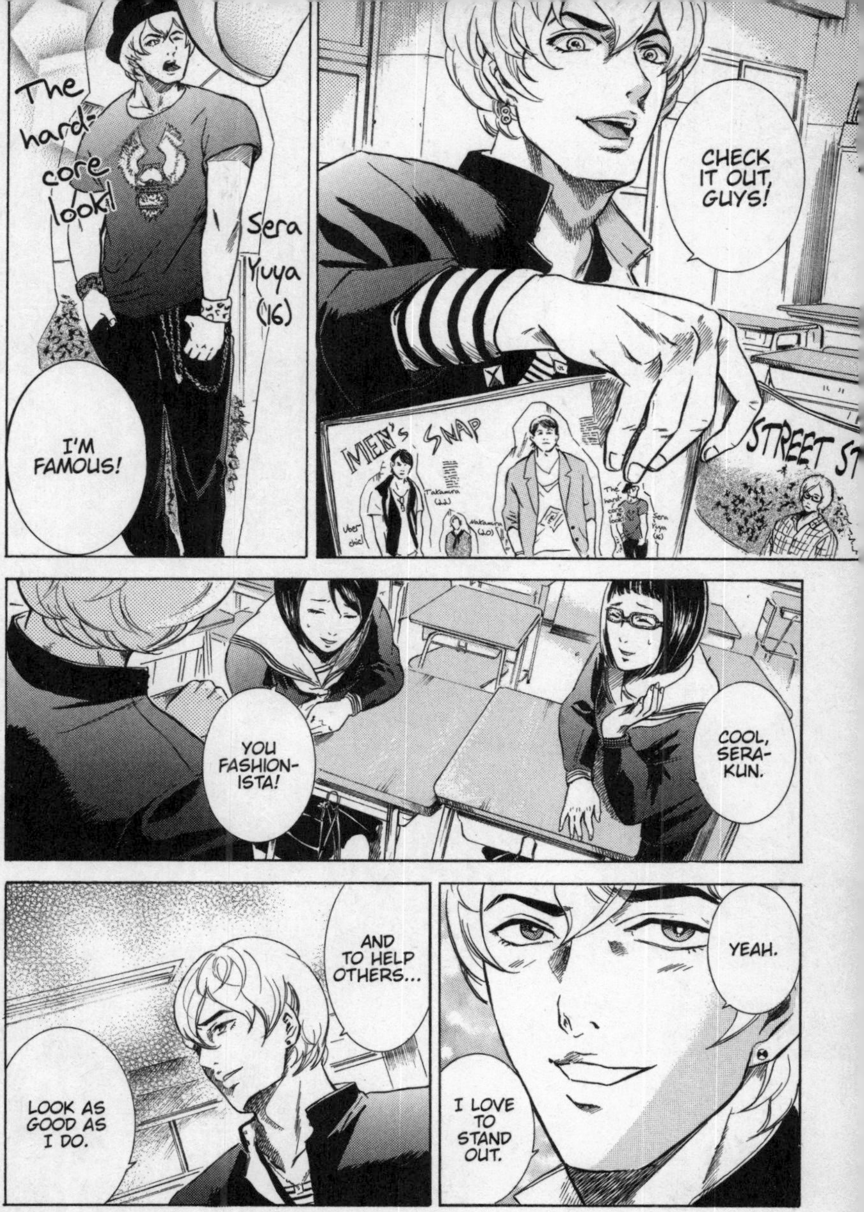
CHECK IT OUT, GUYS!
MEN's SNAP
STREET ST
The hard-core look!
Sera Yuya (16)
I'M FAMOUS!
COOL, SERA-KUN.
YOU FASHION-ISTA!
YEAH.
I LOVE TO STAND OUT.
AND TO HELP OTHERS...
LOOK AS GOOD AS I DO.

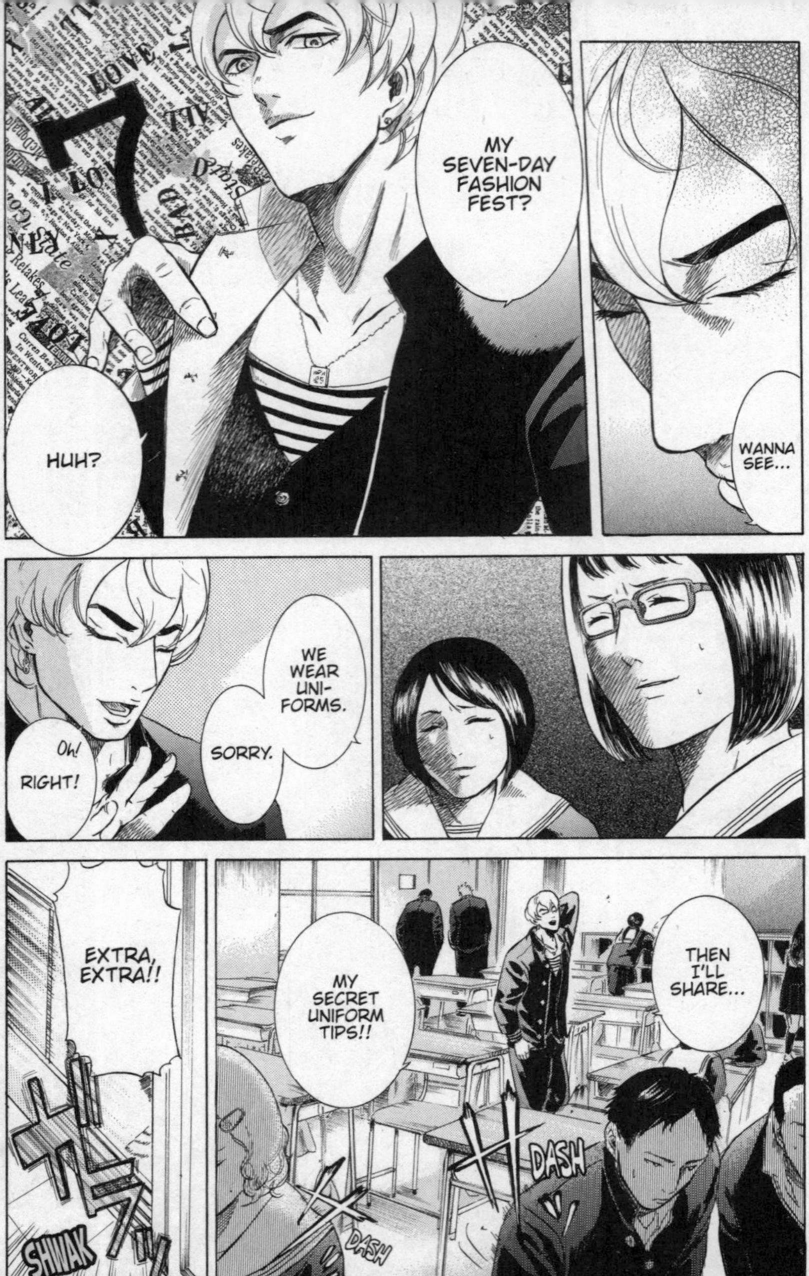
WANNA SEE...
MY SEVEN-DAY FASHION FEST?
HUH?
WE WEAR UNI-FORMS.
SORRY.
Oh! RIGHT!
THEN I'LL SHARE...
MY SECRET UNIFORM TIPS!!
DASH
DASH
EXTRA, EXTRA!!
SHWAK

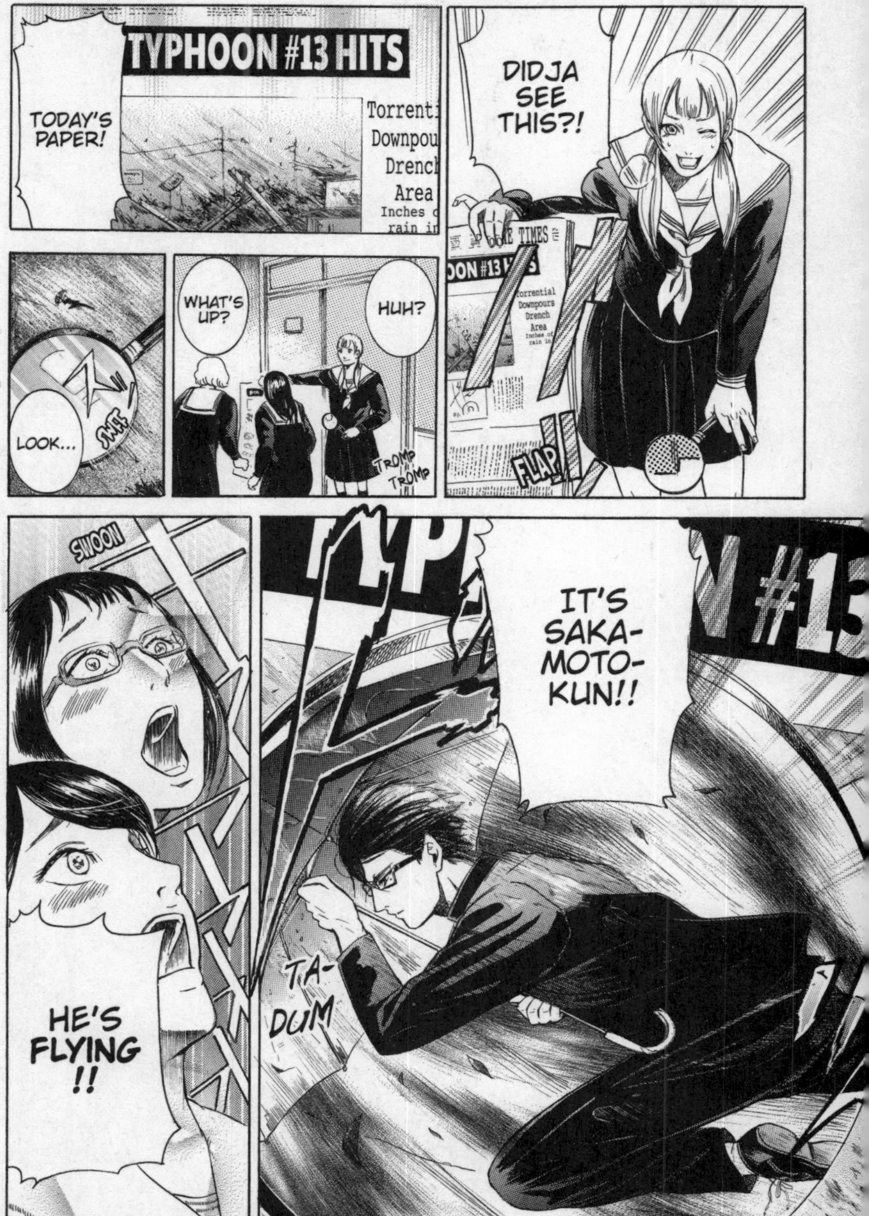
DIDJA SEE THIS?!
TYPHOON #13 HITS
Torrenti
Downpou
Drench
Area
Inches o
rain in
TODAY'S PAPER!
FLAP
HUH?
WHAT'S UP?
TROMP TROMP
SWIFT
LOOK...
IT'S SAKAMOTO-KUN!!
TA-DUM
SWOON
HE'S FLYING!!

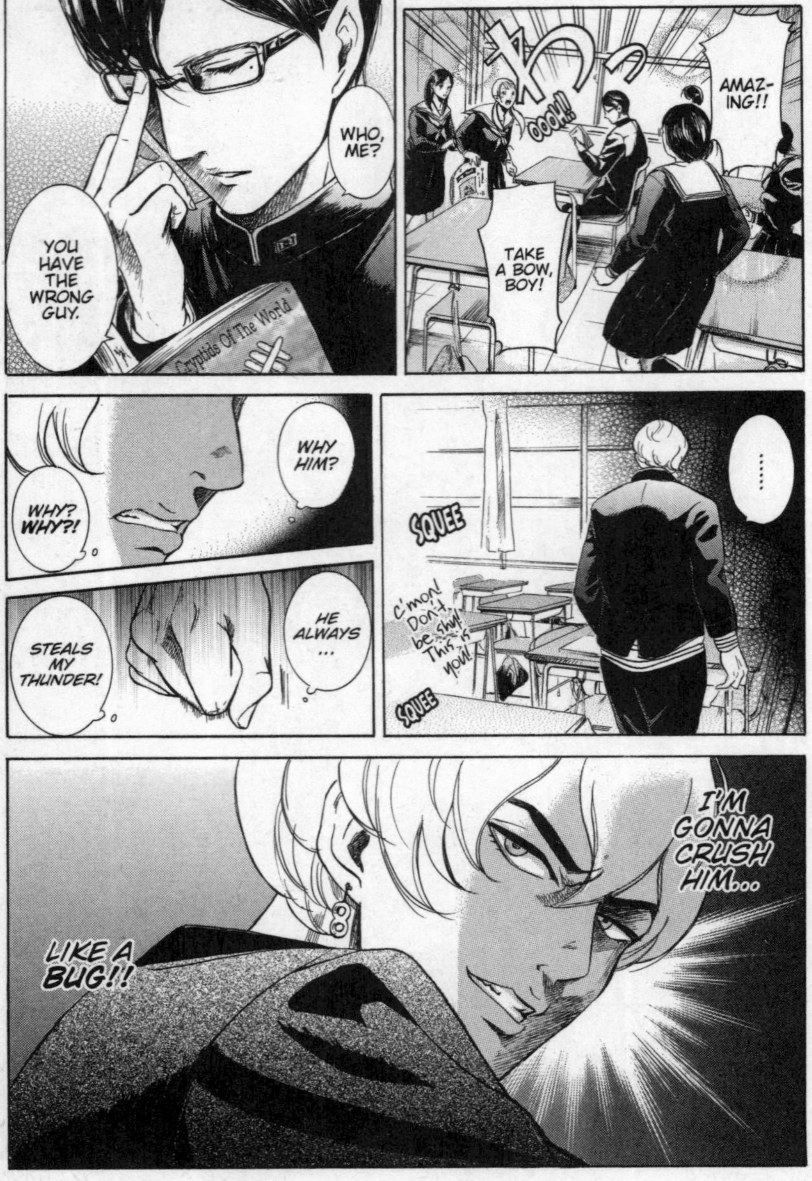
AMAZ-ING!!
OOOH!!
TAKE A BOW, BOY!
WHO, ME?
YOU HAVE THE WRONG GUY.
Cryptids Of The World
......
SQUEE
C'mon! Don't be shy! This is you!
SQUEE
WHY HIM?
WHY? WHY?!
HE ALWAYS ...
STEALS MY THUNDER!
I'M GONNA CRUSH HIM...
LIKE A BUG!!

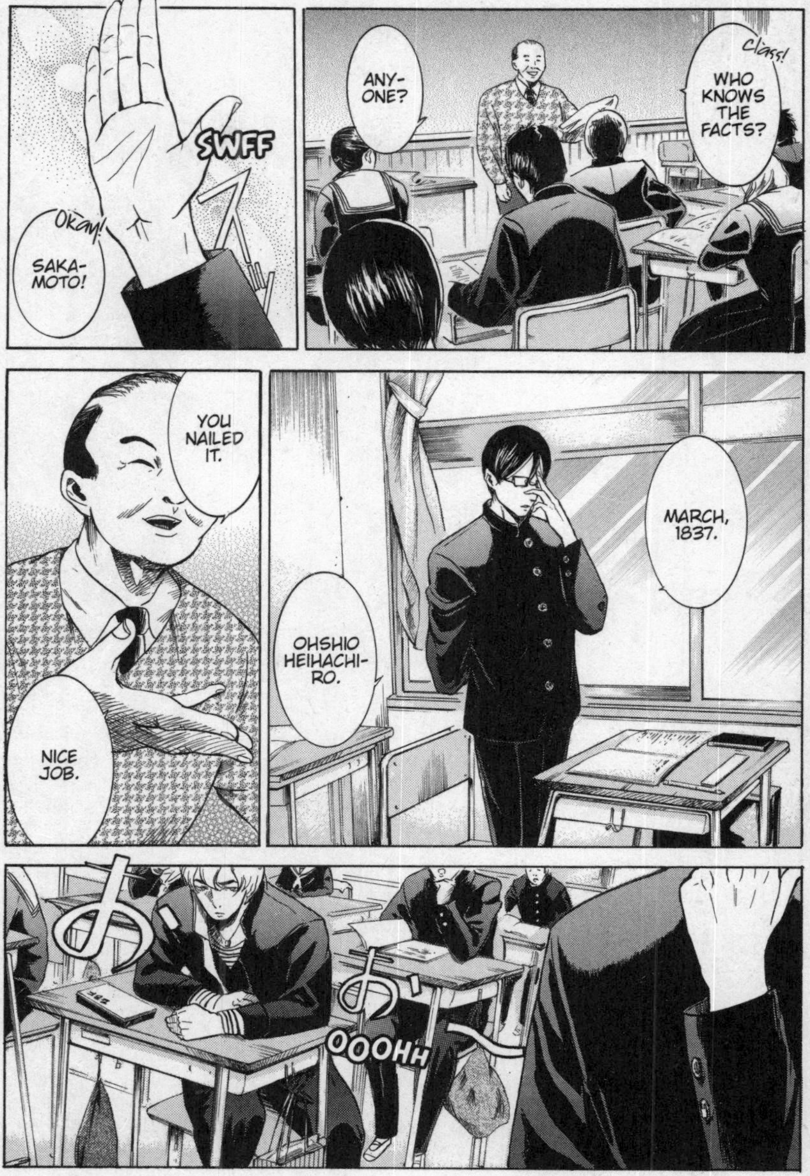
Class!
WHO KNOWS THE FACTS?
ANY-ONE?
SWFF
Okay!
SAKA-MOTO!
MARCH, 1837.
OHSHIO HEIHACHI-RO.
YOU NAILED IT.
NICE JOB.
OOOHH

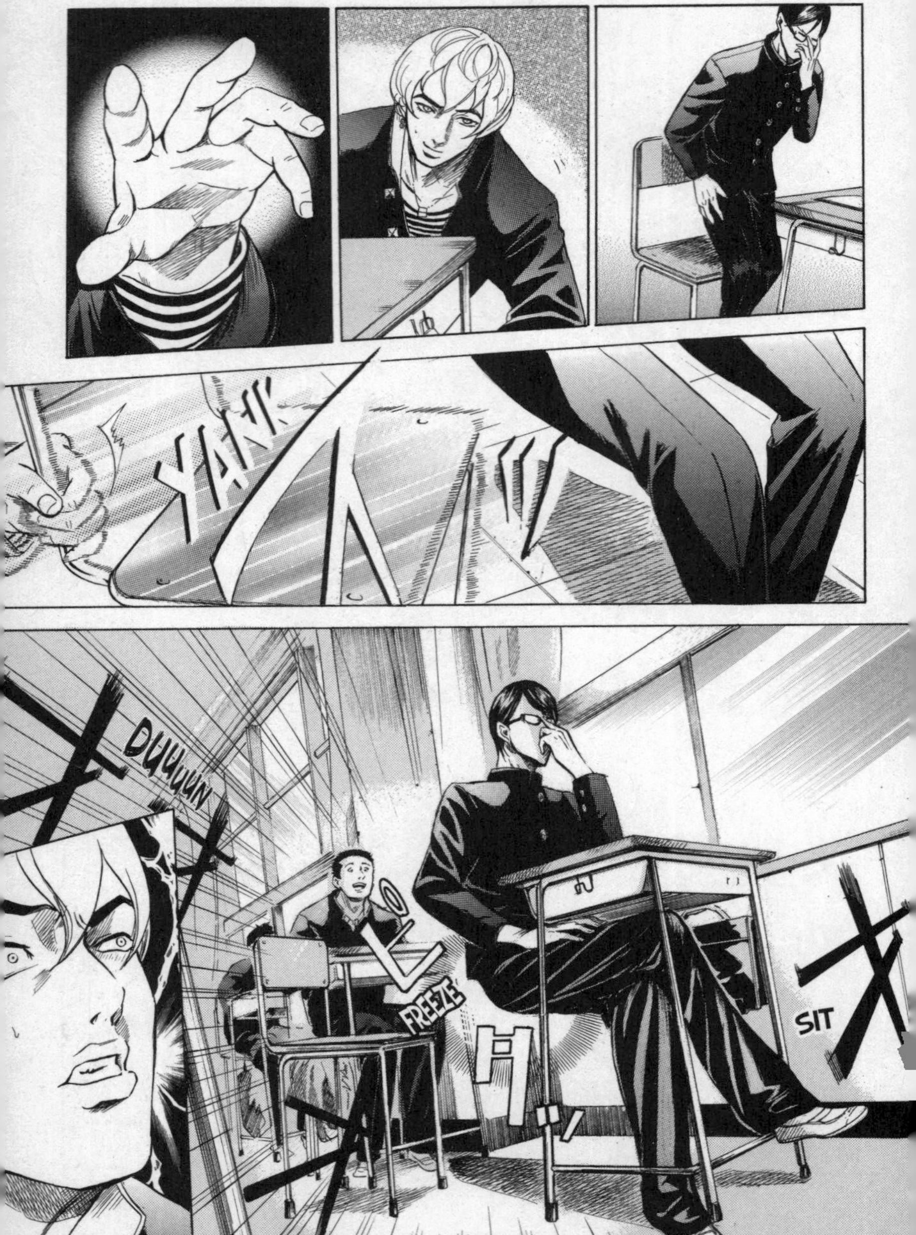
YANK
SIT
FREEZE
Duuuun

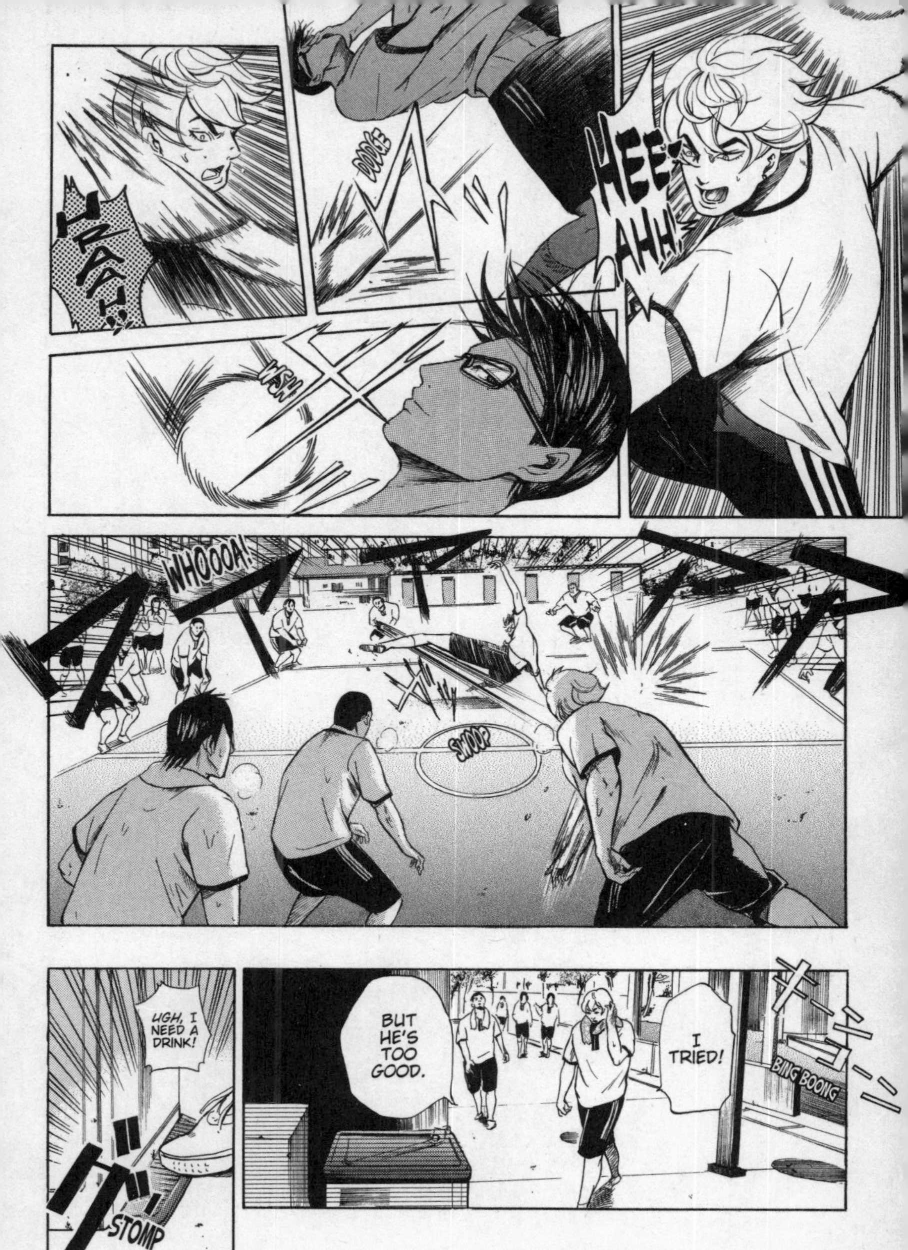
HEE-AHH!
DODGE
YRAAAH!!
WSH
WHOOOA!
SWOOP
BING BOONG
I TRIED!
BUT HE'S TOO GOOD.
UGH, I NEED A DRINK!
STOMP

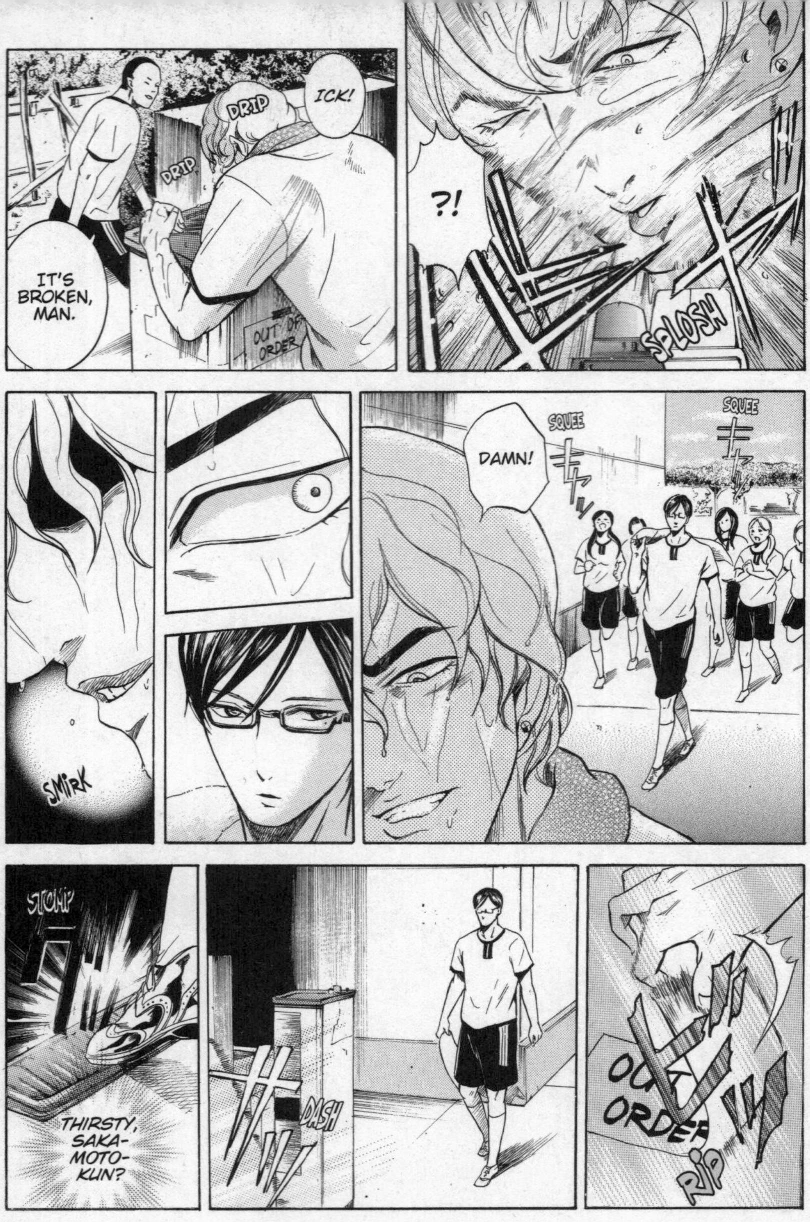
?!
SPLOSH
ICK!
DRIP
DRIP
IT'S BROKEN, MAN.
OUT OF ORDER
SQUEE
DAMN!
SQUEE
SMIRK
ORDER
RIP
DASH
STOMP
THIRSTY, SAKAMOTO-KUN?

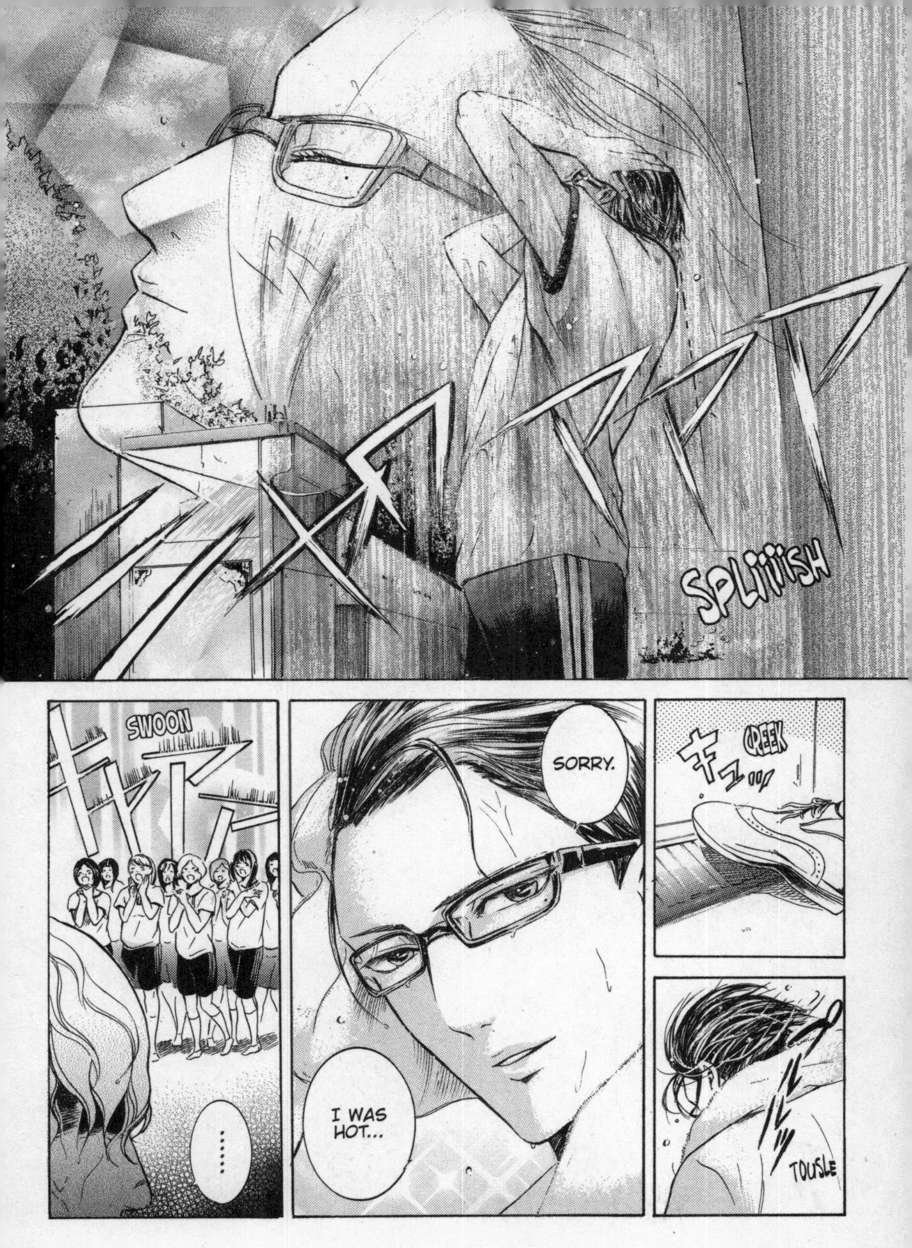
SPLIIIISH
CREEK
TOUSLE
SORRY.
I WAS HOT...
SWOON
......

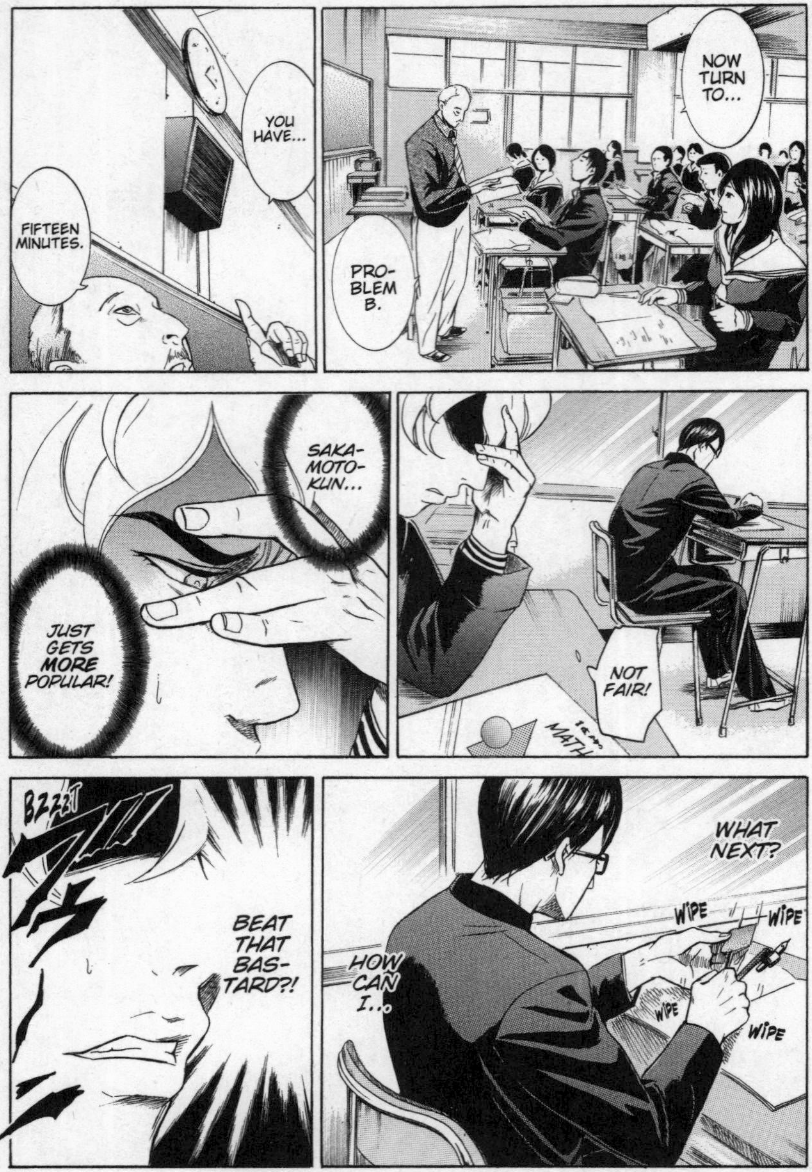
NOW TURN TO...
PRO-BLEM B.
YOU HAVE...
FIFTEEN MINUTES.
NOT FAIR!
MATH
SAKA-MOTO-KUN...
JUST GETS MORE POPULAR!
WHAT NEXT?
WIPE WIPE
WIPE WIPE
HOW CAN I...
BZZZT
BEAT THAT BAS-TARD?!

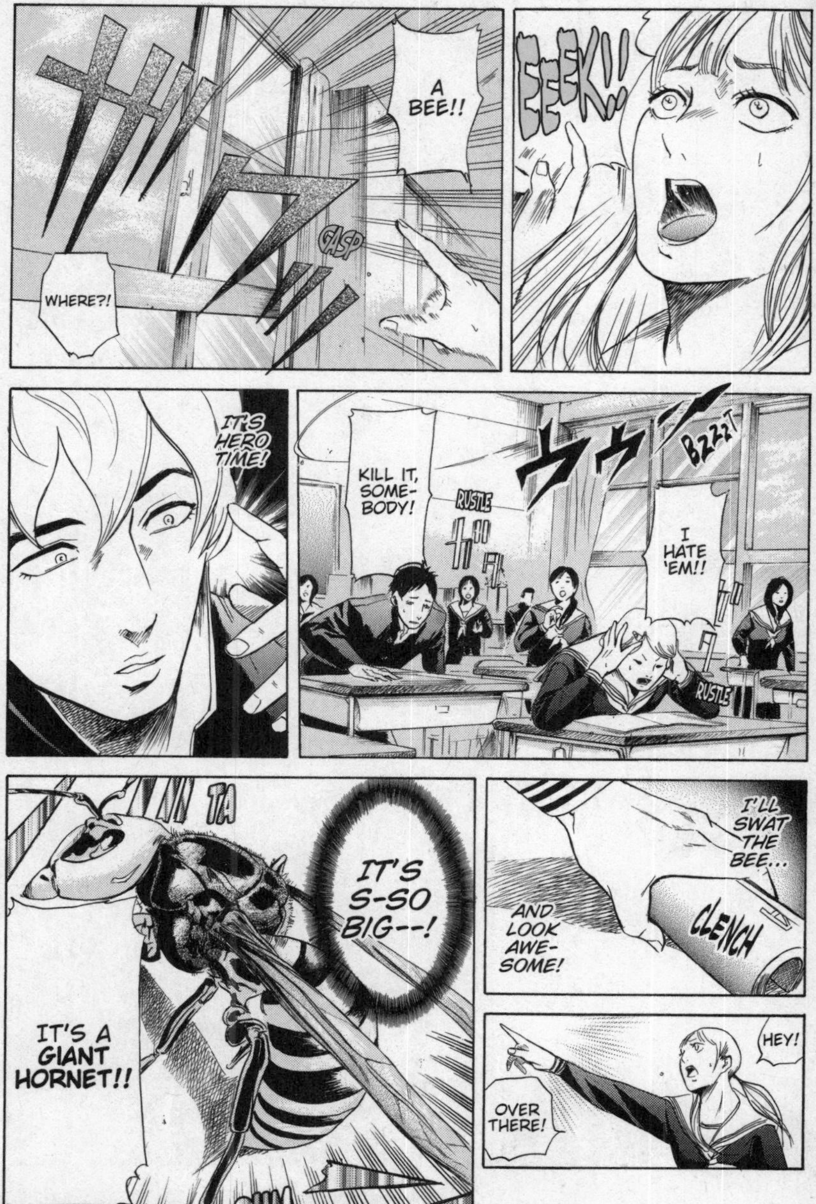
EEEK!!
A BEE!!
GASP
WHERE?!
BZZZT
KILL IT, SOMEBODY!
I HATE 'EM!!
RUSTLE
RUSTLE
IT'S HERO TIME!
I'LL SWAT THE BEE...
AND LOOK AWESOME!
CLENCH
HEY!
OVER THERE!
TA
IT'S S-SO BIG--!
IT'S A GIANT HORNET!!
DUM

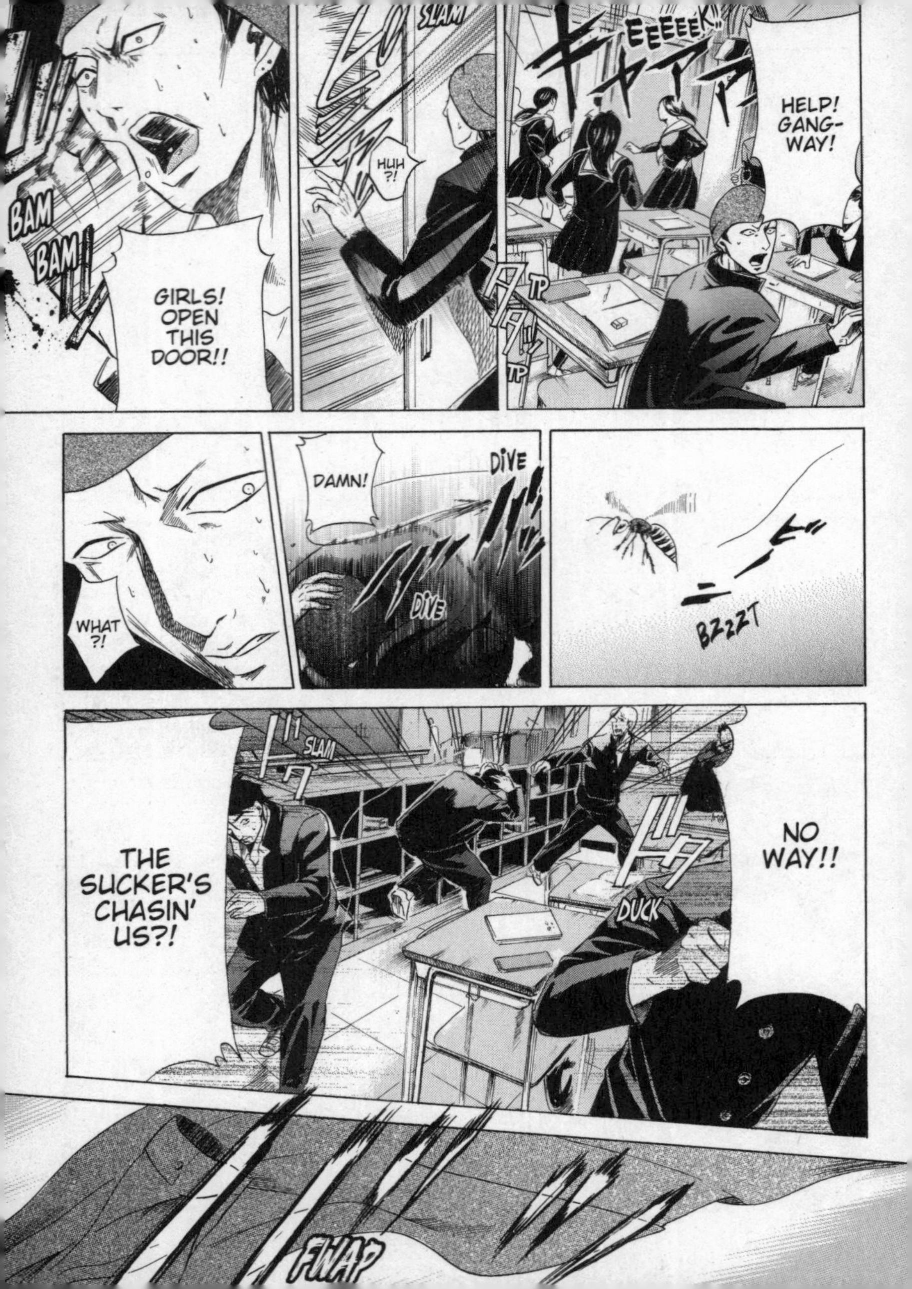
EEEEEK!!
HELP! GANG-WAY!
TP
TP
SLAM
HUH?!
BAM
BAM
GIRLS! OPEN THIS DOOR!!
BZZZT
DAMN!
DIVE
DIVE
WHAT?!
NO WAY!!
SLAM
DUCK
THE SUCKER'S CHASIN' US?!
FWAP

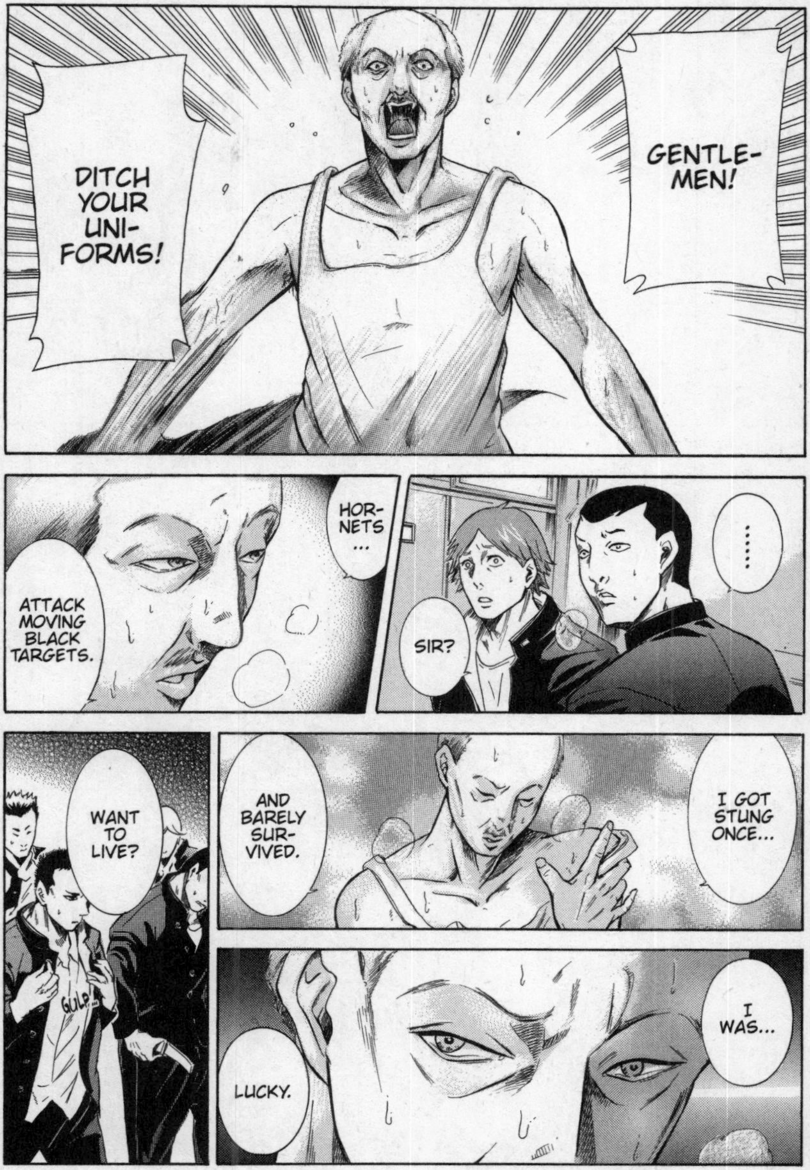
GENTLE-MEN!
DITCH YOUR UNI-FORMS!
......
SIR?
HOR-NETS...
ATTACK MOVING BLACK TARGETS.
I GOT STUNG ONCE...
AND BARELY SUR-VIVED.
I WAS...
LUCKY.
WANT TO LIVE?
GULP...

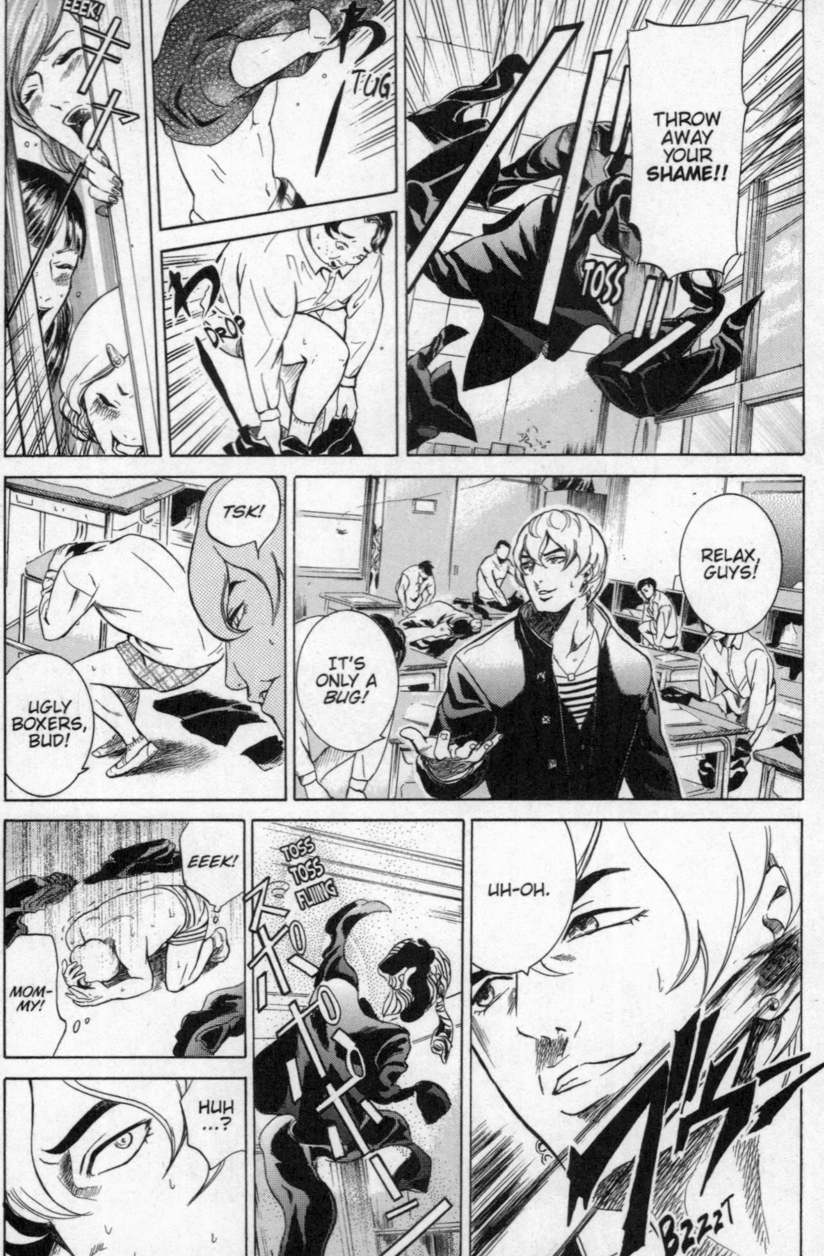
THROW AWAY YOUR SHAME!!
TOSS
TUG
DROP
EEEK!
RELAX, GUYS!
IT'S ONLY A BUG!
TSK!
UGLY BOXERS, BUD!
UH-OH.
BZZZT
TOSS TOSS FLIIING
EEEK!
MOM-MY!
HUH ...?

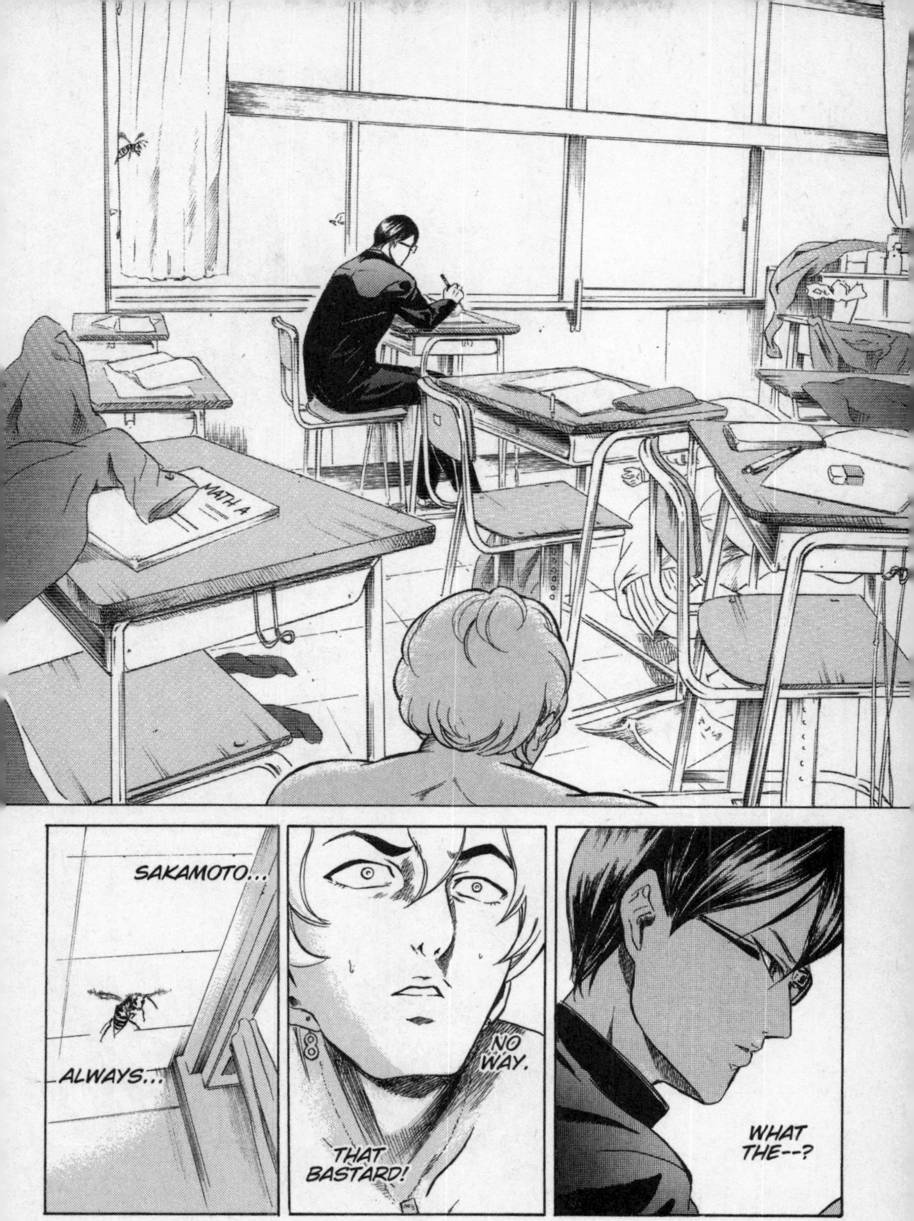
MATH A
WHAT THE--?
NO WAY.
THAT BASTARD!
SAKAMOTO...
ALWAYS...

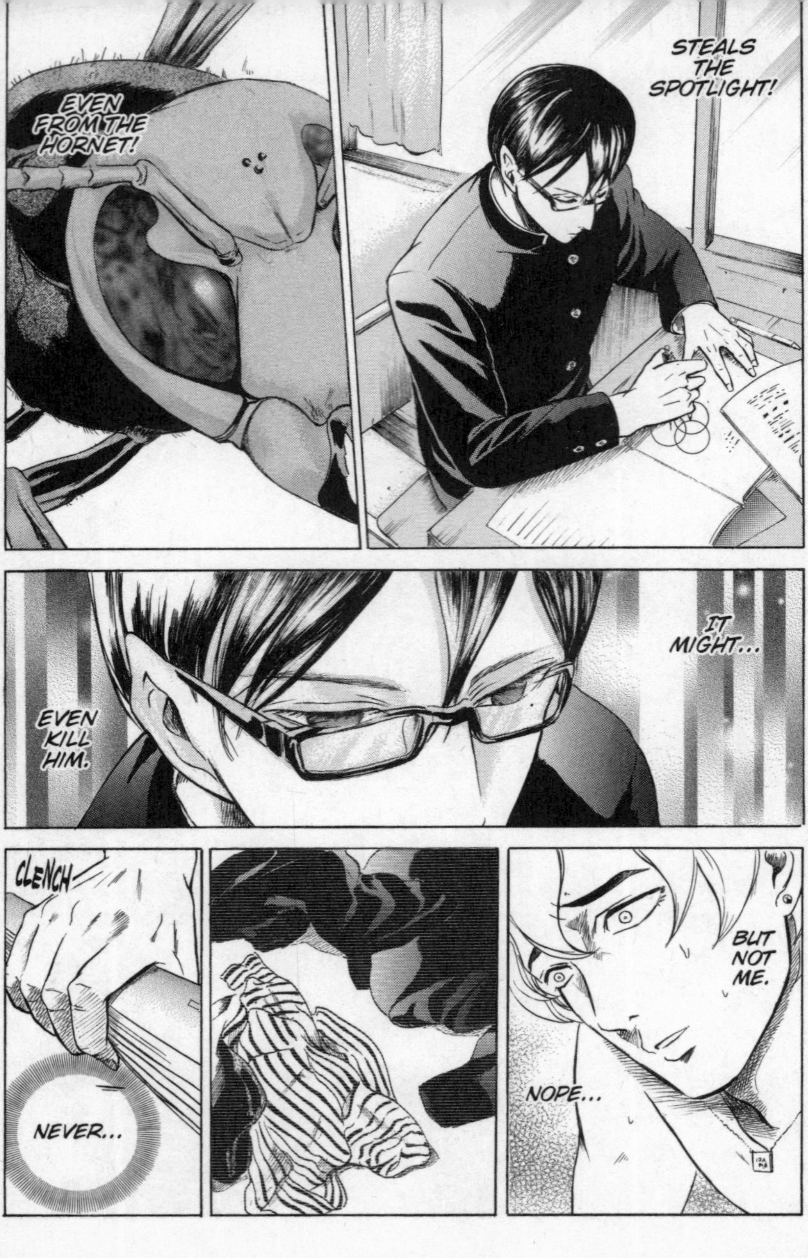
STEALS THE SPOTLIGHT!
EVEN FROM THE HORNET!
IT MIGHT...
EVEN KILL HIM.
BUT NOT ME.
NOPE...
CLENCH
NEVER...

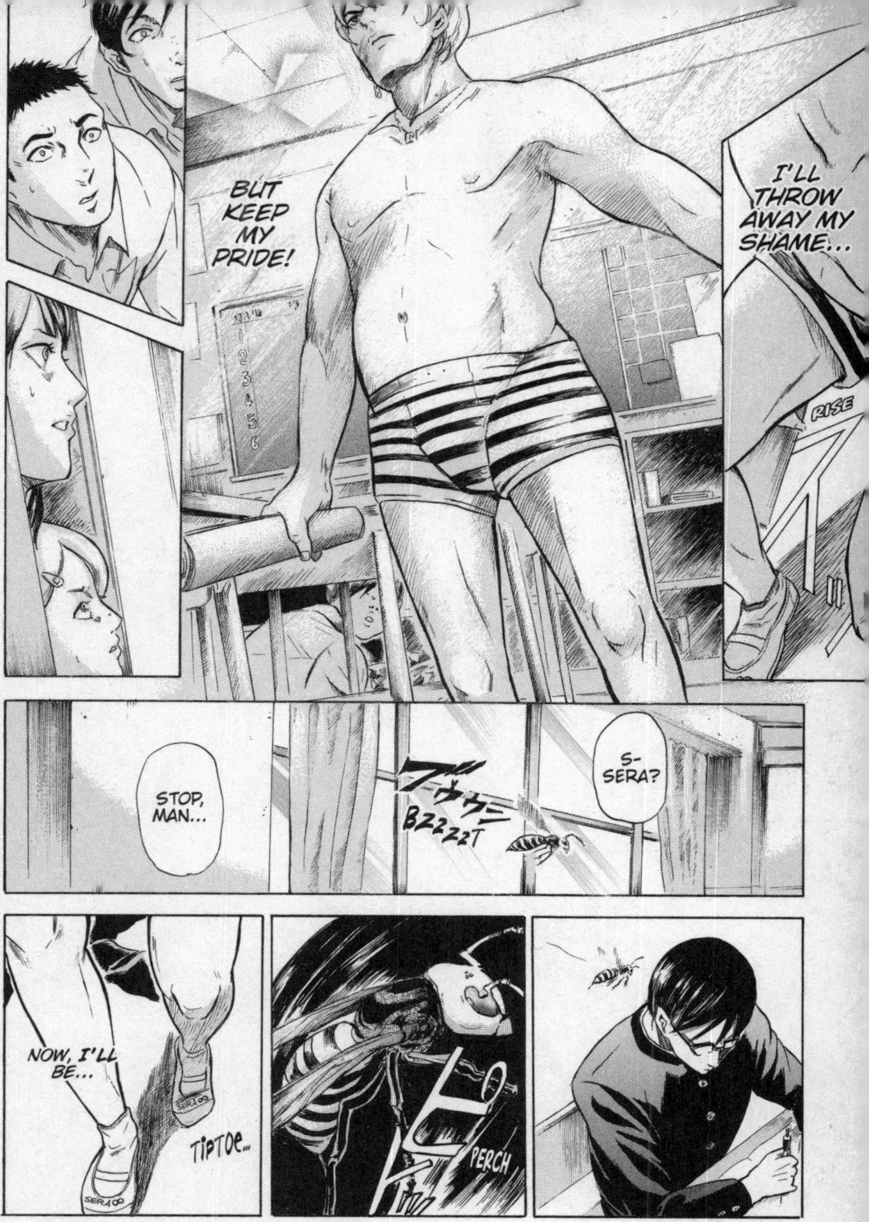
I'LL THROW AWAY MY SHAME...
RISE
BUT KEEP MY PRIDE!
S-SERA?
BZZZZZT
STOP, MAN...
PERCH
NOW, I'LL BE...
SERA∞
TIPTOE...
SERA∞

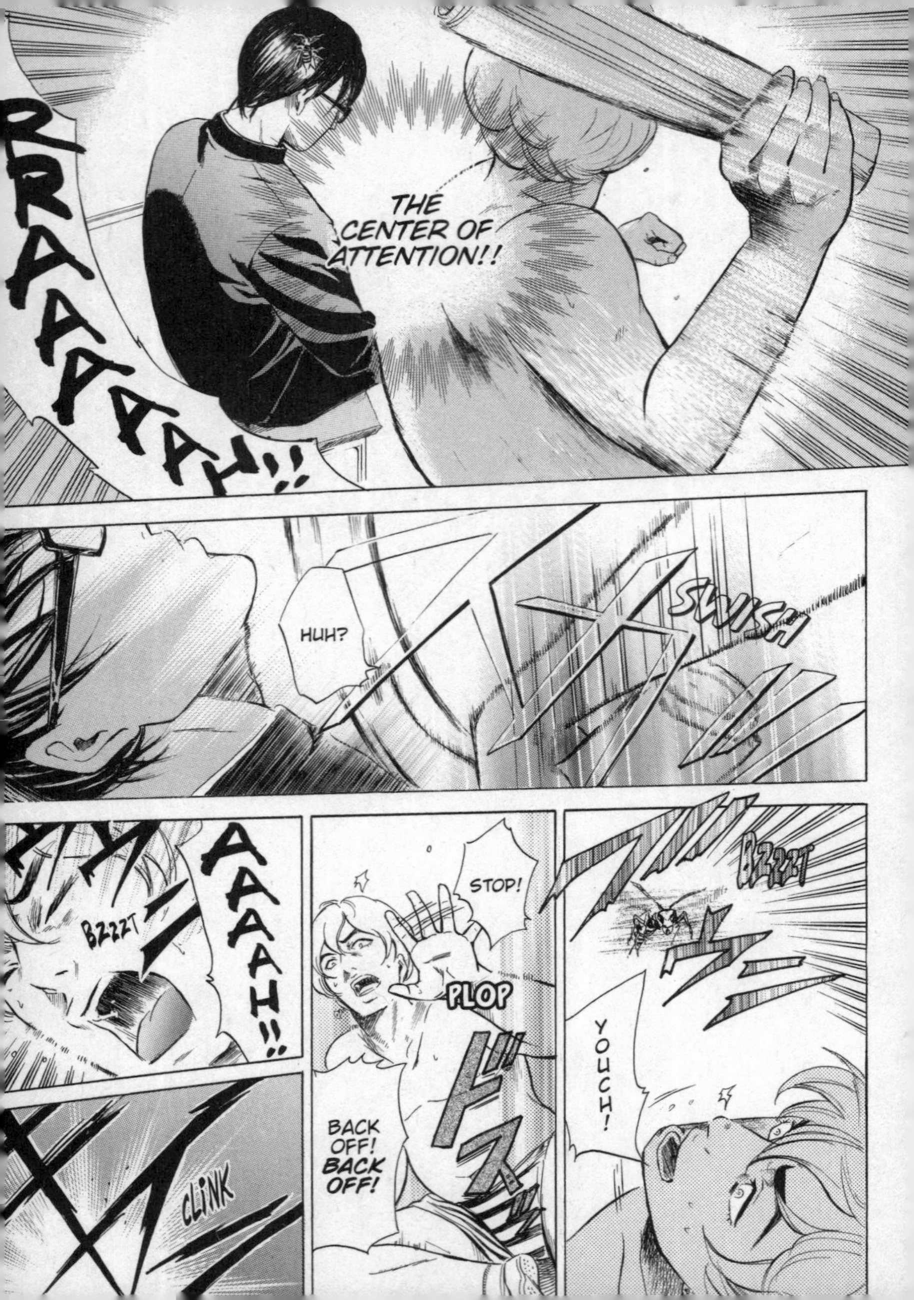
THE CENTER OF ATTENTION!!
RRAAAAAAH!!
SWISH
HUH?
BZZZT
YOUCH!
STOP!
PLOP
BACK OFF! BACK OFF!
AAAAH!!
BZZZT
CLINK

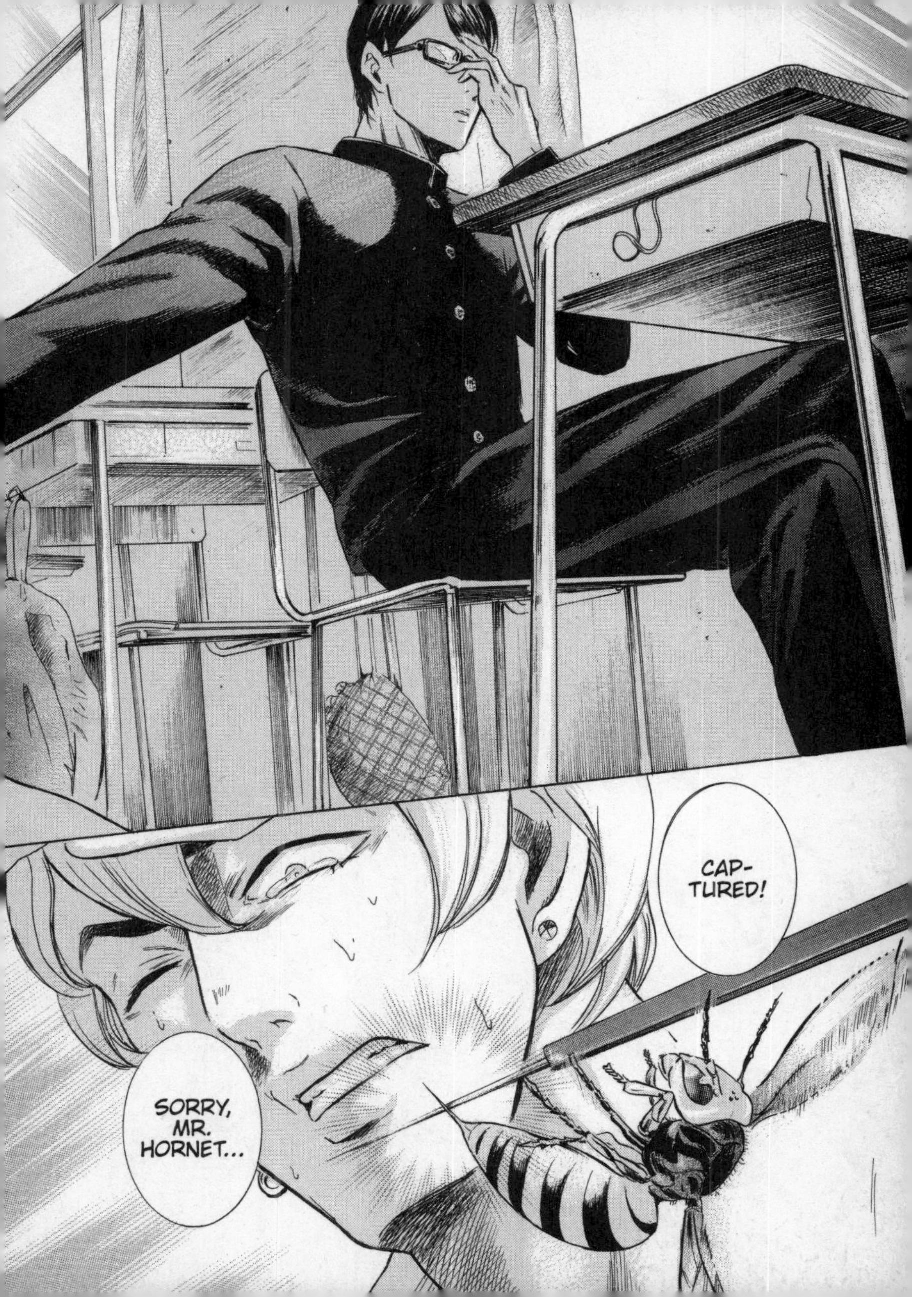
CAP-
TURED!
SORRY,
MR.
HORNET...

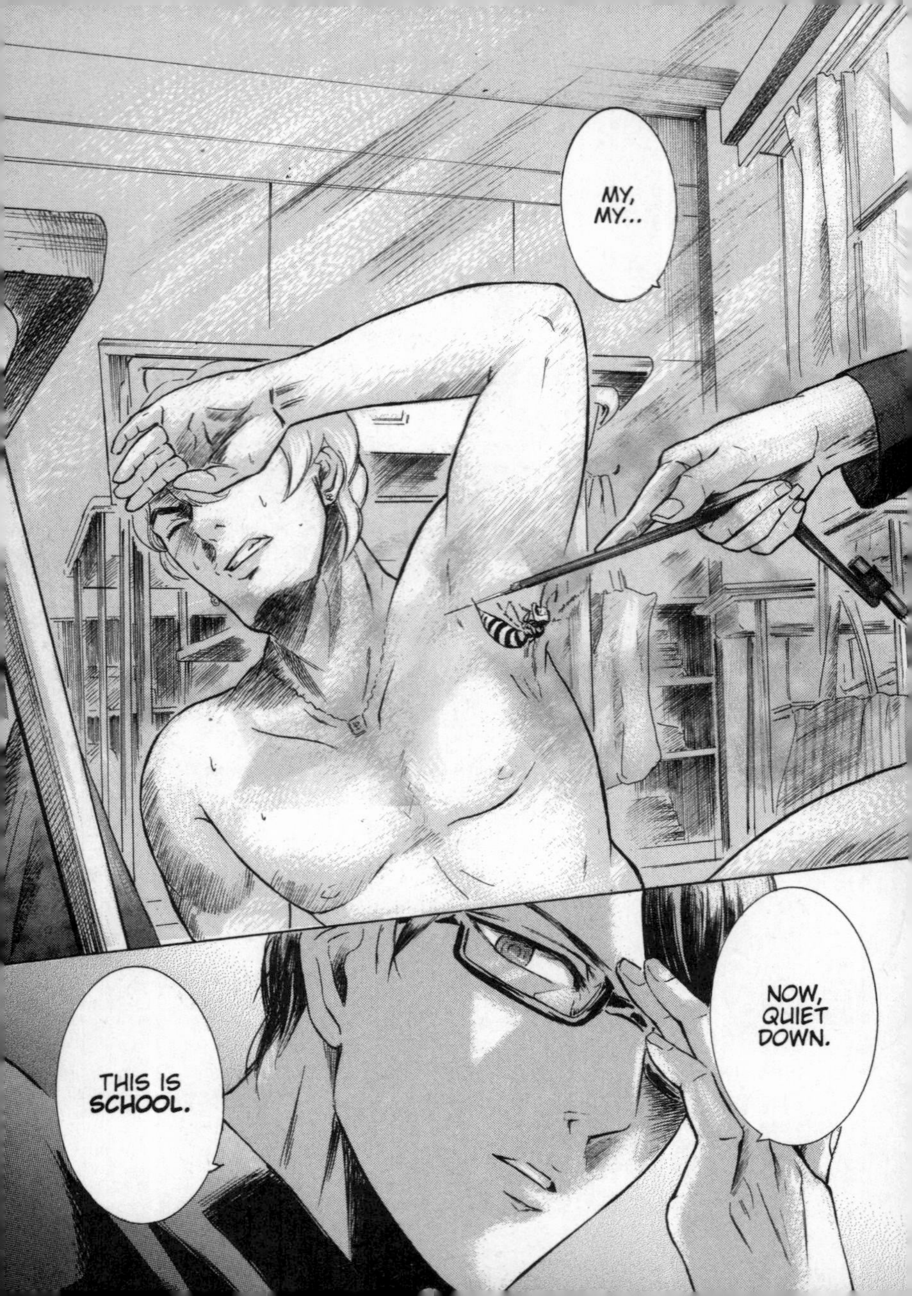
MY, MY...
NOW, QUIET DOWN.
THIS IS SCHOOL.

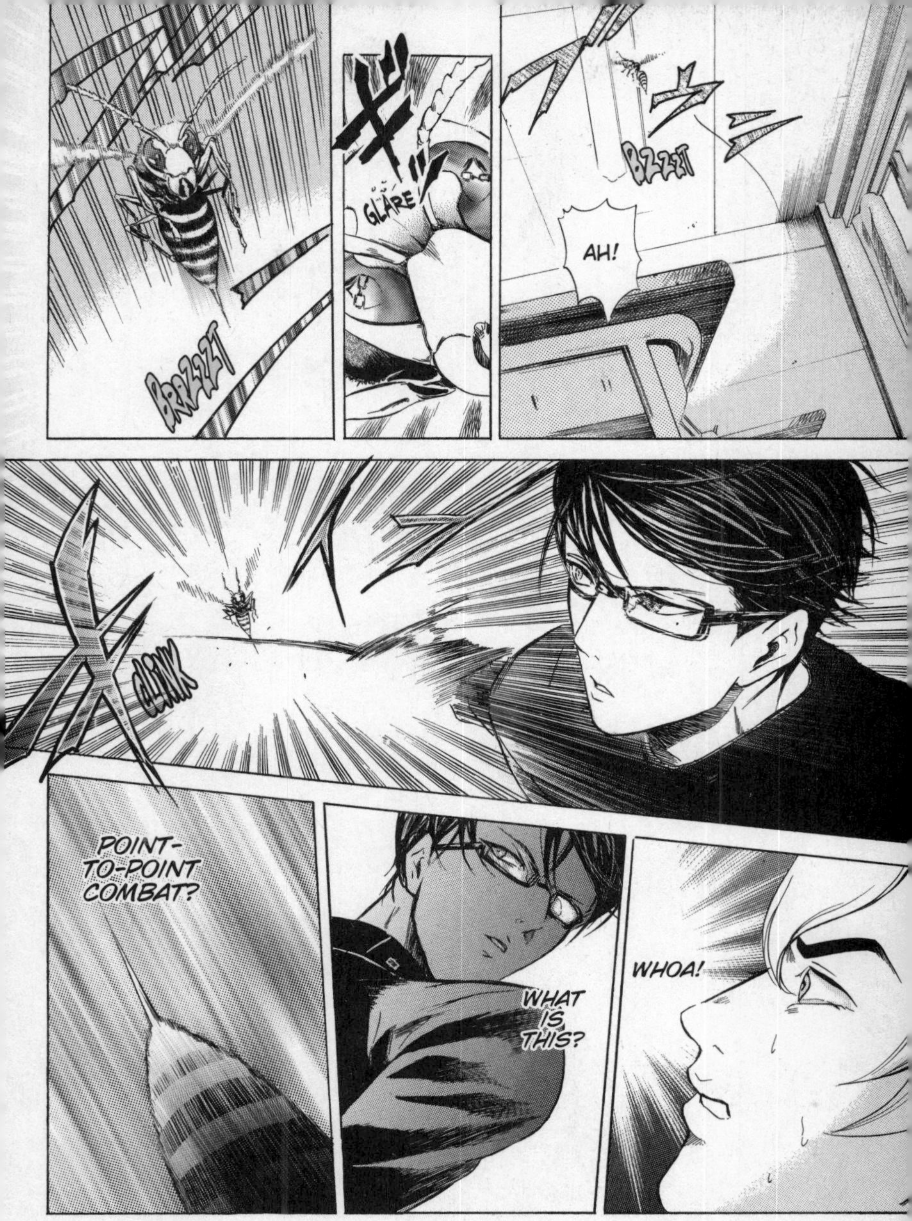
BZZZT
AH!
GLARE
BRRZZZT
CLINK
WHOA!
WHAT IS THIS?
POINT-TO-POINT COMBAT?

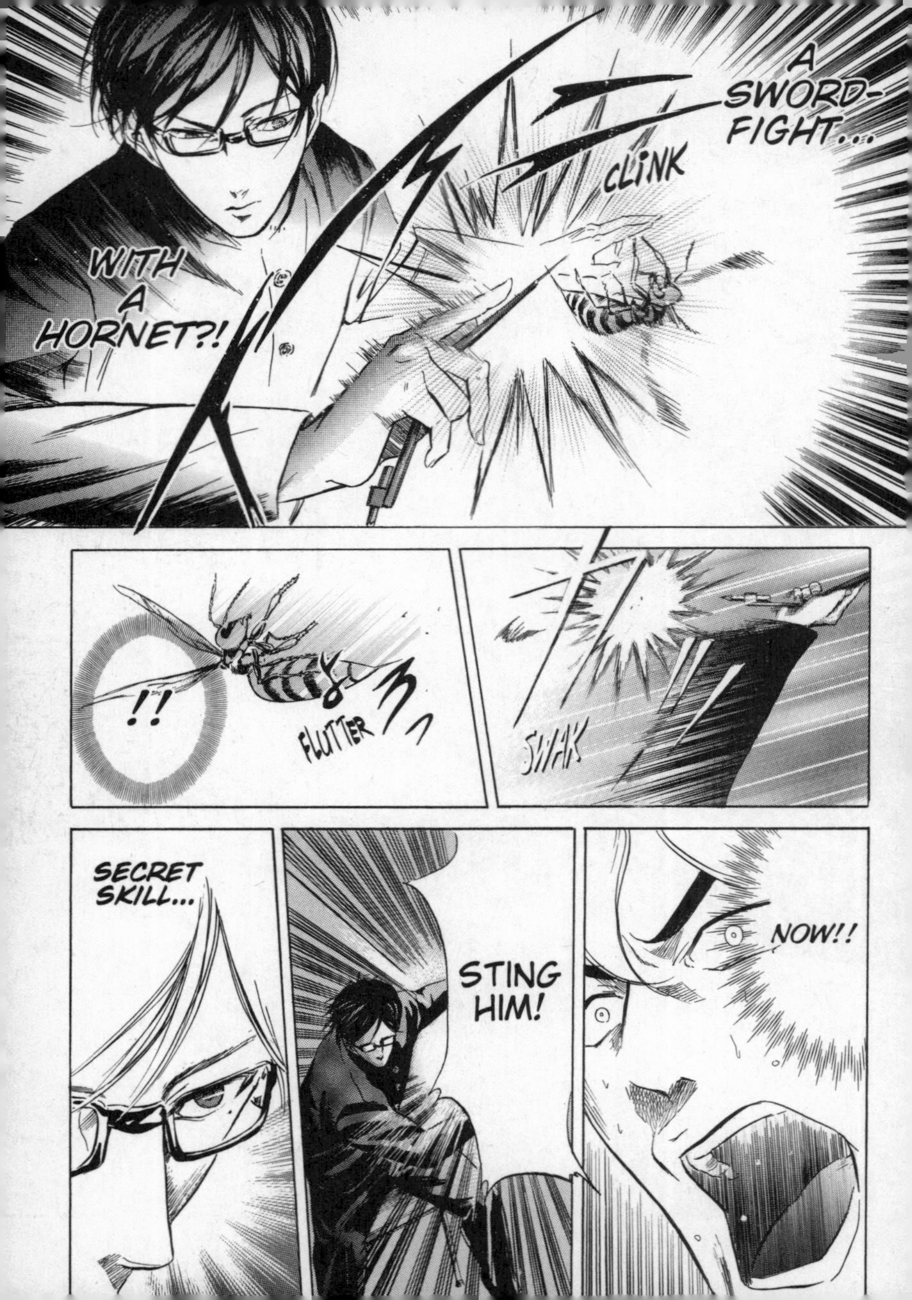
A SWORD-FIGHT...
CLINK
WITH A HORNET?!
SWAK
!!
FLUTTER
NOW!!
STING HIM!
SECRET SKILL...

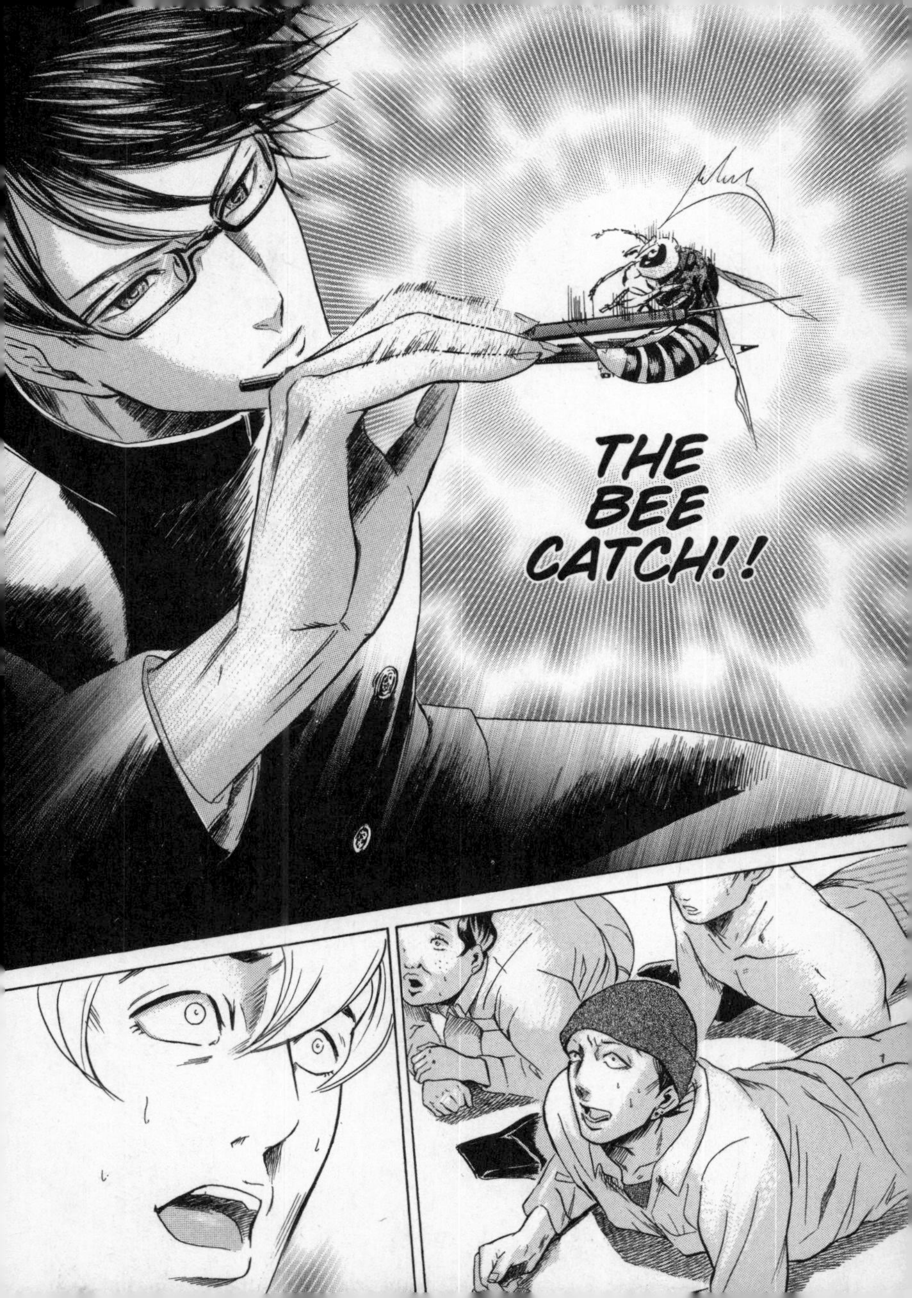
THE BEE CATCH!!

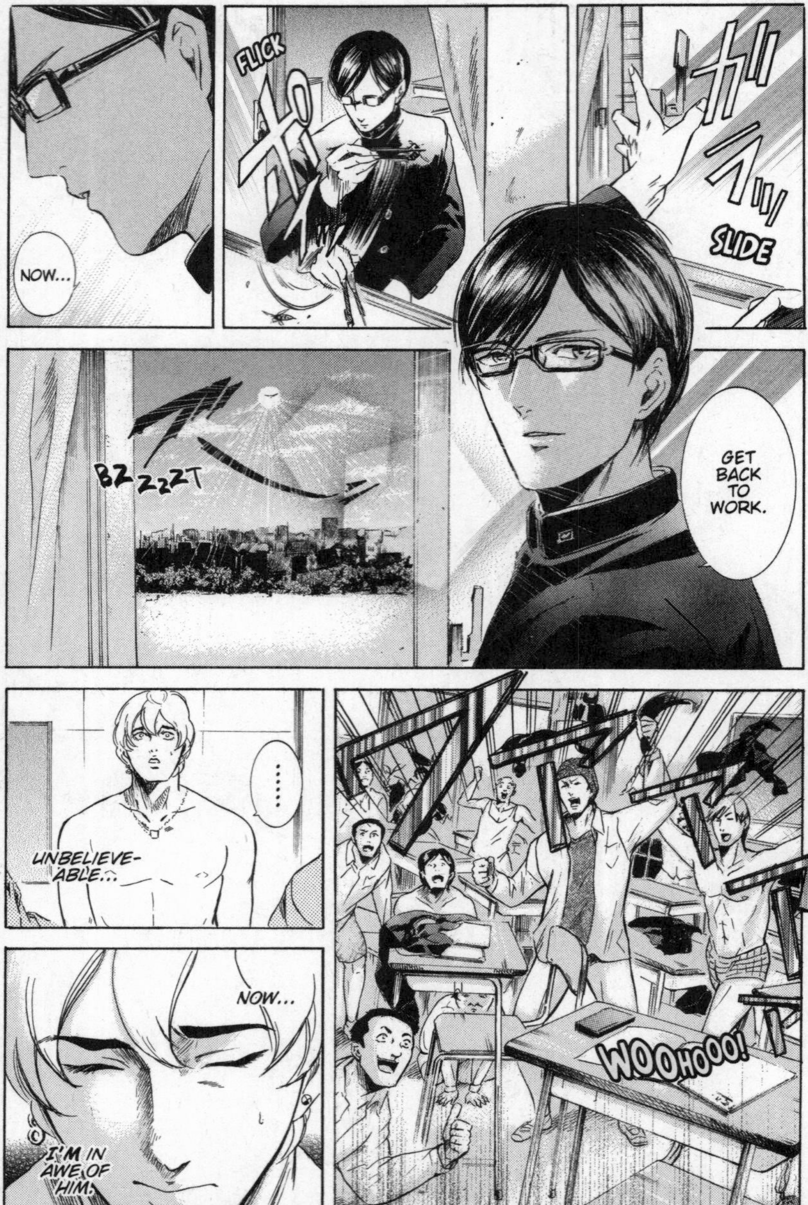
SLIDE
FLICK
NOW...
GET BACK TO WORK.
BZZZZT
WOOHOOO!
......
UNBELIEVE-ABLE...
NOW...
I'M IN AWE OF HIM.

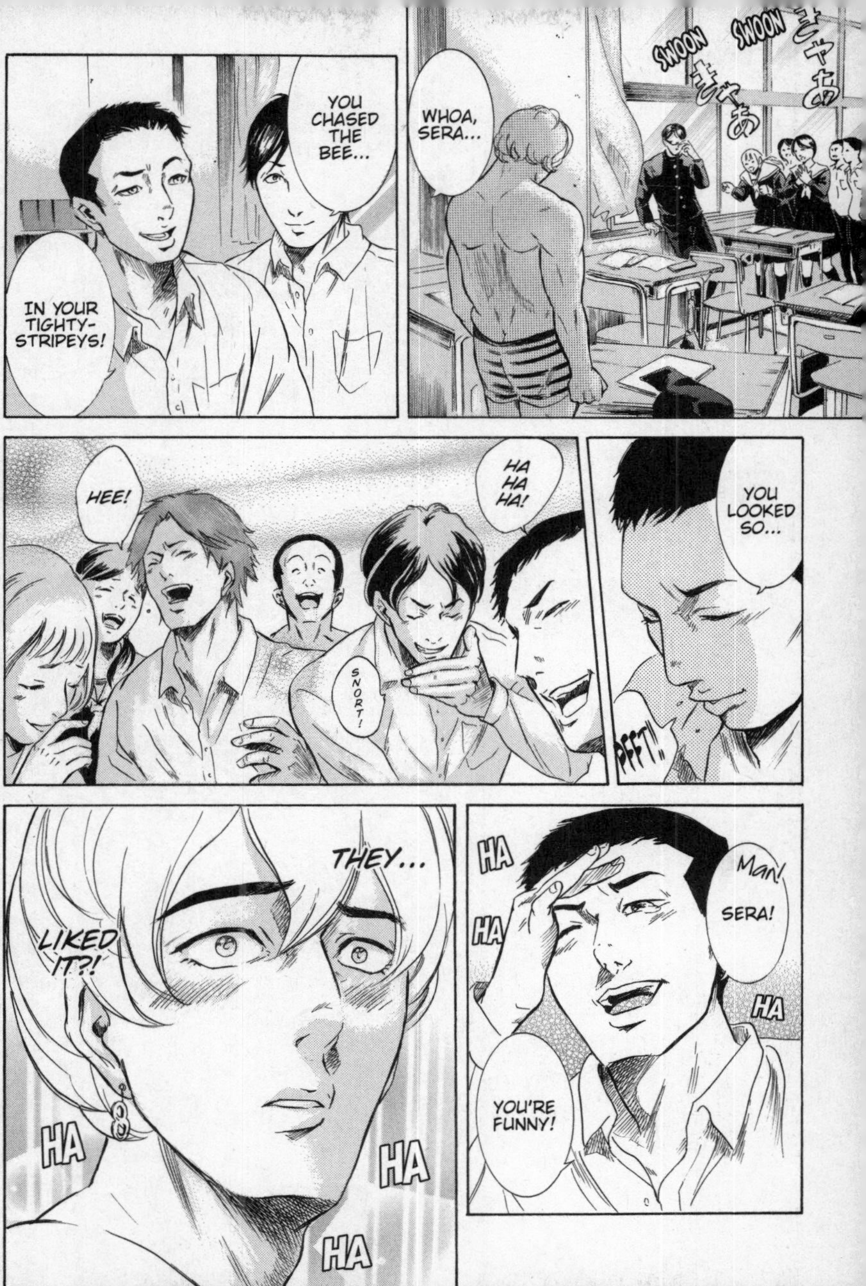

SWOON
SWOON
きゃあ
きゃあ
WHOA, SERA...
YOU CHASED THE BEE...
IN YOUR TIGHTY-STRIPEYS!
YOU LOOKED SO...
PFFT!
HA HA HA!
HEE!
SNORT!
HA
HA
Man! SERA!
HA
YOU'RE FUNNY!
THEY...
LIKED IT?!
HA
HA
HA

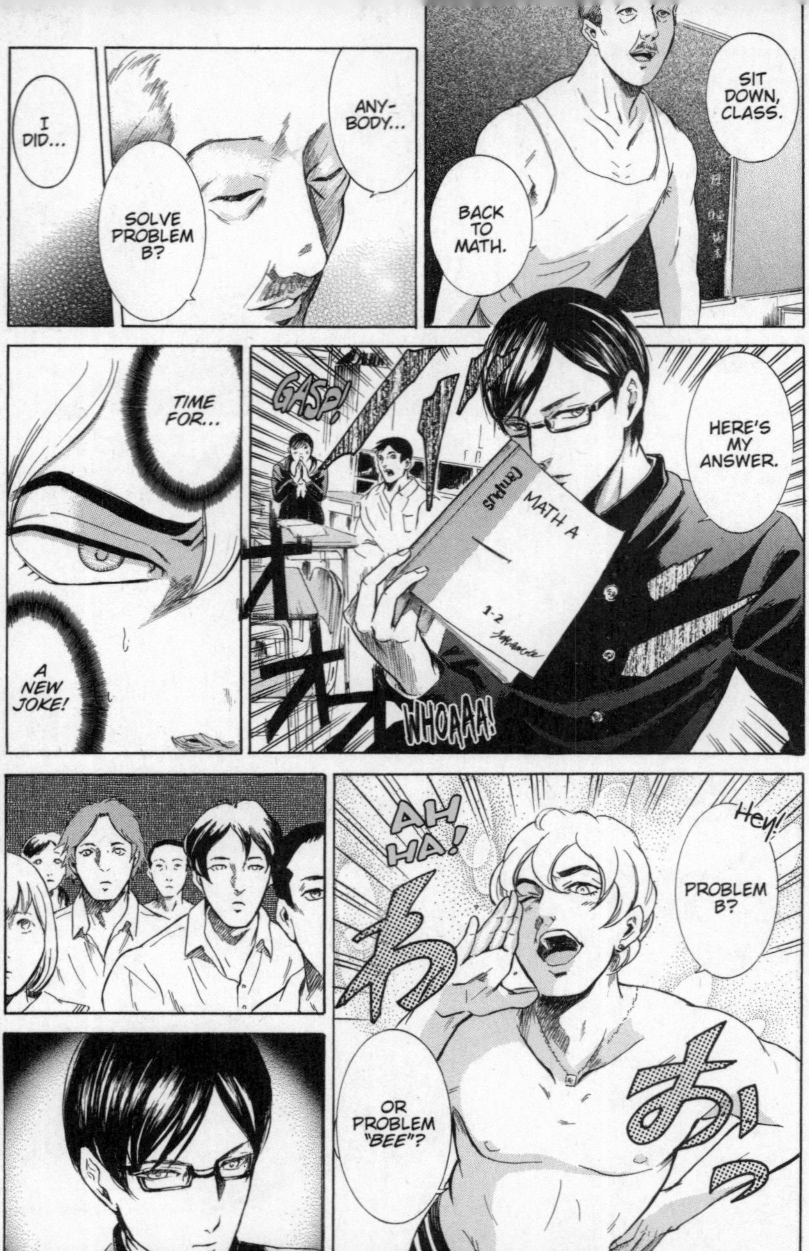
SIT DOWN, CLASS.
BACK TO MATH.
ANY-BODY...
SOLVE PROBLEM B?
I DID...
HERE'S MY ANSWER.
GASP!
Campus
MATH A
1-2
WHOAAA!
TIME FOR...
A NEW JOKE!
Hey!
PROBLEM B?
AH HA!
OR PROBLEM "BEE"?

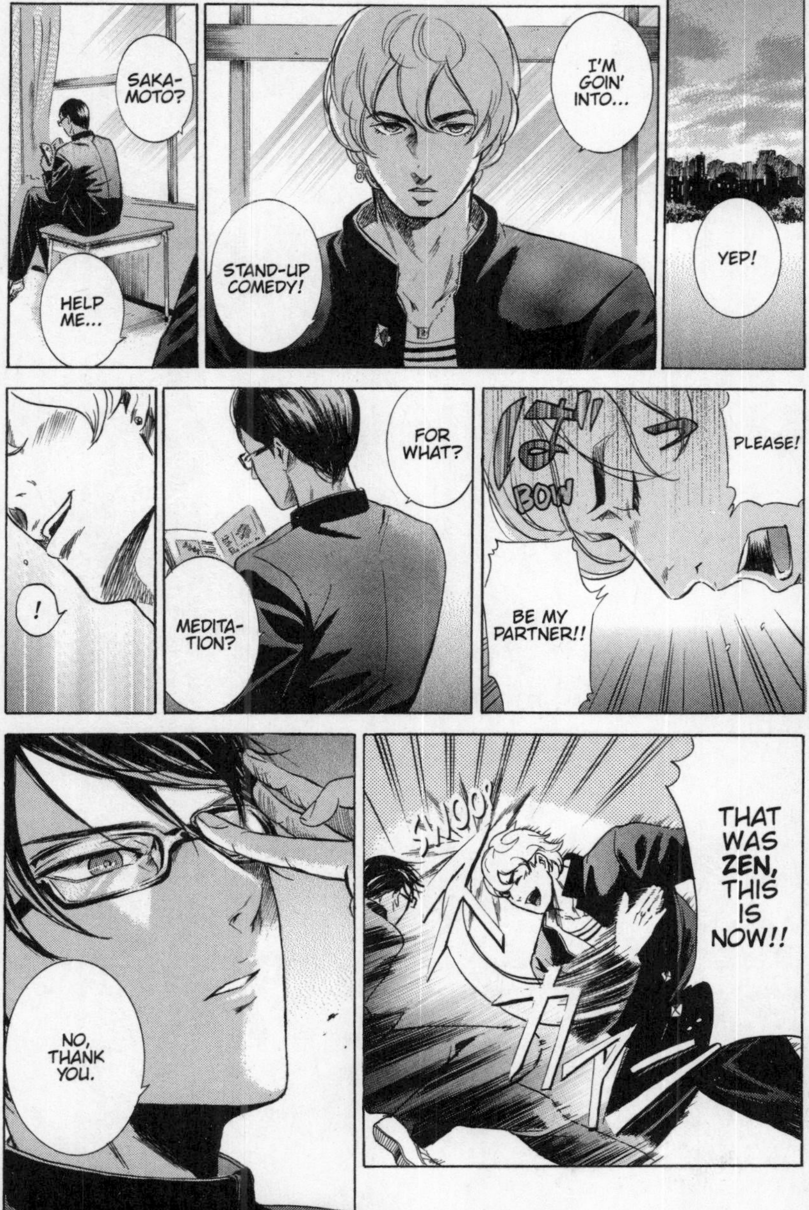
YEP!
I'M GOIN' INTO...
STAND-UP COMEDY!
SAKA-MOTO?
HELP ME...
PLEASE!
BOW
BE MY PARTNER!!
FOR WHAT?
MEDITA-TION?
!
SWOOP
THAT WAS ZEN, THIS IS NOW!!
NO, THANK YOU.

End of Chapter 2

P.E. Test #2:
   Standing
   Broad Jump

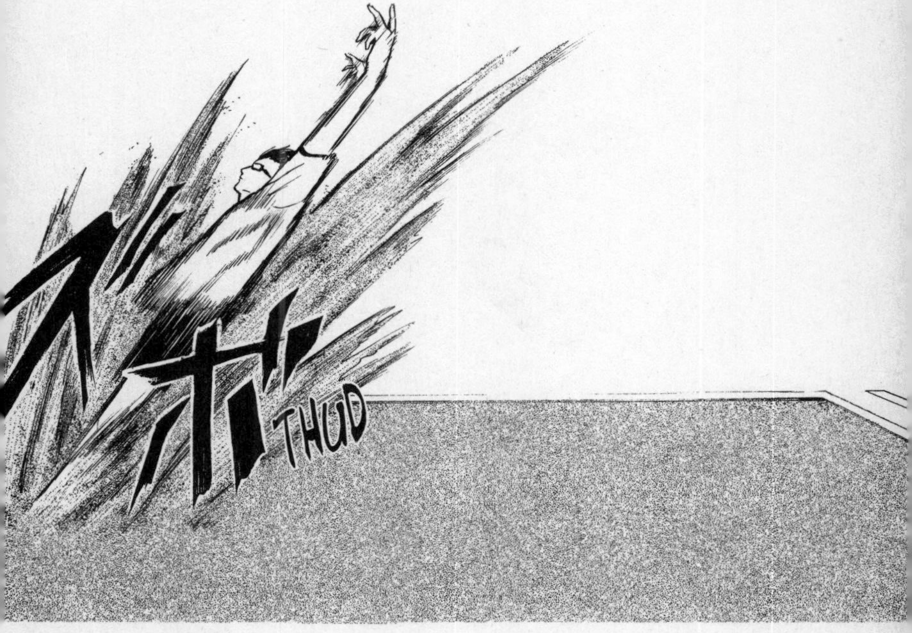
THUD

CHAPTER 3: PROTECTION

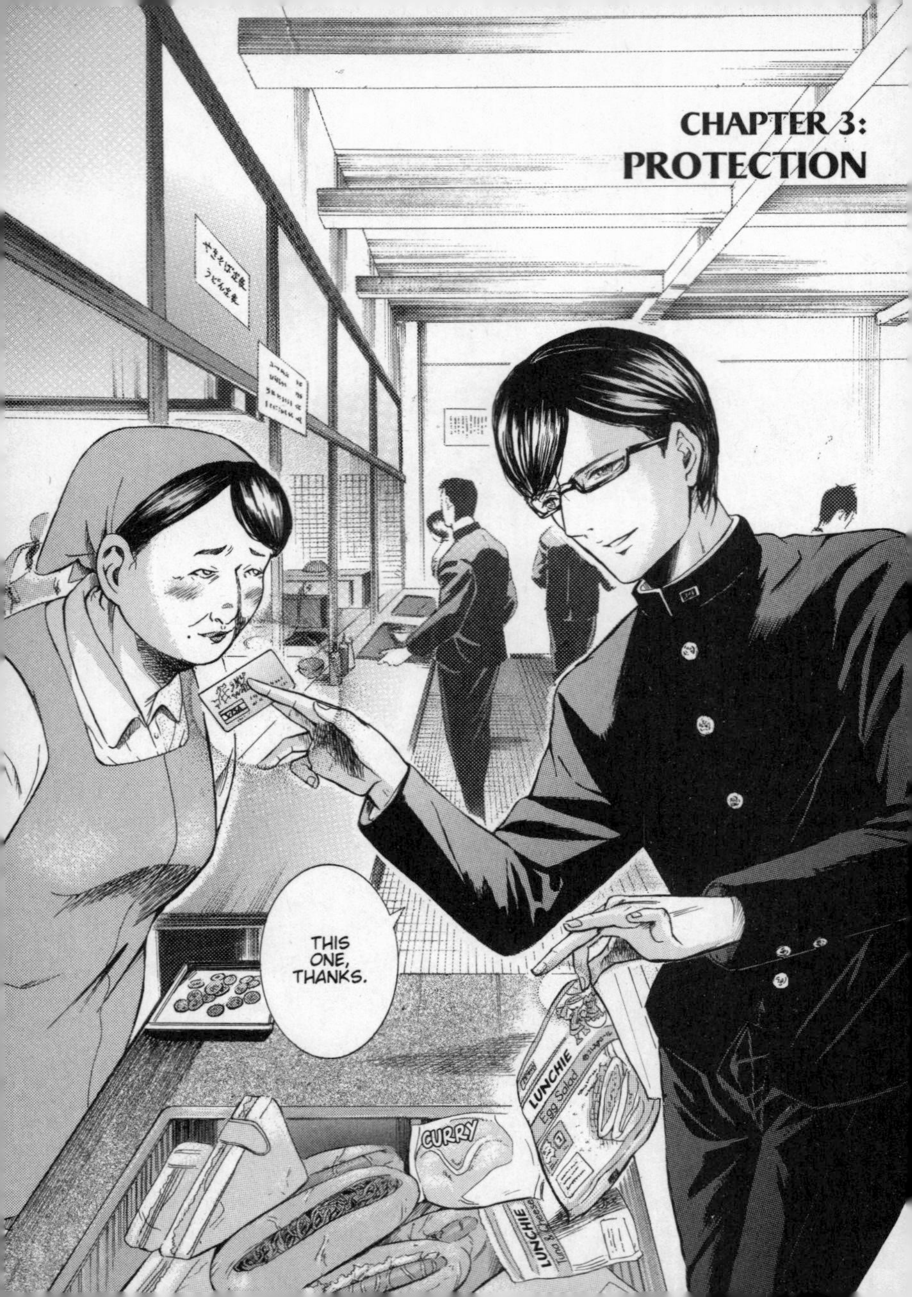
THIS ONE, THANKS.
LUNCHIE
Egg Salad
CURRY
LUNCHIE
Tuna & Cheese

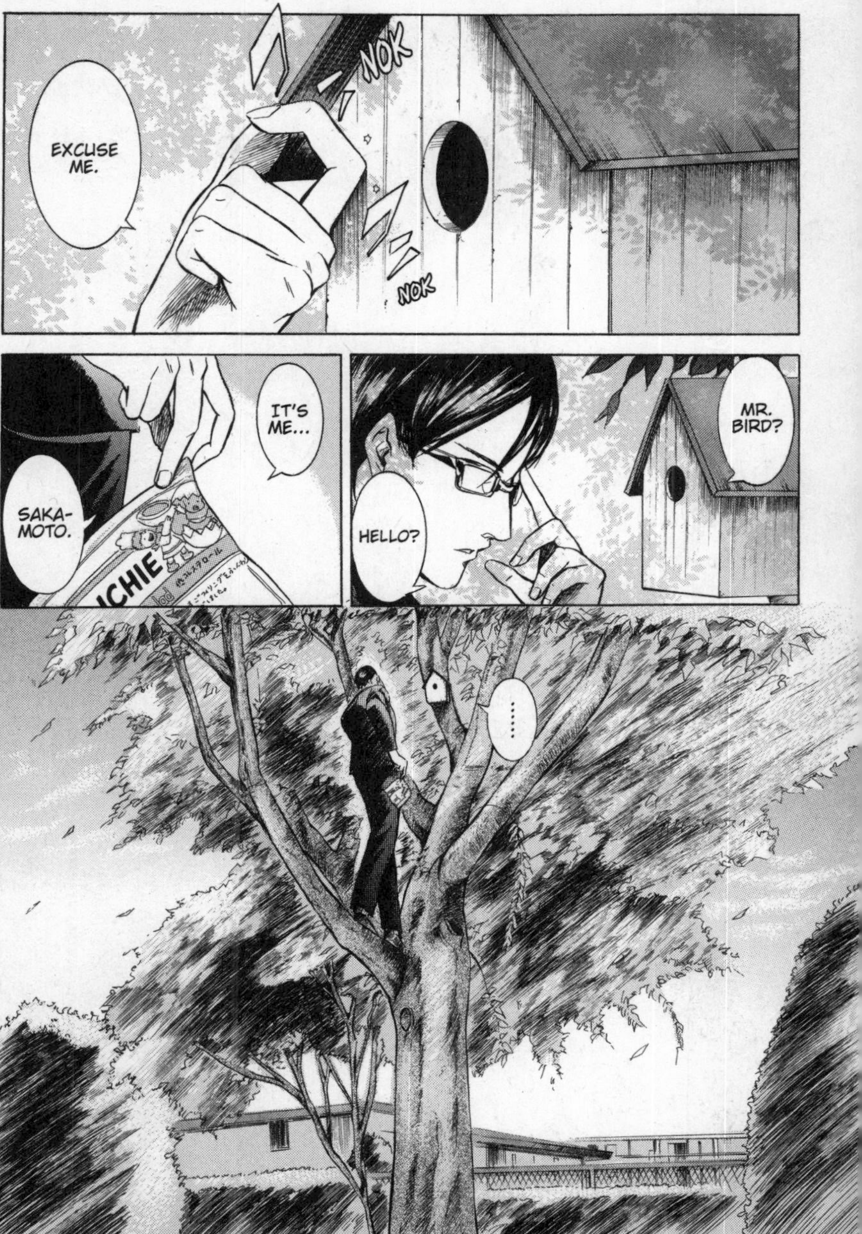
NOK
NOK
EXCUSE ME.
MR. BIRD?
HELLO?
IT'S ME...
SAKAMOTO.
......

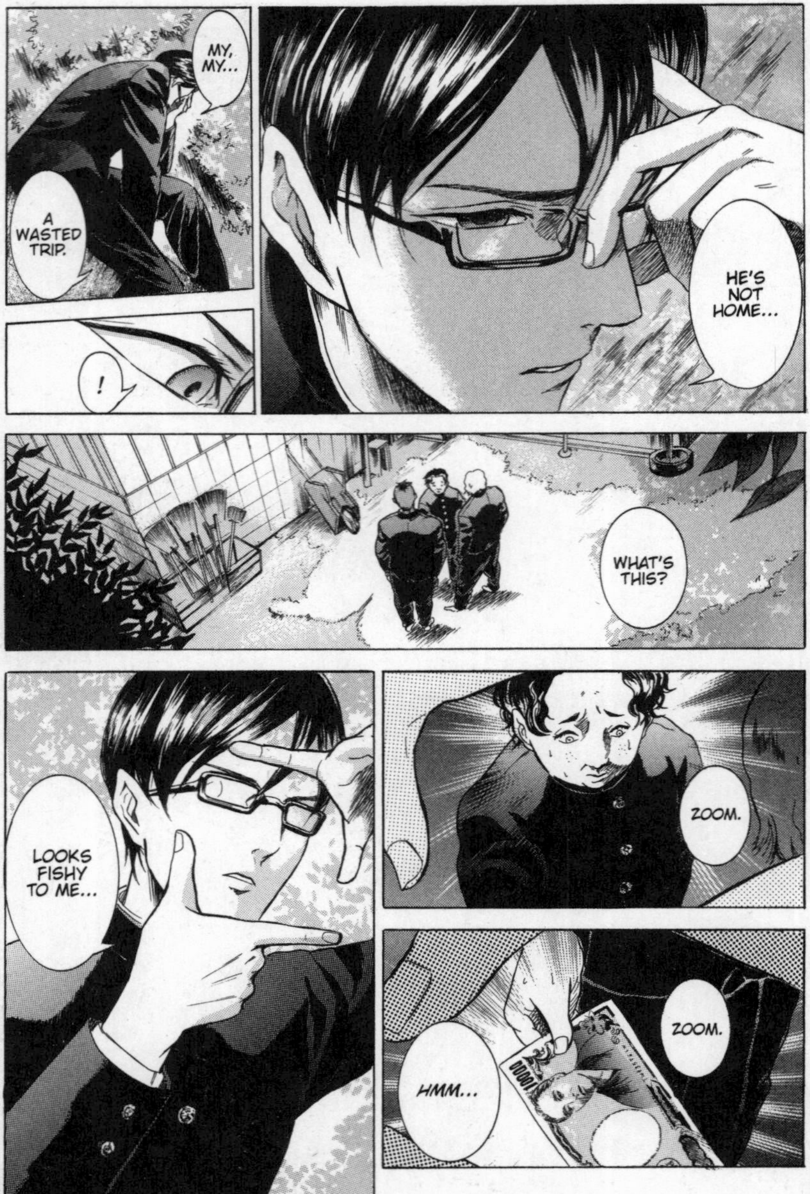
HE'S NOT HOME...
MY, MY...
A WASTED TRIP.
!
WHAT'S THIS?
ZOOM.
ZOOM.
HMM...
LOOKS FISHY TO ME...

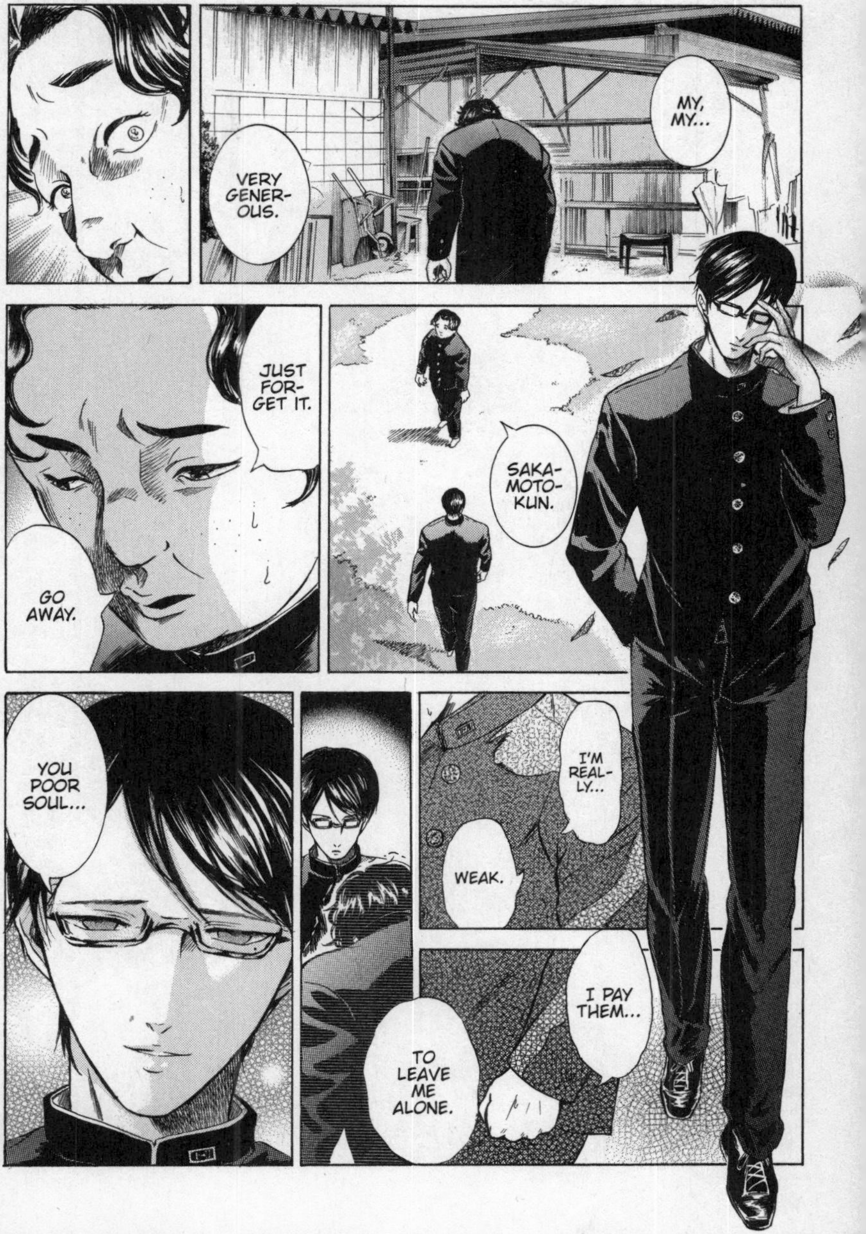
MY, MY...
VERY GENEROUS.
SAKAMOTO-KUN.
JUST FORGET IT.
GO AWAY.
I'M REALLY...
WEAK.
I PAY THEM...
TO LEAVE ME ALONE.
YOU POOR SOUL...

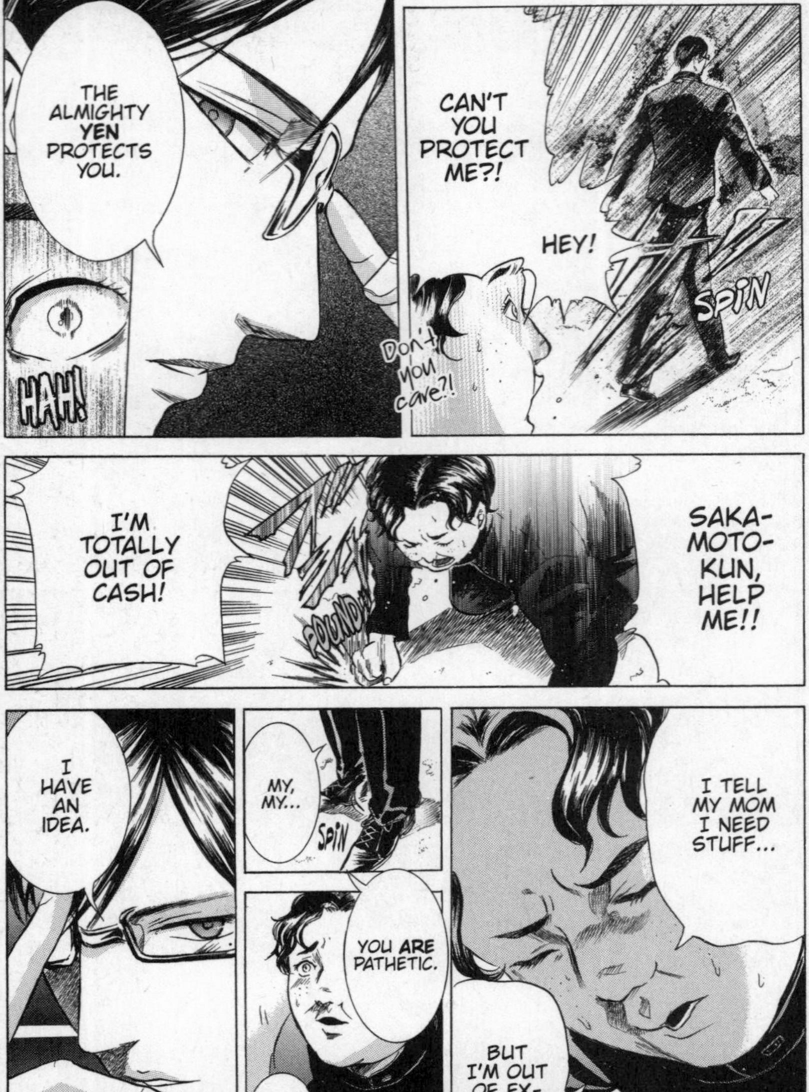
CAN'T YOU PROTECT ME?!
HEY!
SPIN
Don't you care?!
THE ALMIGHTY **YEN** PROTECTS YOU.
HAH!
SAKA-MOTO-KUN, HELP ME!!
POUND
I'M TOTALLY OUT OF CASH!
I TELL MY MOM I NEED STUFF...
BUT I'M OUT OF EX-CUSES!
MY, MY...
SPIN
YOU **ARE** PATHETIC.
SO?
I HAVE AN IDEA.

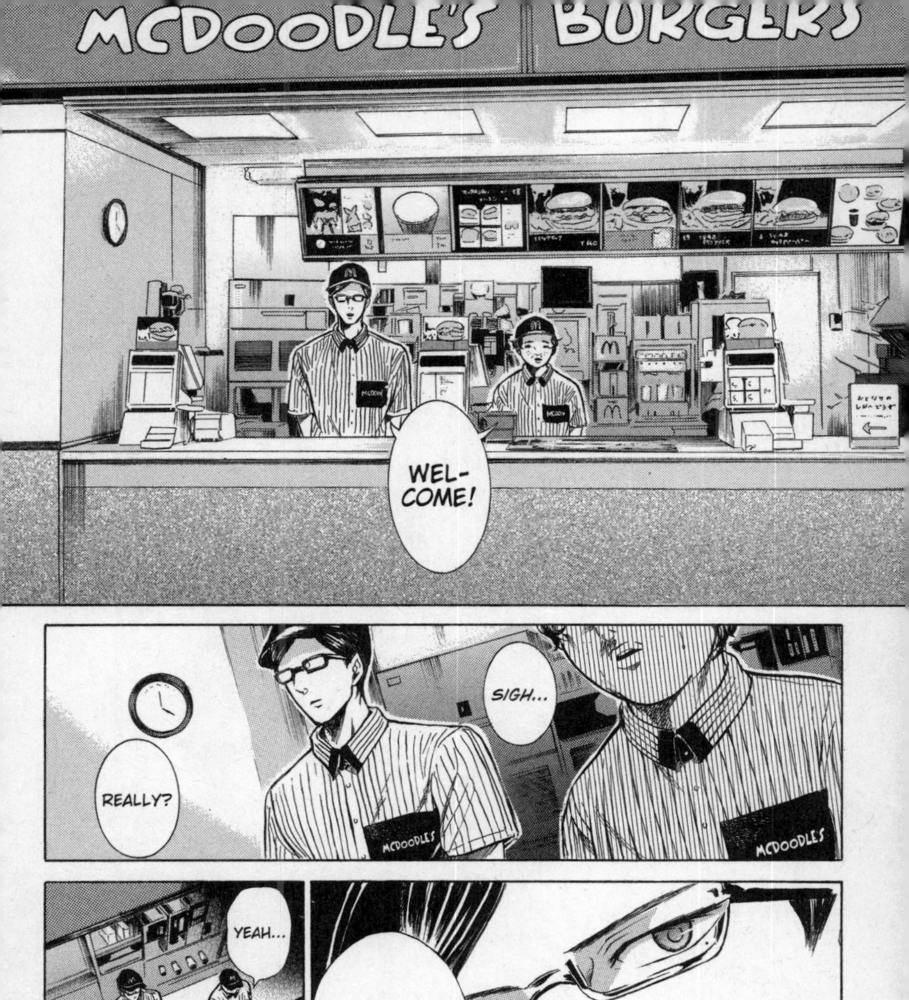
MCDOODLE'S BURGERS
WEL-COME!
SIGH...
MCDOODLE'S
MCDOODLE'S
REALLY?
YOU NEED MONEY, RIGHT?
YEAH...
I GUESS SO...

※KITCHEN.

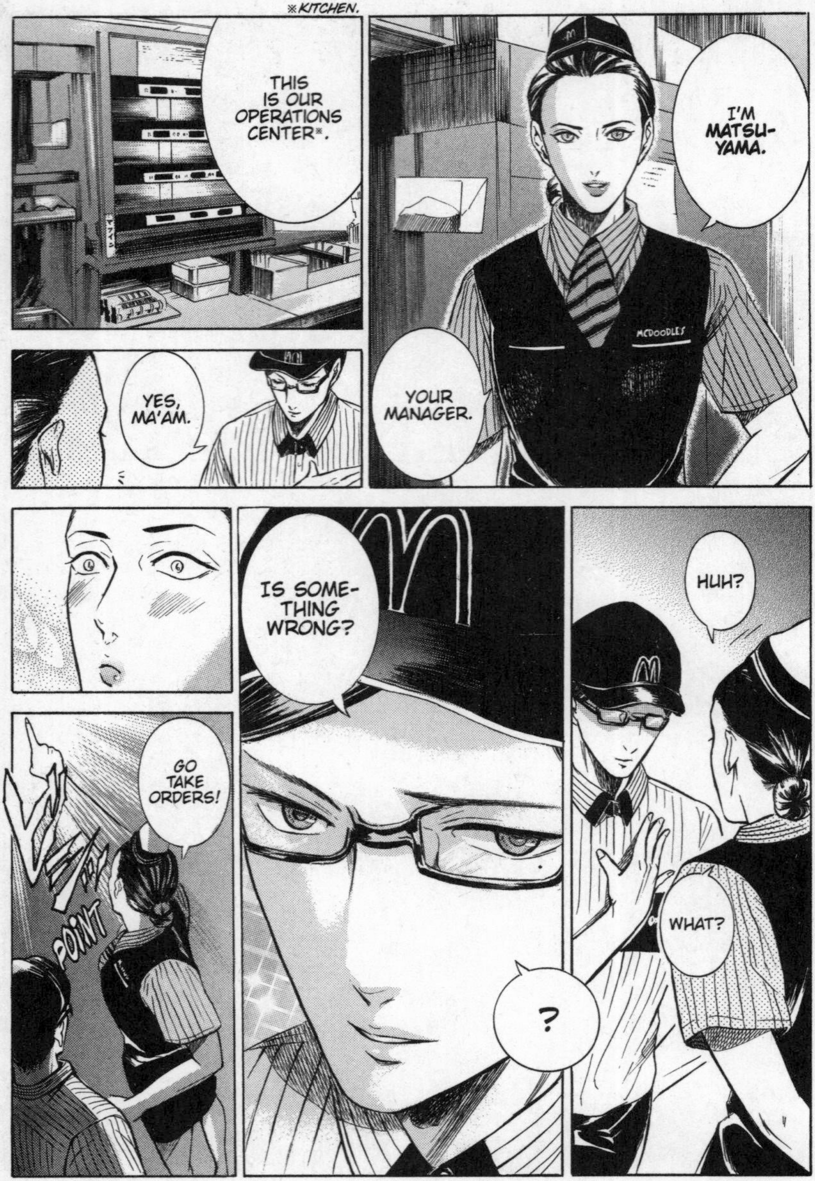
I'M MATSU-YAMA.
YOUR MANAGER.
THIS IS OUR OPERATIONS CENTER※.
YES, MA'AM.
HUH?
WHAT?
IS SOME-THING WRONG?
?
GO TAKE ORDERS!
POINT

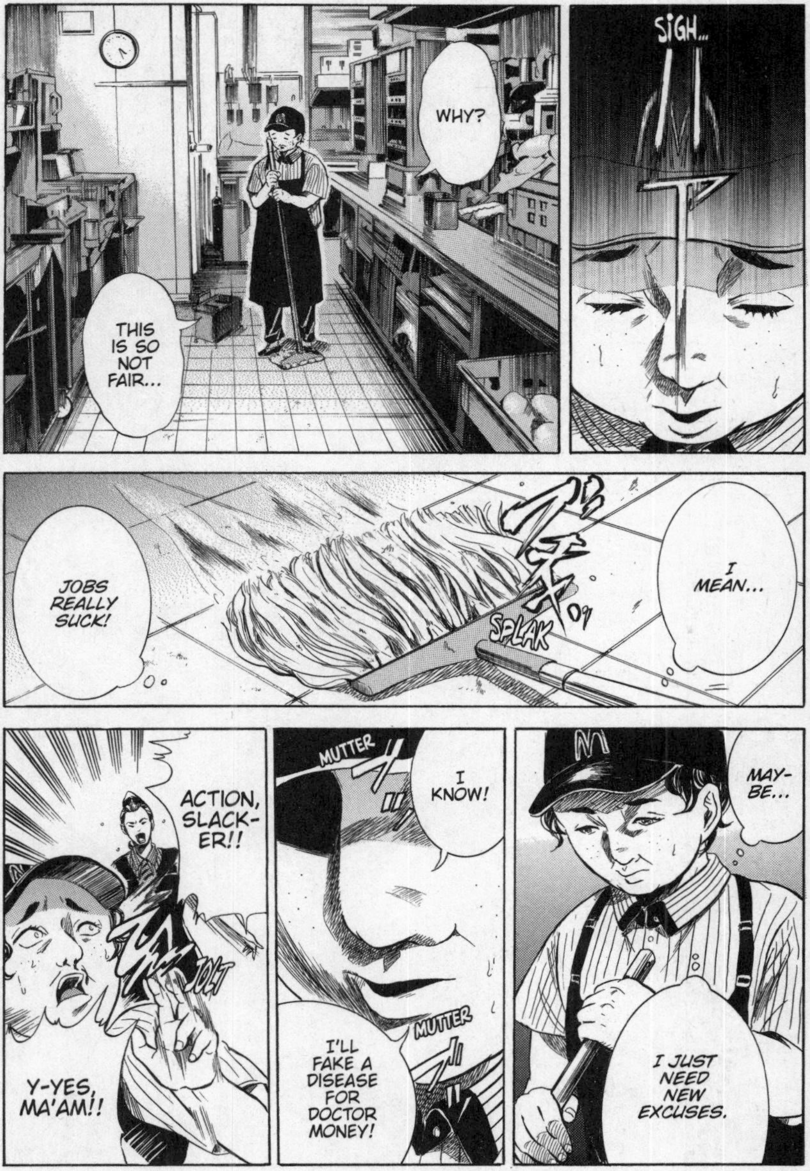
SIGH...
WHY?
THIS IS SO NOT FAIR...
I MEAN...
SPLAK
JOBS REALLY SUCK!
MAY-BE...
I JUST NEED NEW EXCUSES.
MUTTER
I KNOW!
MUTTER
I'LL FAKE A DISEASE FOR DOCTOR MONEY!
ACTION, SLACK-ER!!
JOLT
Y-YES, MA'AM!!

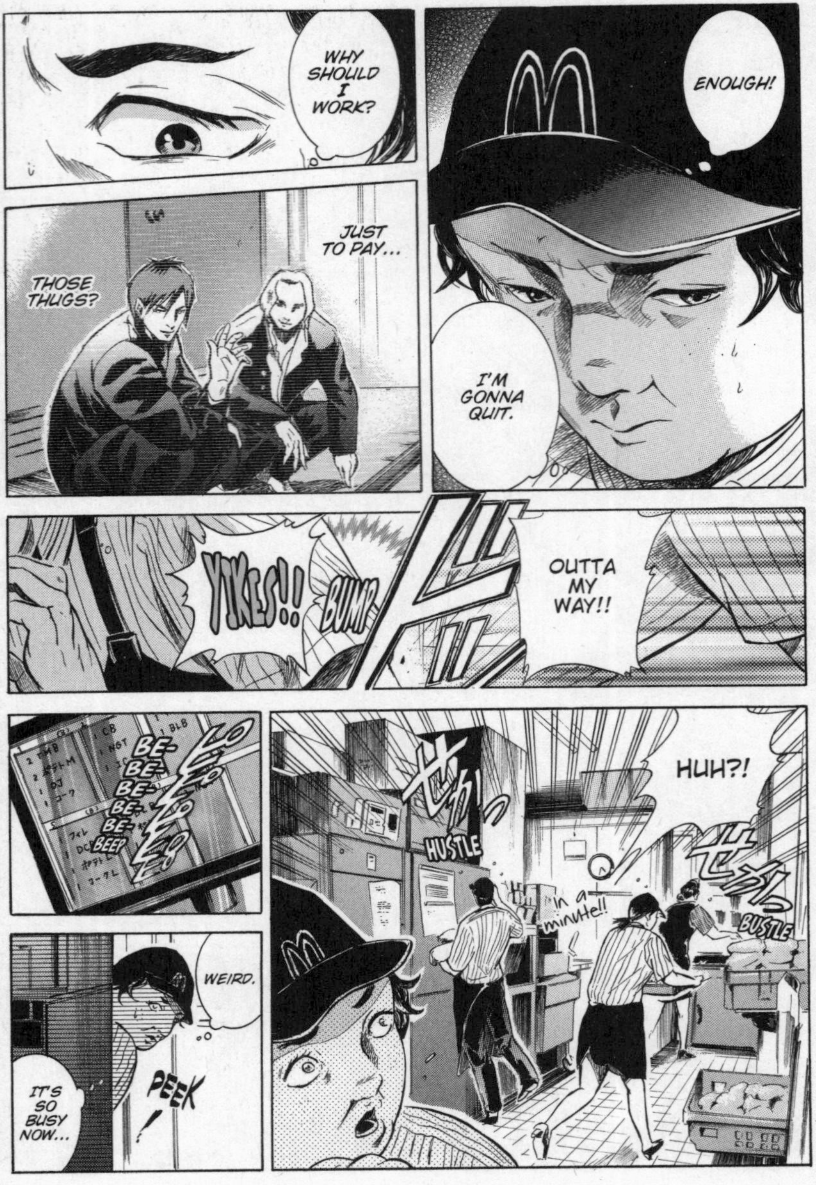

ENOUGH!
I'M GONNA QUIT.
WHY SHOULD I WORK?
JUST TO PAY...
THOSE THUGS?
OUTTA MY WAY!!
BUMP
YIKES!!
HUH?!
BUSTLE
in a minute!!
HUSTLE
BE-BE-BE-BE-BE-BEEP
WEIRD.
PEEK
IT'S SO BUSY NOW...

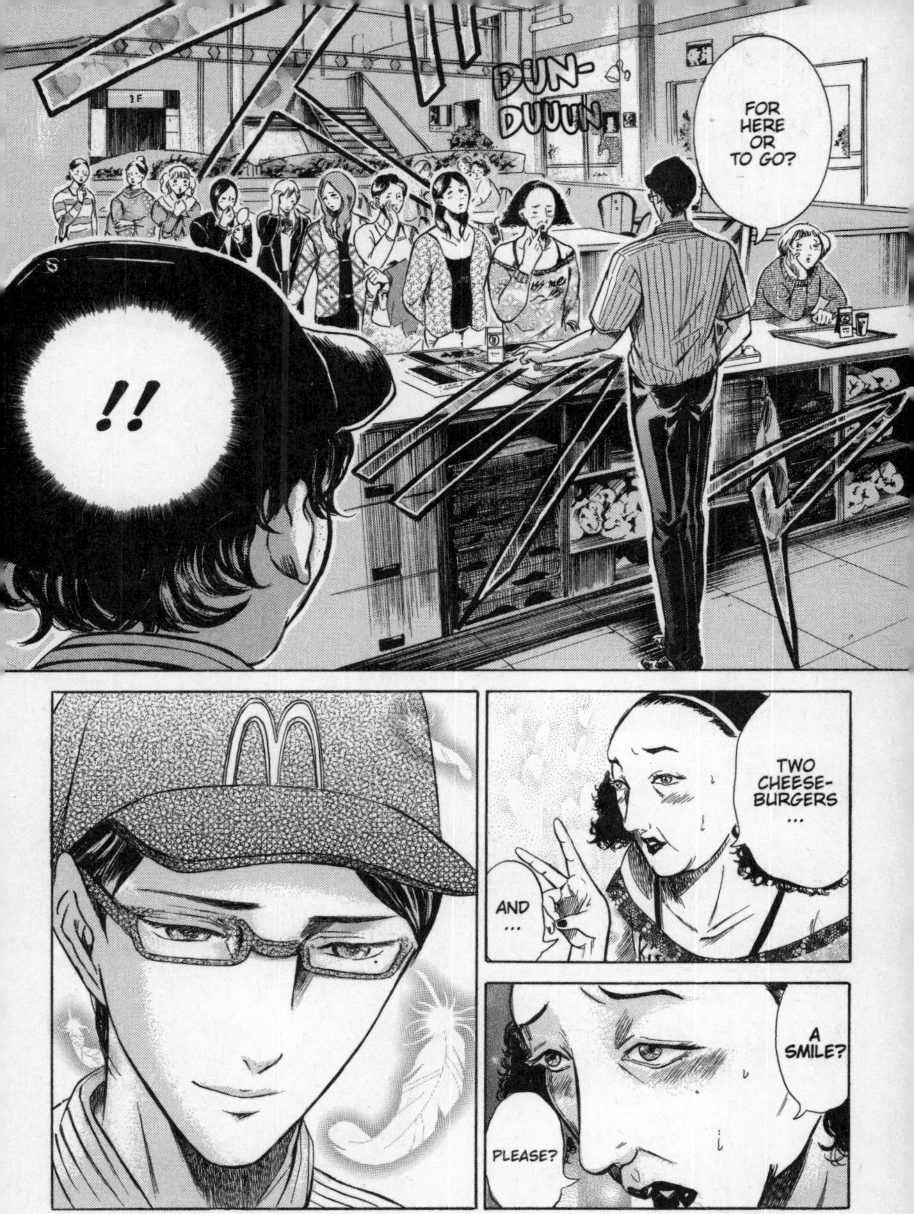
FOR HERE OR TO GO?
DUN-DUUUN
!!
TWO CHEESE-BURGERS ...
AND ...
A SMILE?
PLEASE?

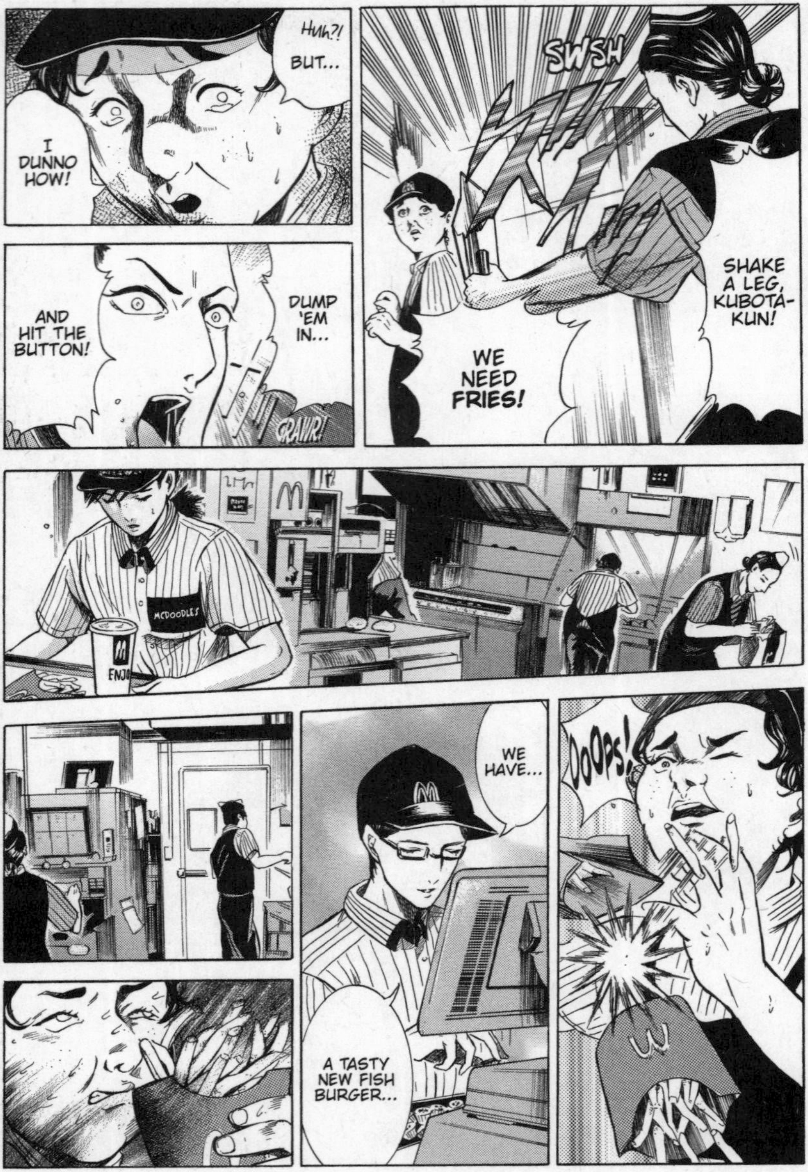
SWSH
SHAKE A LEG, KUBOTA-KUN!
WE NEED FRIES!
Huh?!
BUT...
I DUNNO HOW!
DUMP 'EM IN...
AND HIT THE BUTTON!
GRAWR!
MCDOODLES
OOOPS!
WE HAVE...
A TASTY NEW FISH BURGER...

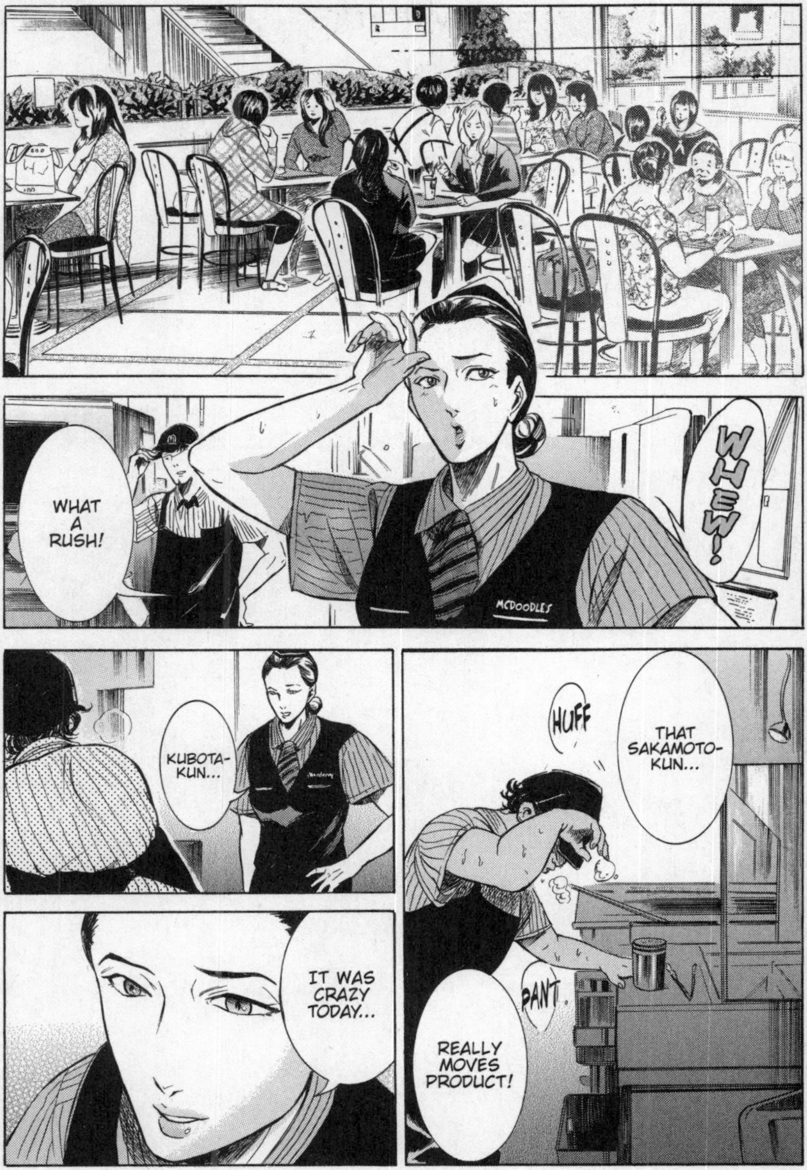
WHEW!
MCDOODLES
WHAT A RUSH!
HUFF
THAT SAKAMOTO-KUN...
PANT
REALLY MOVES PRODUCT!
KUBOTA-KUN...
IT WAS CRAZY TODAY...

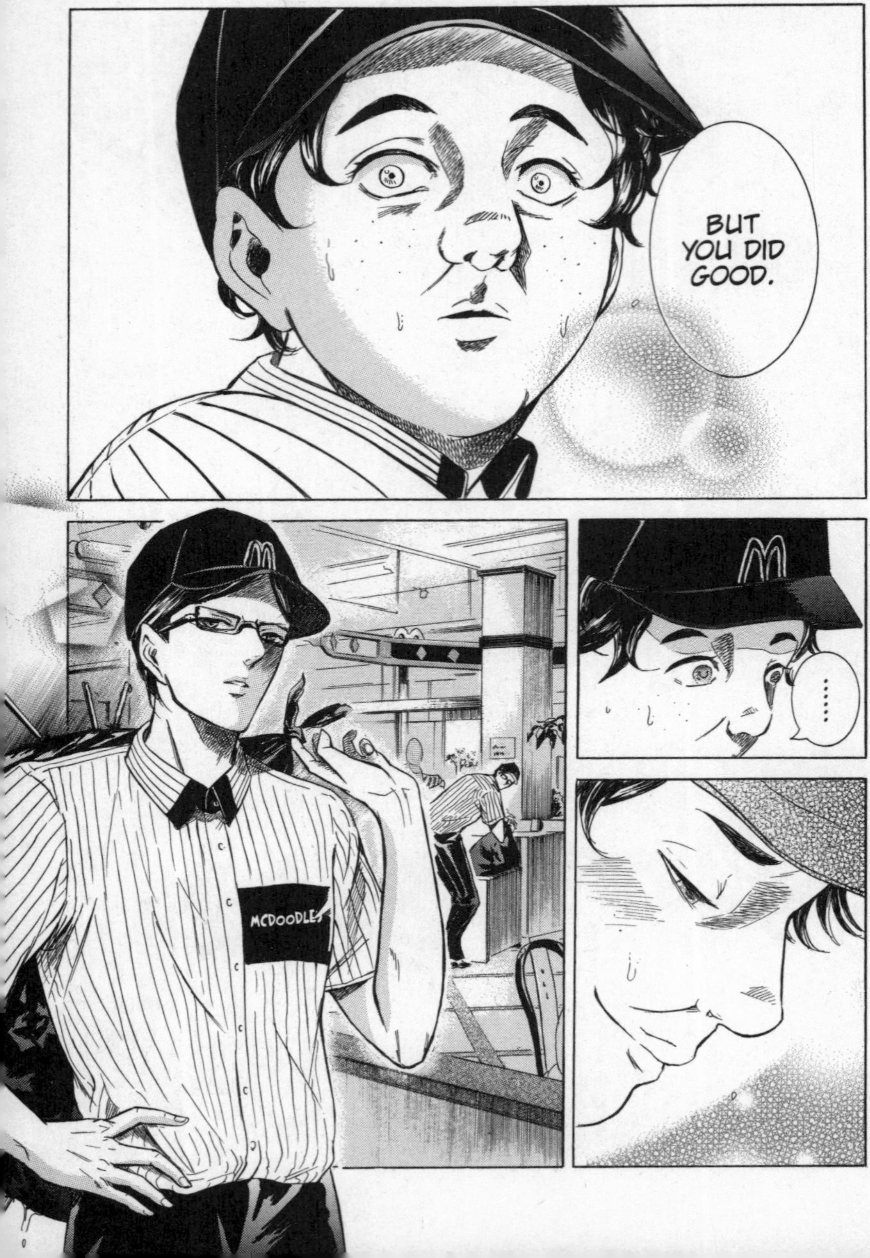
BUT YOU DID GOOD.
......
MCDOODLES

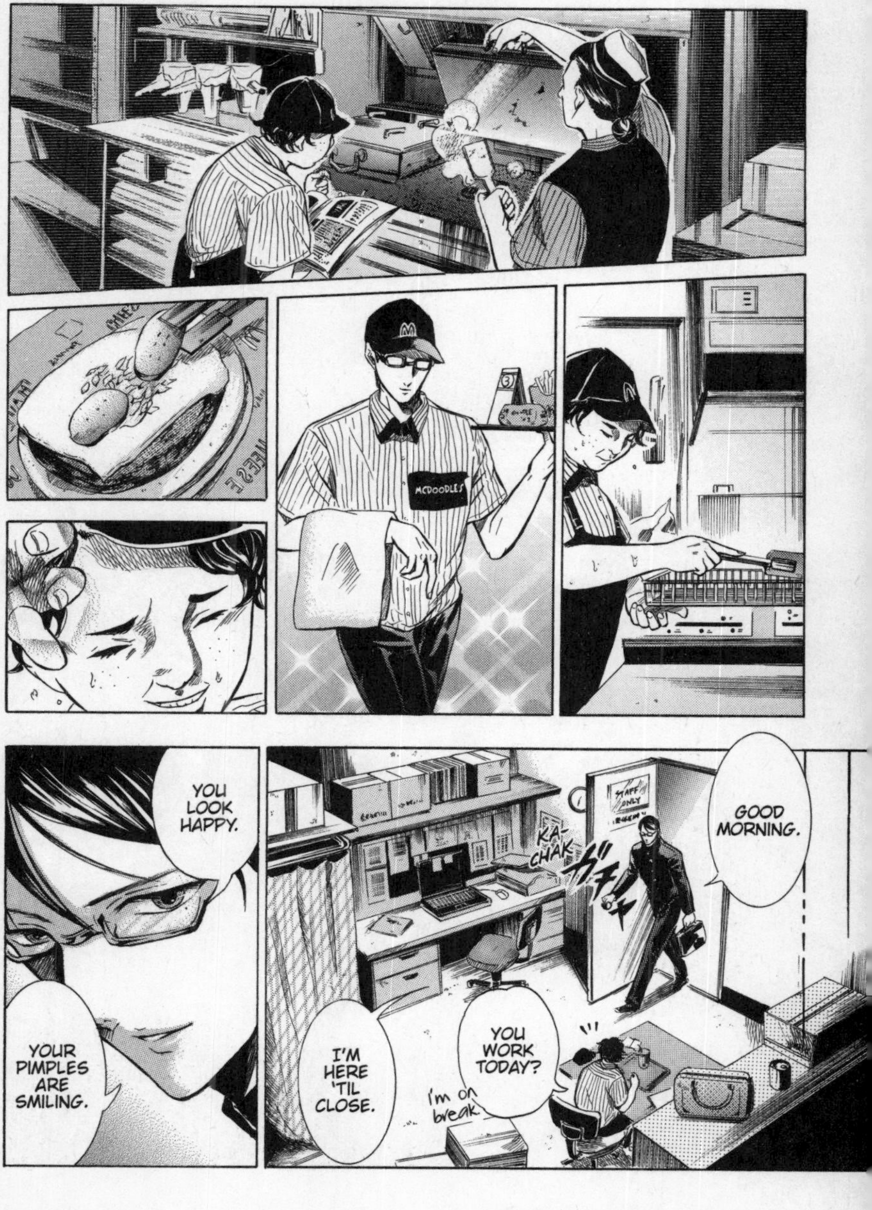
MCDOODLES
STAFF ONLY
GOOD MORNING.
KA-CHAK
YOU WORK TODAY?
I'm on break.
I'M HERE 'TIL CLOSE.
YOU LOOK HAPPY.
YOUR PIMPLES ARE SMILING.

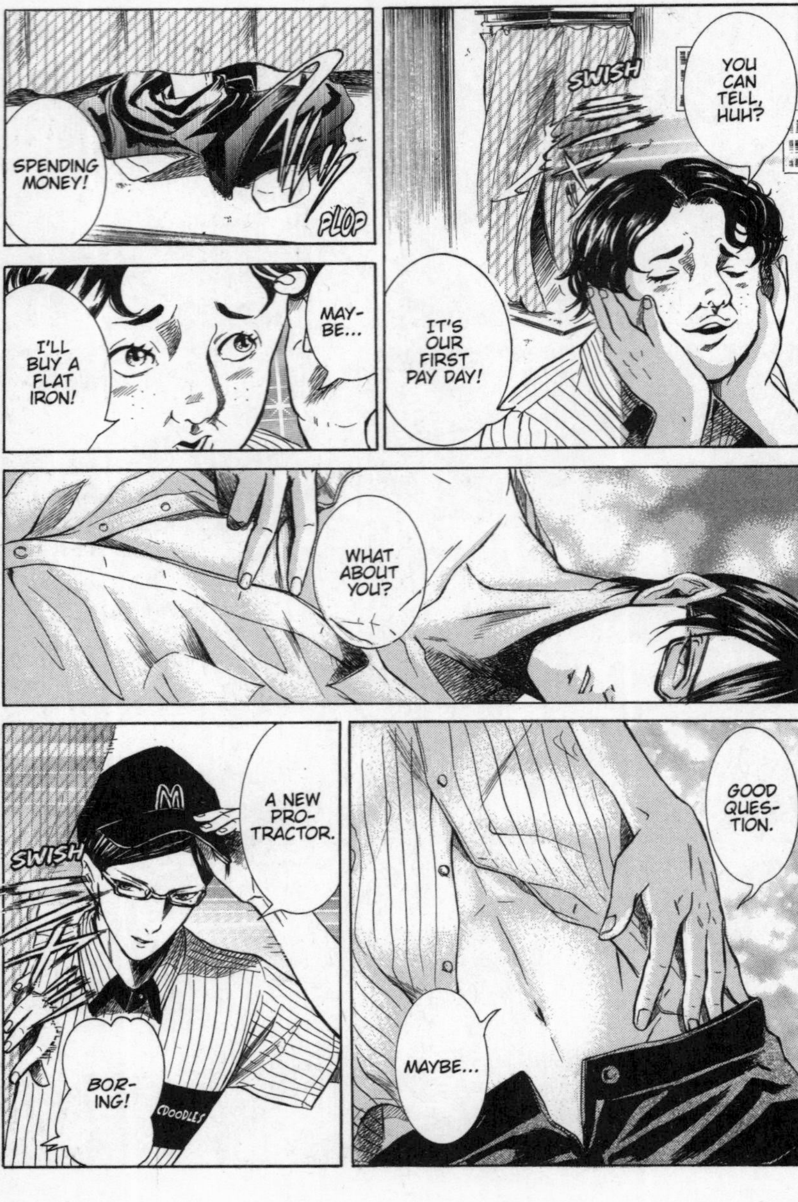
SWISH
YOU CAN TELL, HUH?
IT'S OUR FIRST PAY DAY!
SPENDING MONEY!
PLOP
MAY-BE...
I'LL BUY A FLAT IRON!
WHAT ABOUT YOU?
GOOD QUES-TION.
MAYBE...
A NEW PRO-TRACTOR.
SWISH
BOR-ING!
DOODLES

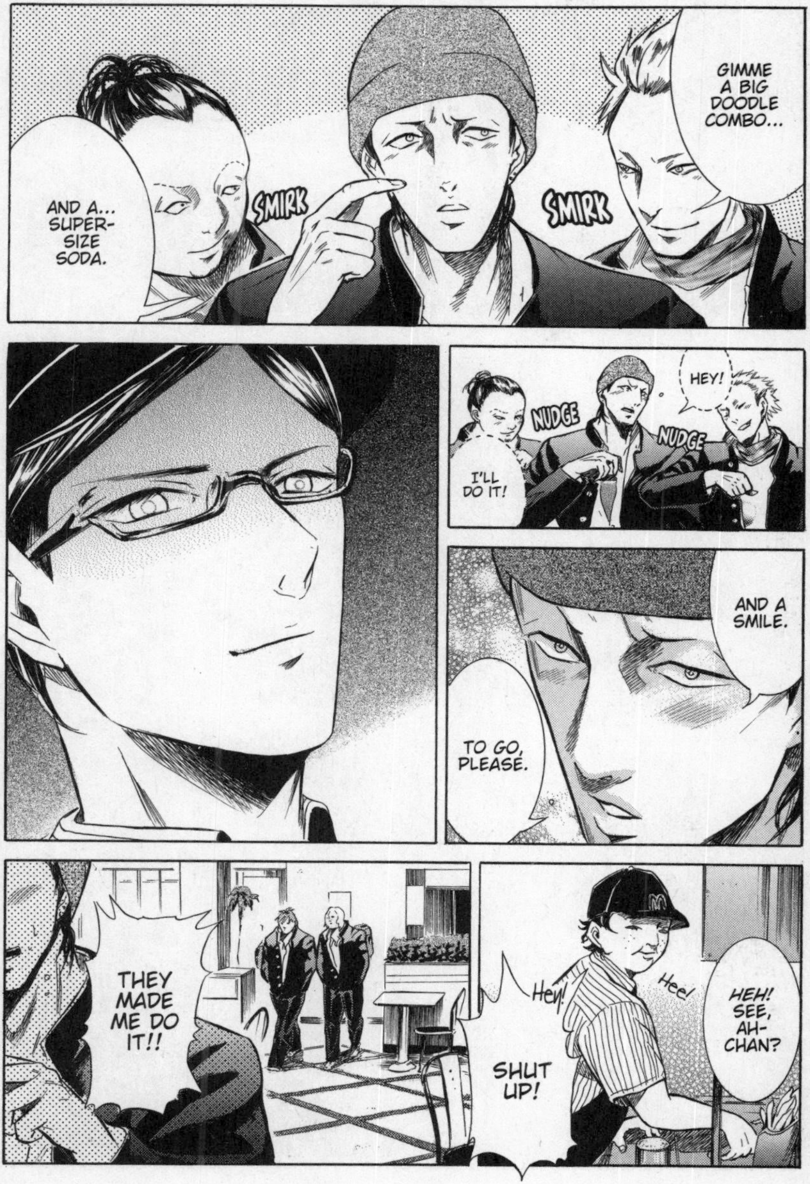
GIMME A BIG DOODLE COMBO...
SMIRK
SMIRK
AND A... SUPER-SIZE SODA.
HEY!
NUDGE
NUDGE
I'LL DO IT!
AND A SMILE.
TO GO, PLEASE.
HEH! SEE, AH-CHAN?
Hee!
Heh!
SHUT UP!
THEY MADE ME DO IT!!

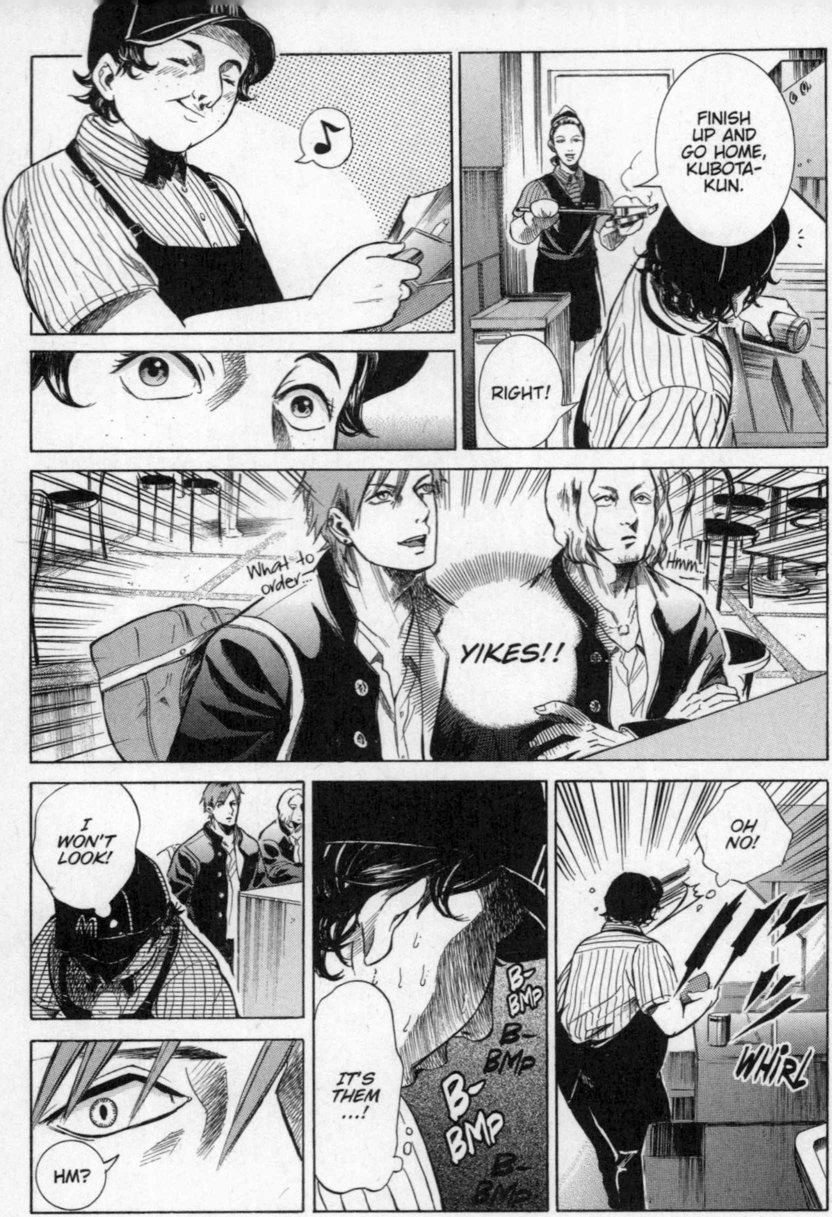
FINISH UP AND GO HOME, KUBOTA-KUN.
RIGHT!
♪
Hmm...
What to order...
YIKES!!
OH NO!
WHIRL
B-BMP
B-BMP
B-BMP
B-BMP
IT'S THEM ...!
I WON'T LOOK!
HM?

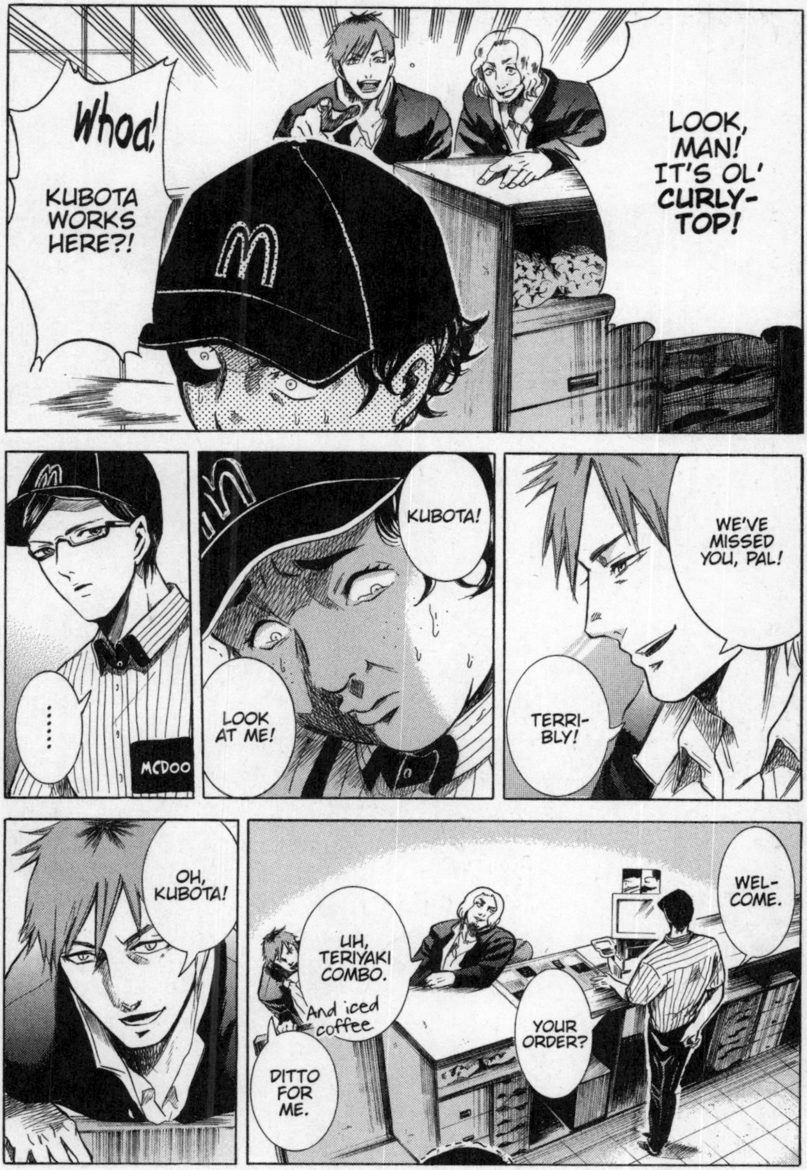
LOOK, MAN! IT'S OL' CURLY-TOP!
Whoa!
KUBOTA WORKS HERE?!
WE'VE MISSED YOU, PAL!
TERRI-BLY!
KUBOTA!
LOOK AT ME!
......
MCDOO
WEL-COME.
YOUR ORDER?
UH, TERIYAKI COMBO.
And iced coffee
DITTO FOR ME.
OH, KUBOTA!

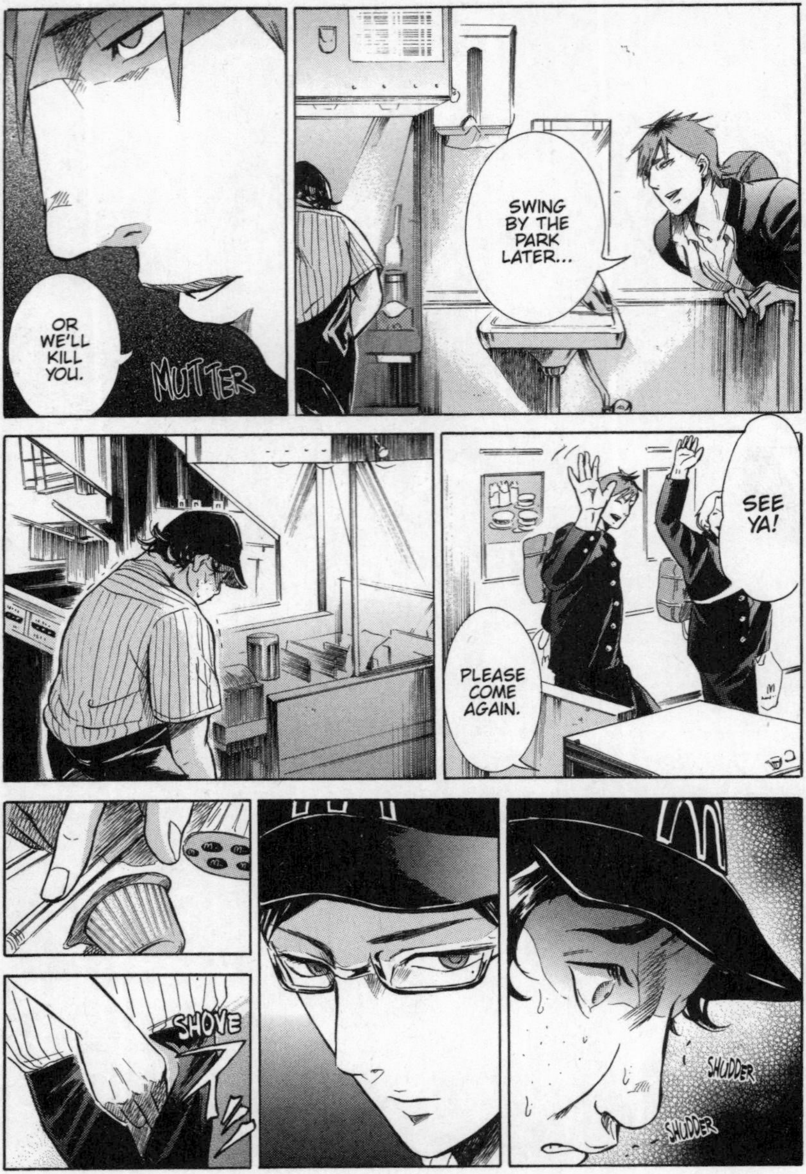
SWING BY THE PARK LATER...
OR WE'LL KILL YOU.
MUTTER
SEE YA!
PLEASE COME AGAIN.
SHUDDER
SHUDDER
SHOVE

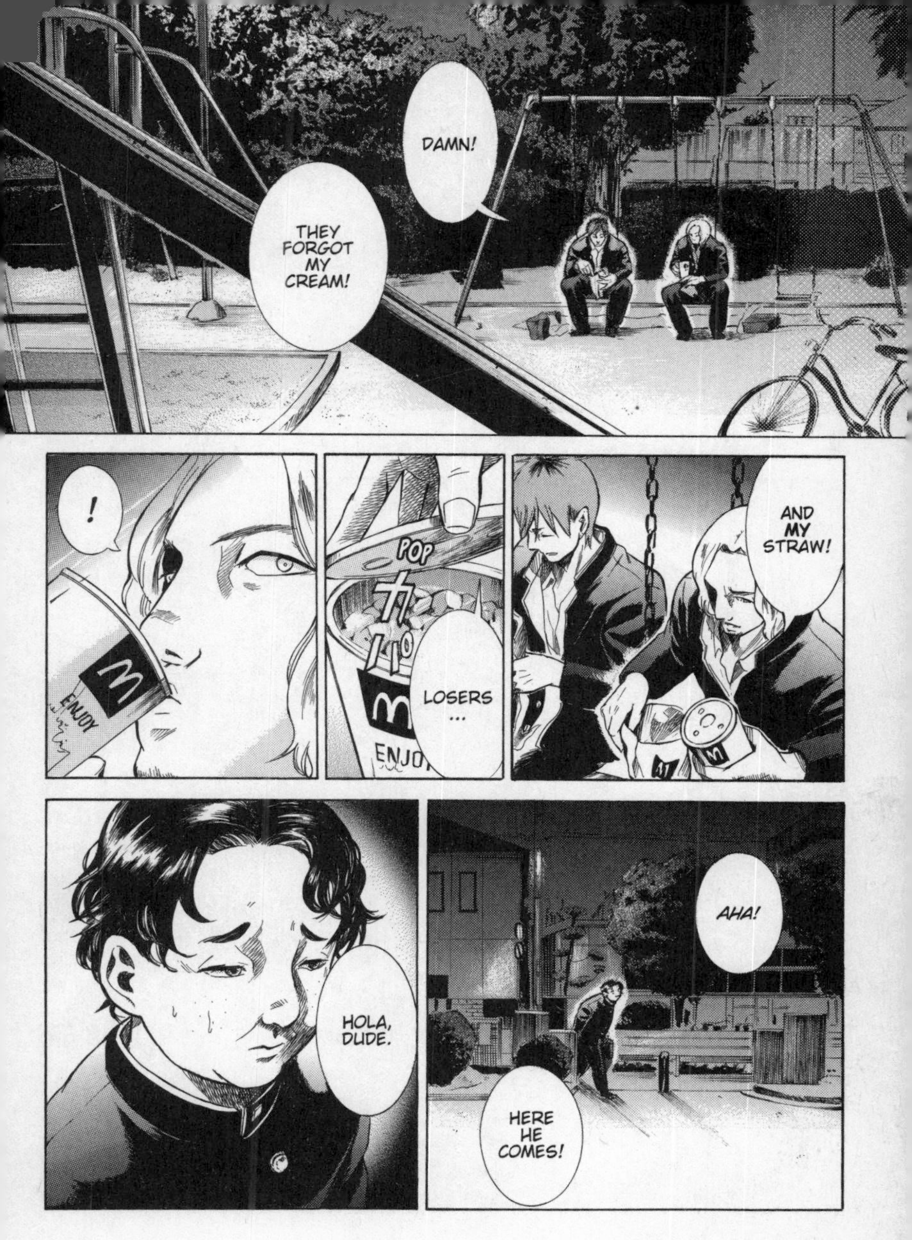
DAMN!
THEY FORGOT MY CREAM!
AND MY STRAW!
POP
カパ
LOSERS ...
ENJOY
!
ENJOY
AHA!
HERE HE COMES!
HOLA, DUDE.

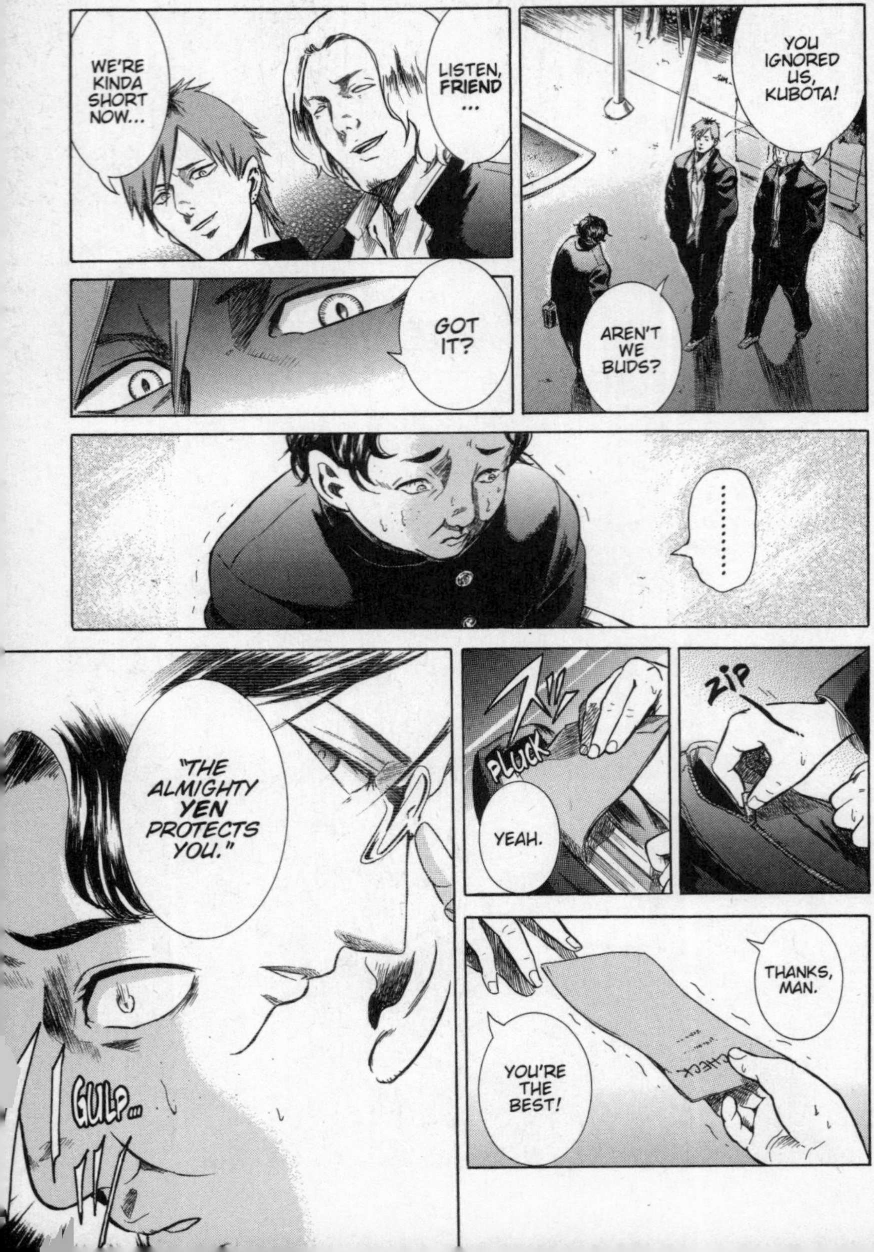
YOU IGNORED US, KUBOTA!
AREN'T WE BUDS?
LISTEN, FRIEND ...
WE'RE KINDA SHORT NOW...
GOT IT?
......
ZIP
PLUCK
YEAH.
THANKS, MAN.
YOU'RE THE BEST!
"THE ALMIGHTY YEN PROTECTS YOU."
GULP...

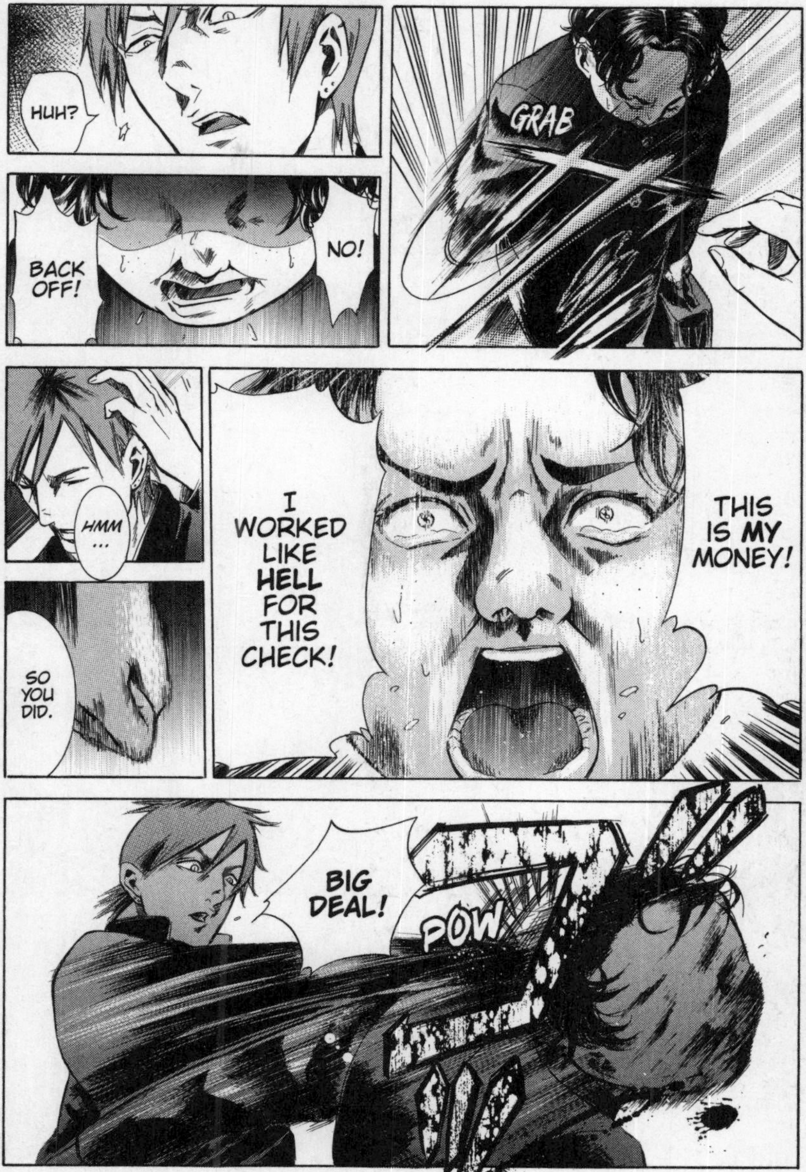
GRAB
HUH?
NO!
BACK OFF!
THIS IS MY MONEY!
I WORKED LIKE HELL FOR THIS CHECK!
HMM...
SO YOU DID.
BIG DEAL!
POW

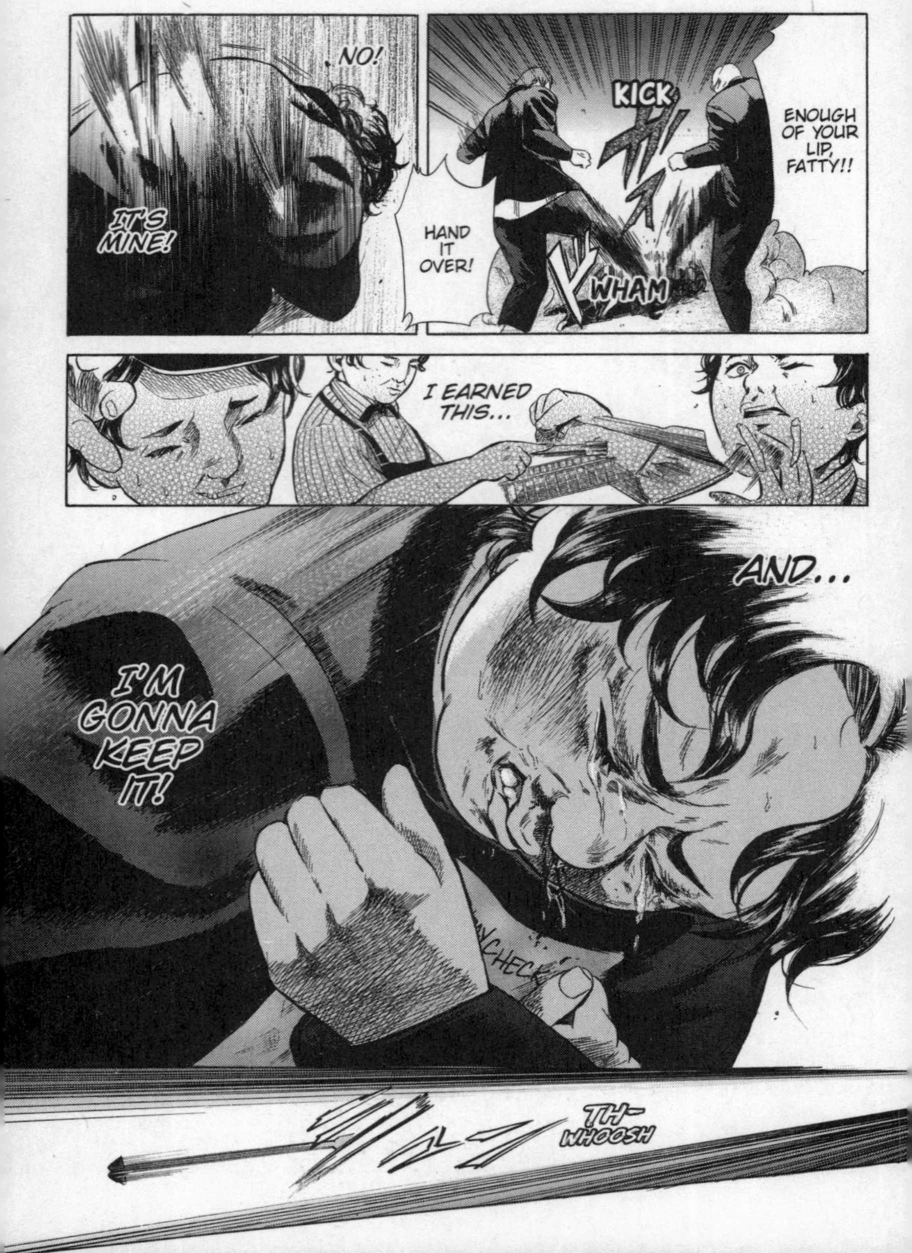
ENOUGH OF YOUR LIP, FATTY!!
KICK
WHAM
HAND IT OVER!
NO!
IT'S MINE!
I EARNED THIS...
AND...
I'M GONNA KEEP IT!
TH-WHOOSH

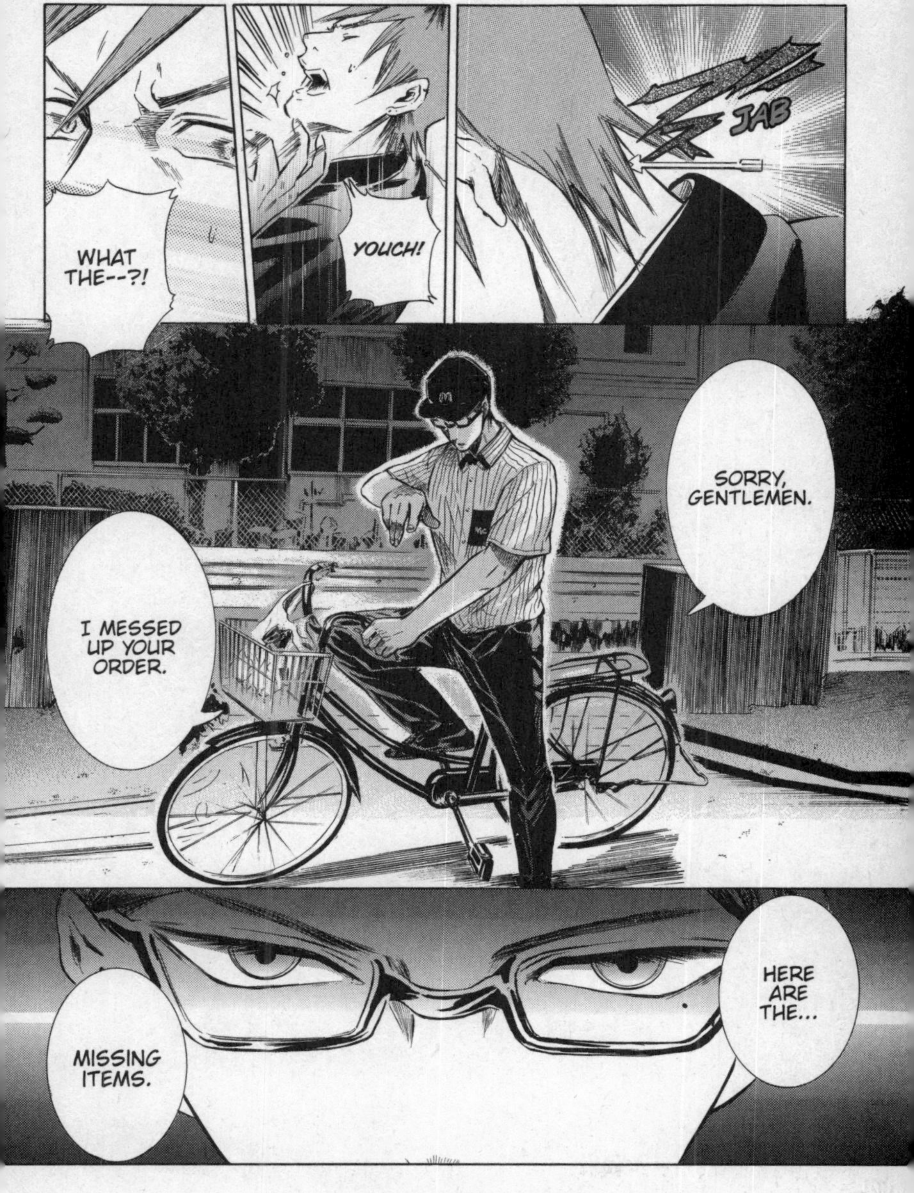
JAB
YOUCH!
WHAT THE--?!
SORRY, GENTLEMEN.
I MESSED UP YOUR ORDER.
HERE ARE THE...
MISSING ITEMS.

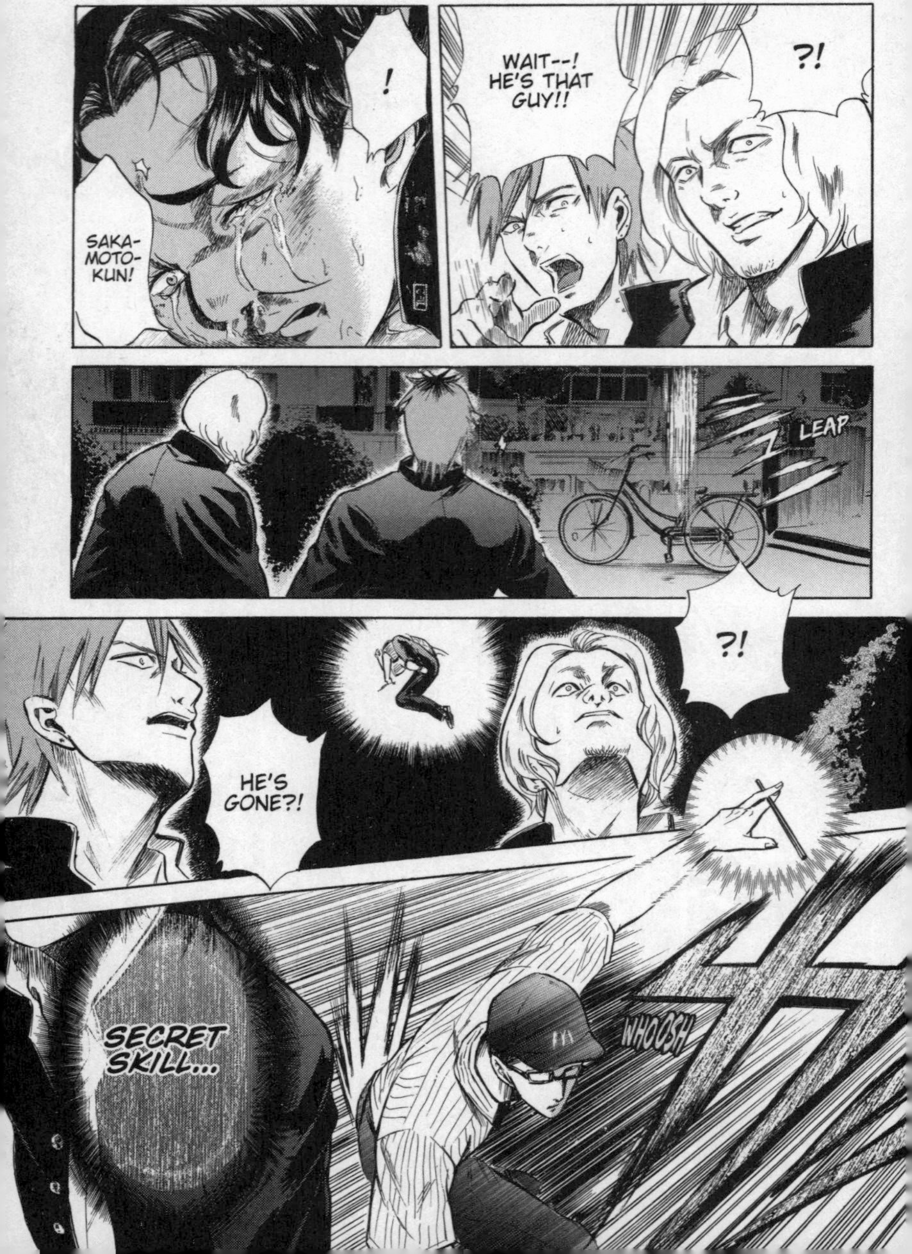
?!
WAIT--! HE'S THAT GUY!!
!
SAKA-MOTO-KUN!
LEAP
?!
HE'S GONE?!
WHOOSH
SECRET SKILL...

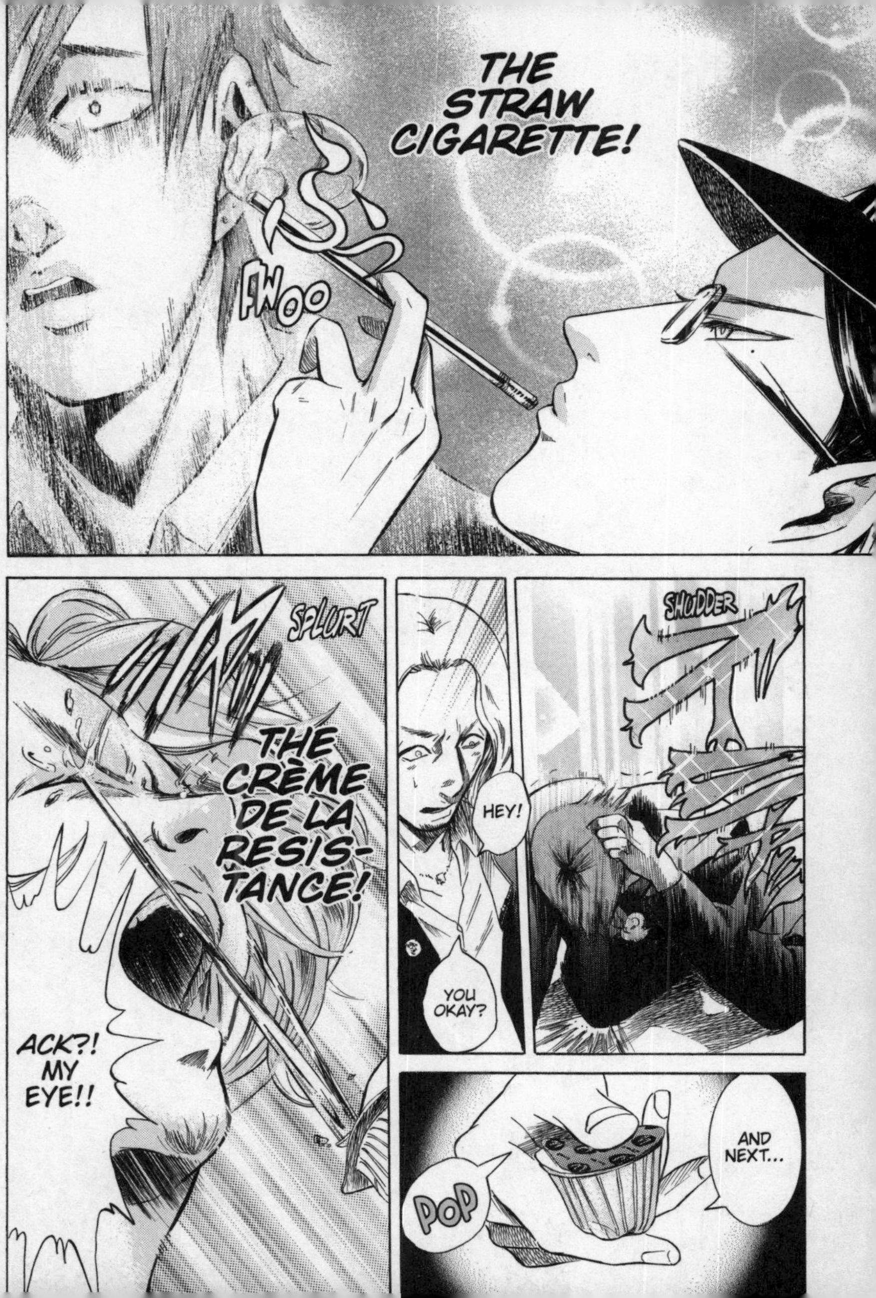
THE STRAW CIGARETTE!
FWOO
SHUDDER
HEY!
YOU OKAY?
AND NEXT...
POP
SPLURT
THE CRÈME DE LA RESIS-TANCE!
ACK?! MY EYE!!

THE REST...

IS UP TO YOU.

I'VE DONE MY PART.

WELL, KUBOTA...

ONLY YOU CAN DO.

SOME THINGS...

QUIVER.

SECRET...

SKILL...

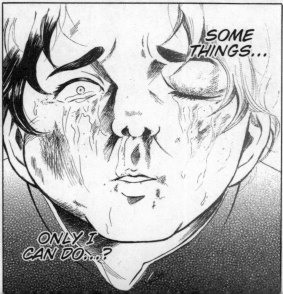

SOME THINGS...

ONLY I CAN DO....?

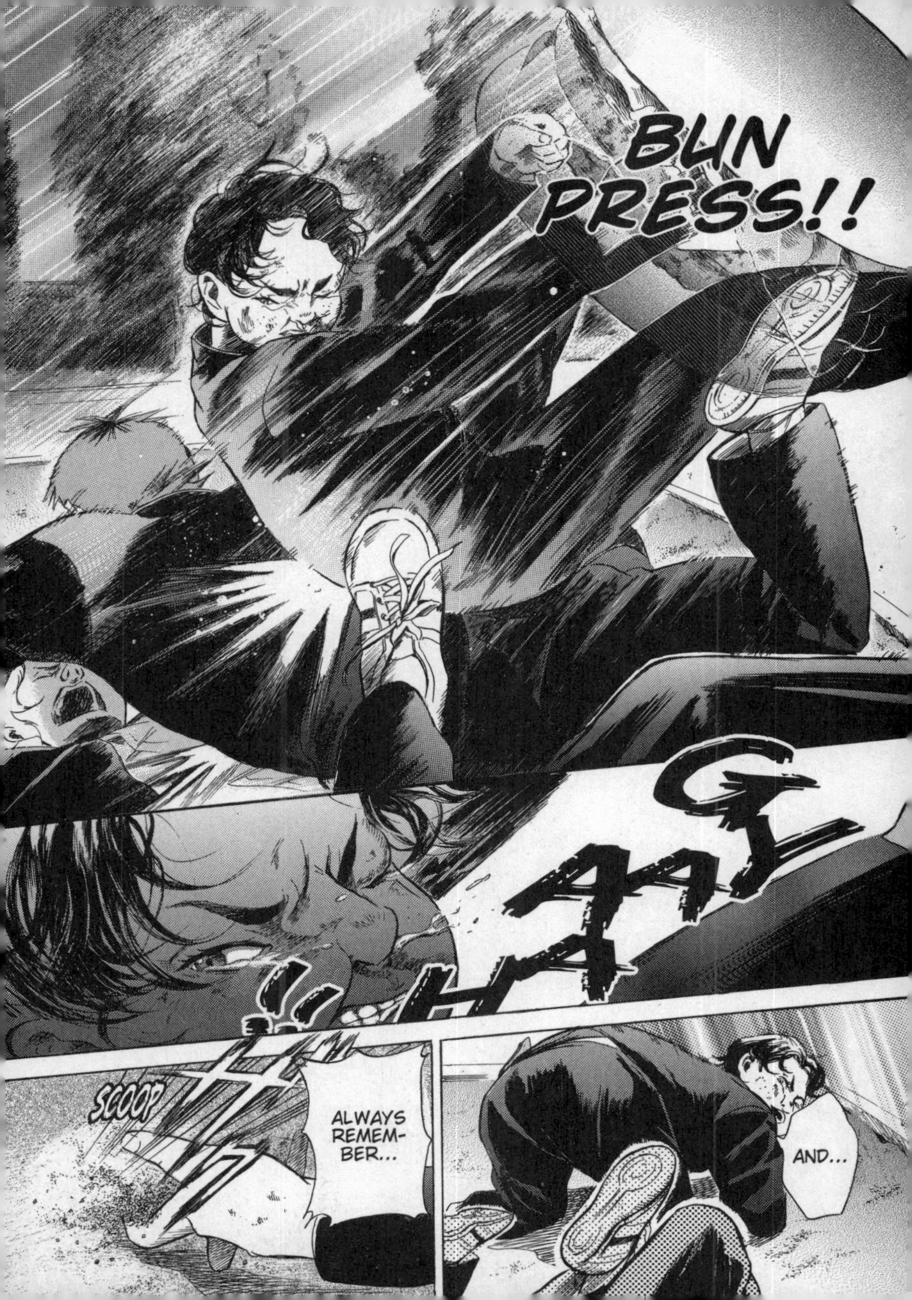
BUN PRESS!!
AND...
SCOOP
ALWAYS REMEM-BER...

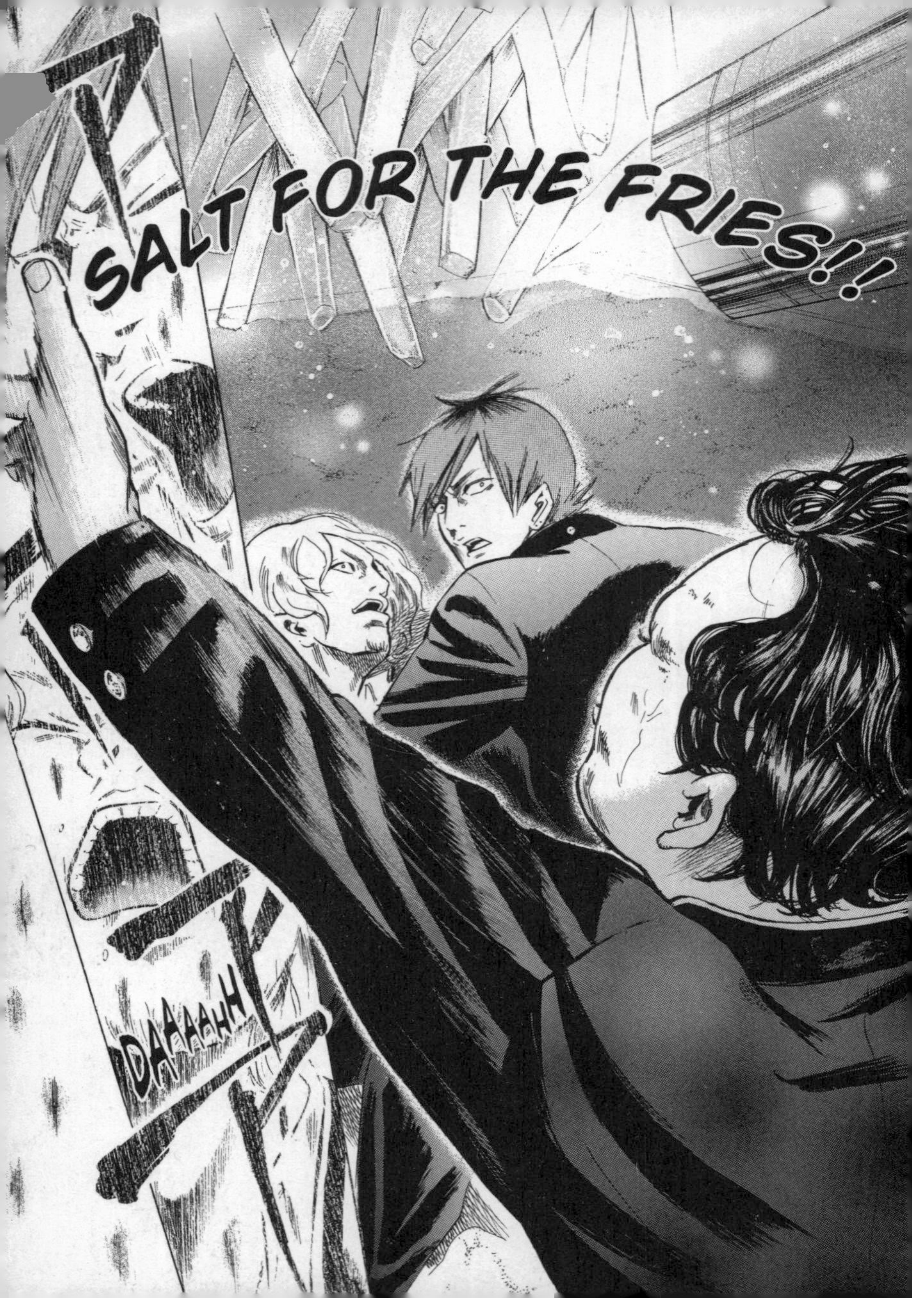
SALT FOR THE FRIES!!
DAAAAAH

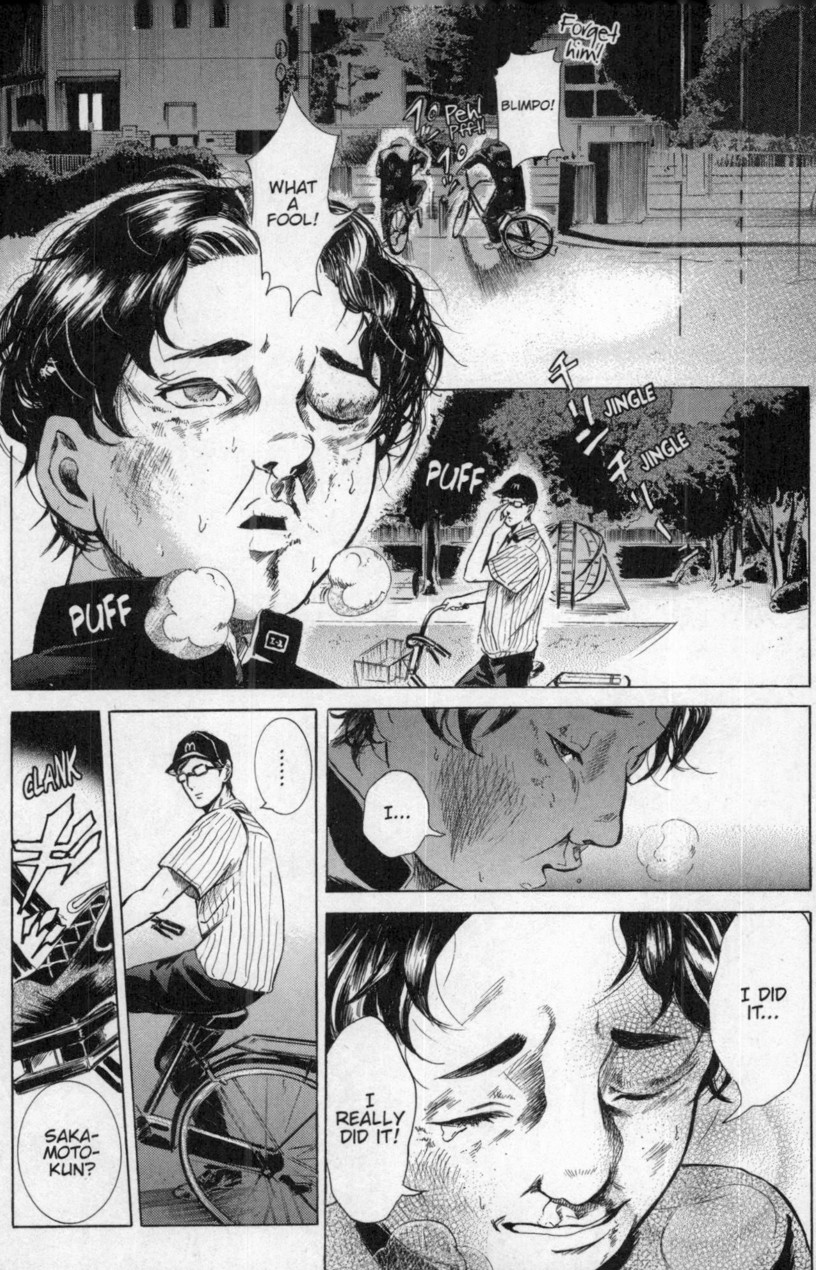
Forget him!
BLIMPO!
Peh! Pfff!
WHAT A FOOL!
JINGLE
JINGLE
PUFF
PUFF
I...
I DID IT...
I REALLY DID IT!
......
CLANK
SAKA-MOTO-KUN?

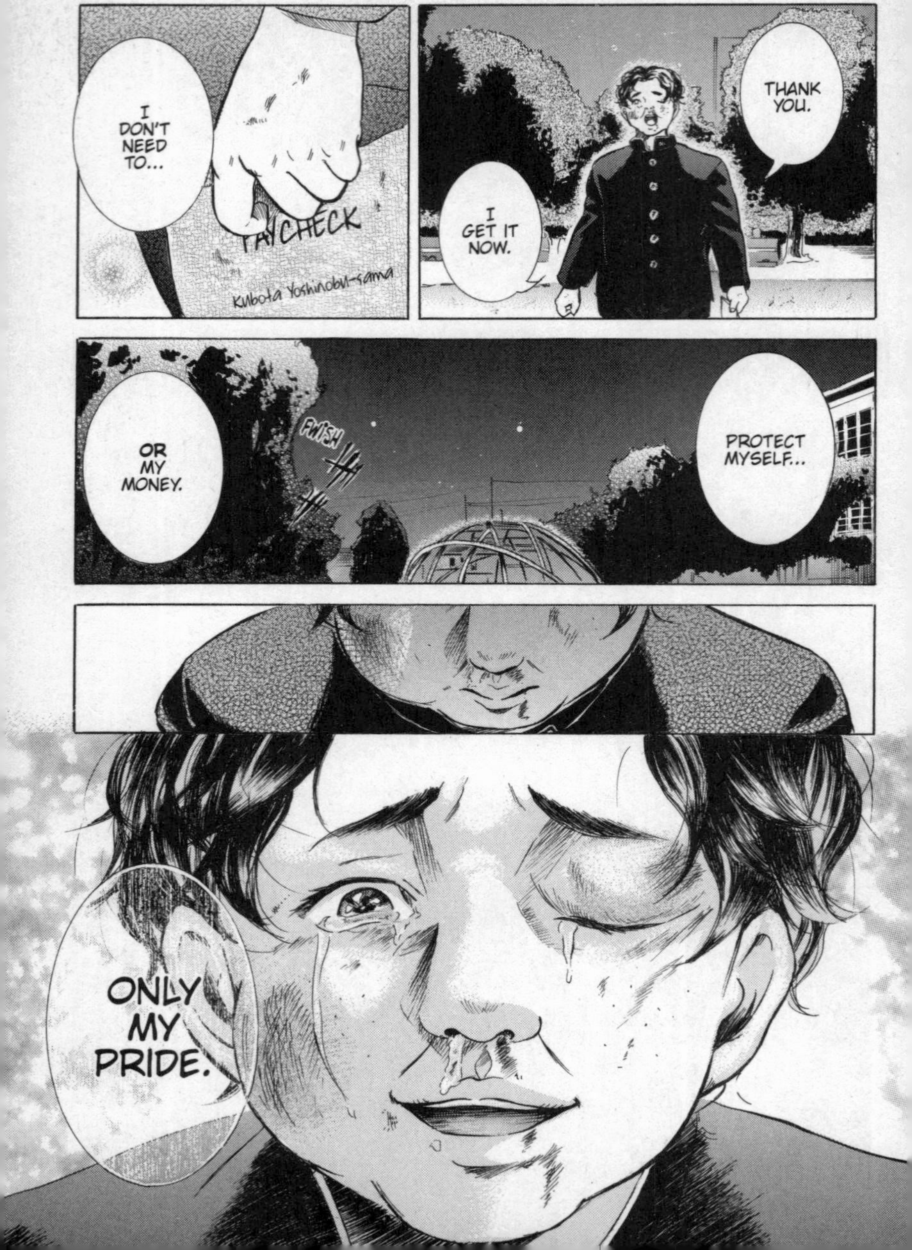
THANK YOU.
I GET IT NOW.
I DON'T NEED TO...
PAYCHECK
Kubota Yoshinobu-sama
PROTECT MYSELF...
FWISH
OR MY MONEY.
ONLY MY PRIDE.

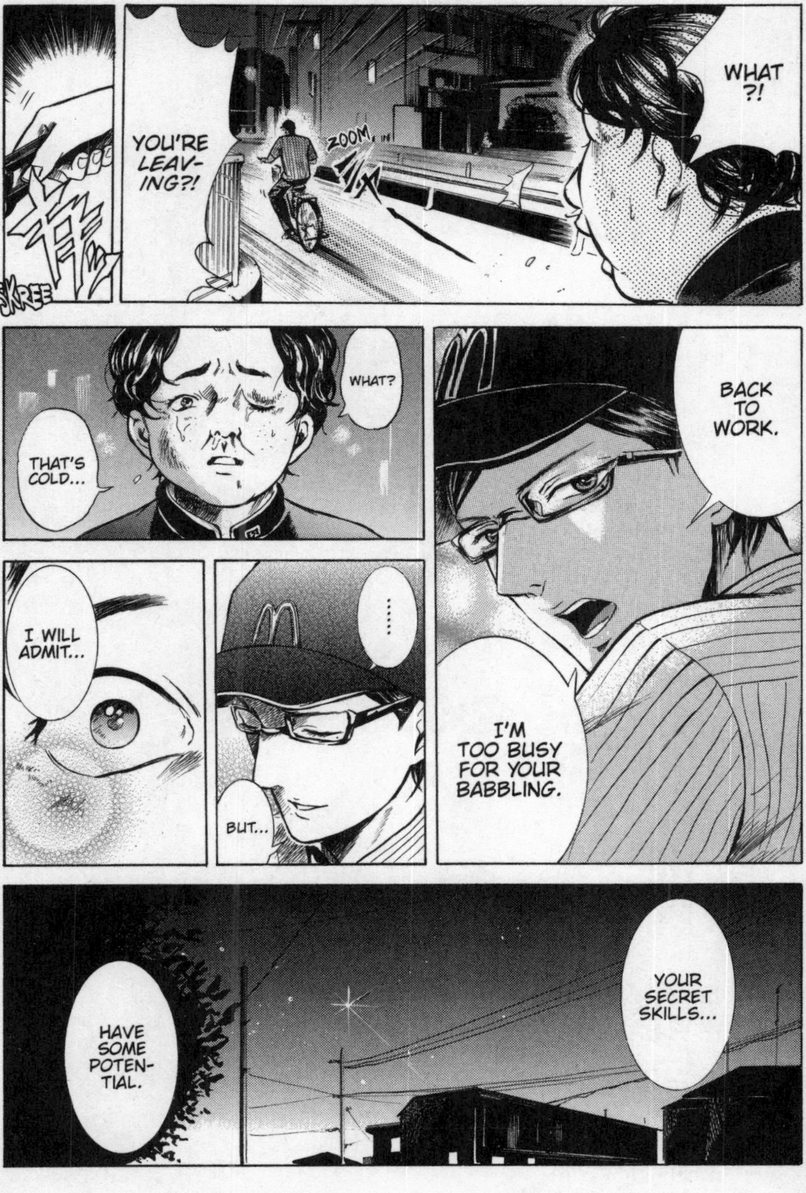
WHAT ?!
YOU'RE LEAV-ING?!
ZOOM
SKREE
BACK TO WORK.
I'M TOO BUSY FOR YOUR BABBLING.
WHAT?
THAT'S COLD...
......
BUT...
I WILL ADMIT...
YOUR SECRET SKILLS...
HAVE SOME POTEN-TIAL.

End of Chapter 3

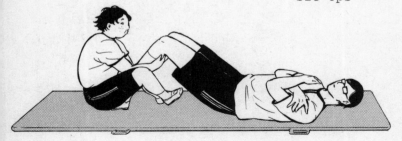

P.E. Test #3:
   Sit-Ups

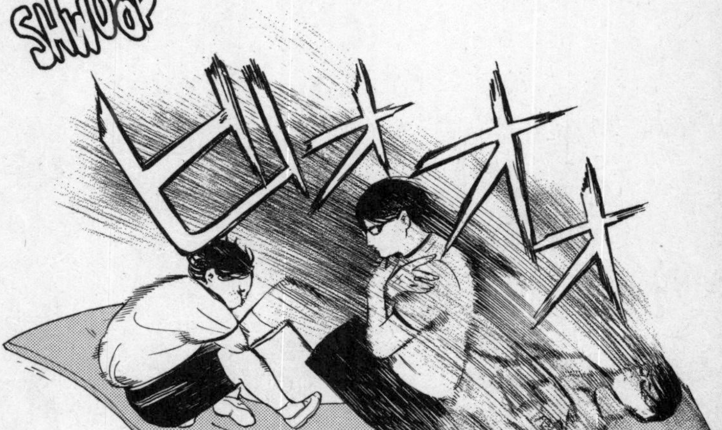
SHWOOP

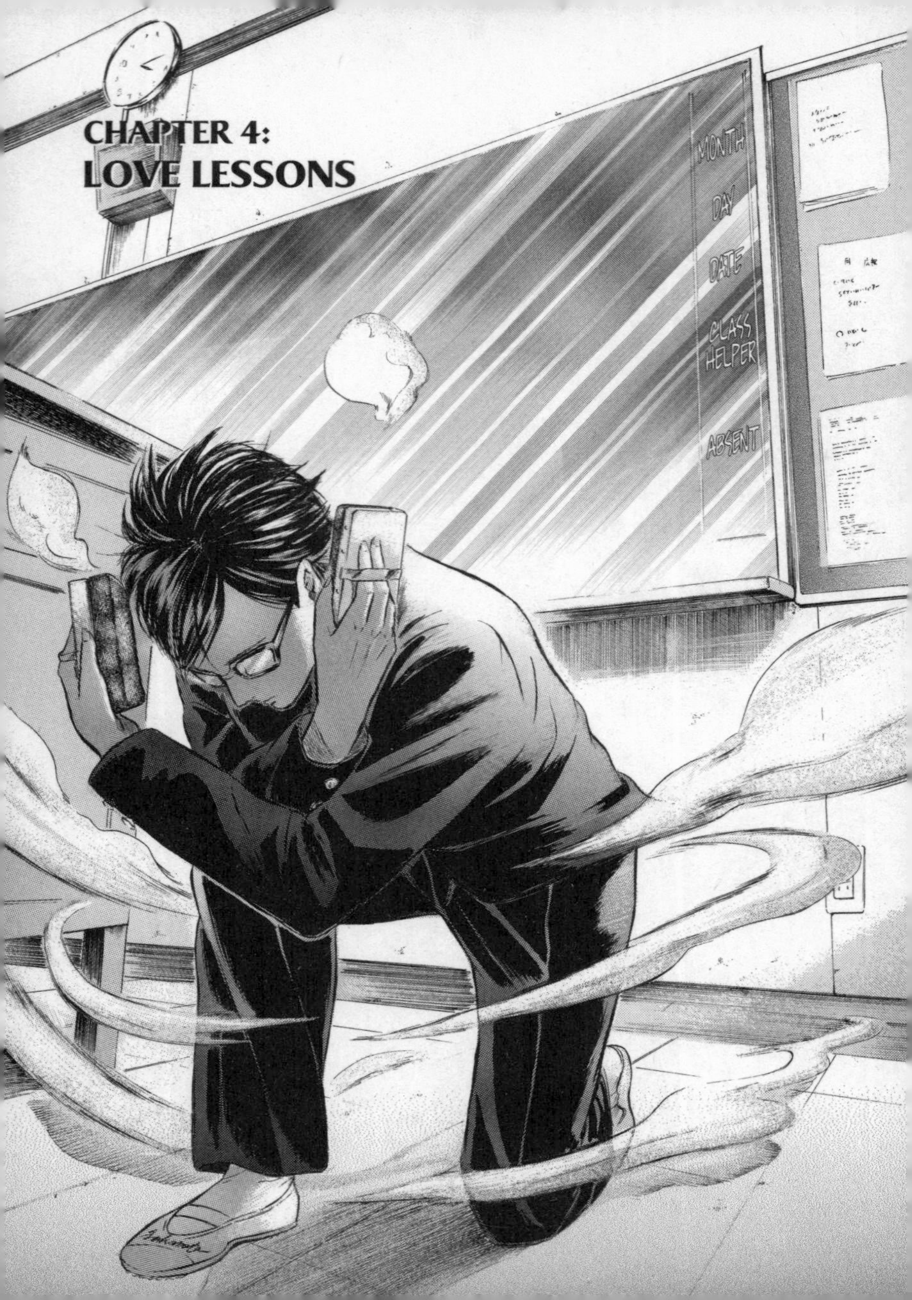
CHAPTER 4:
LOVE LESSONS
MONTH
DAY
DATE
CLASS HELPER
ABSENT

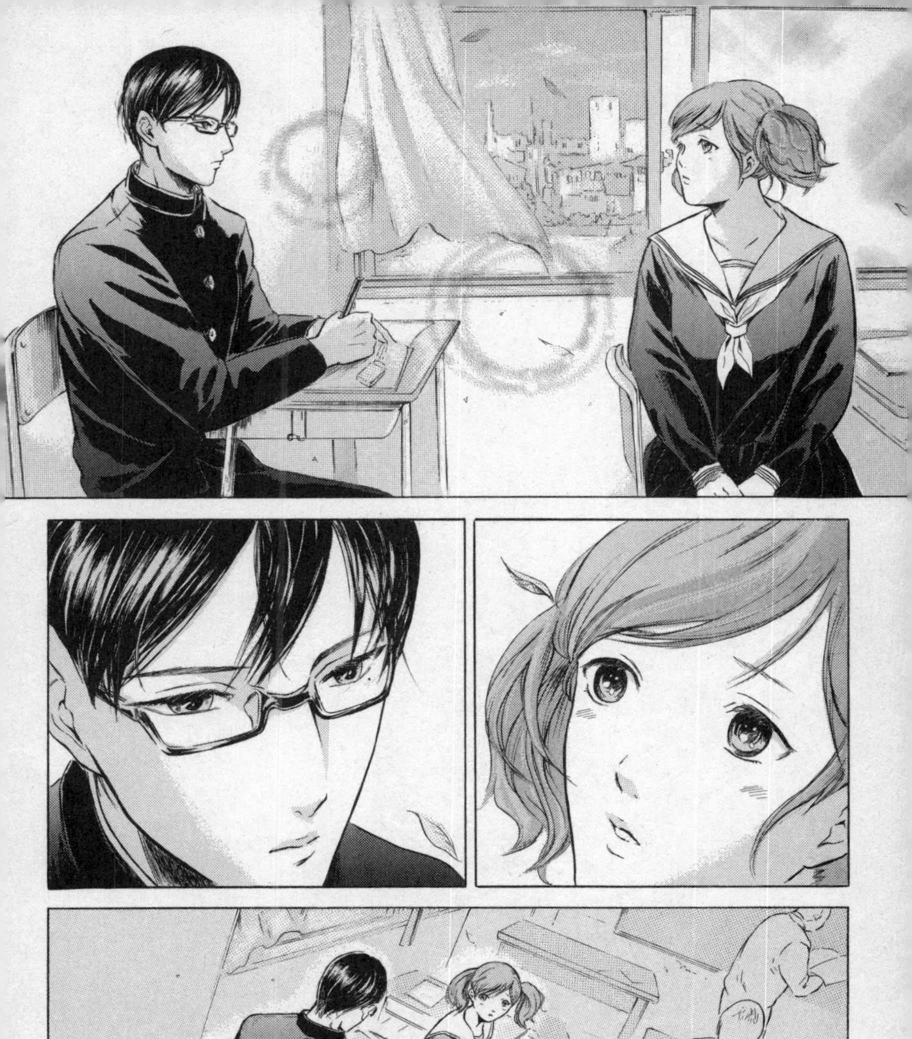

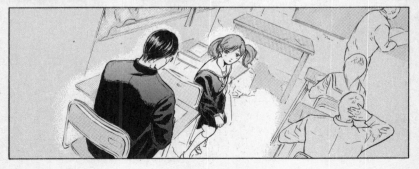

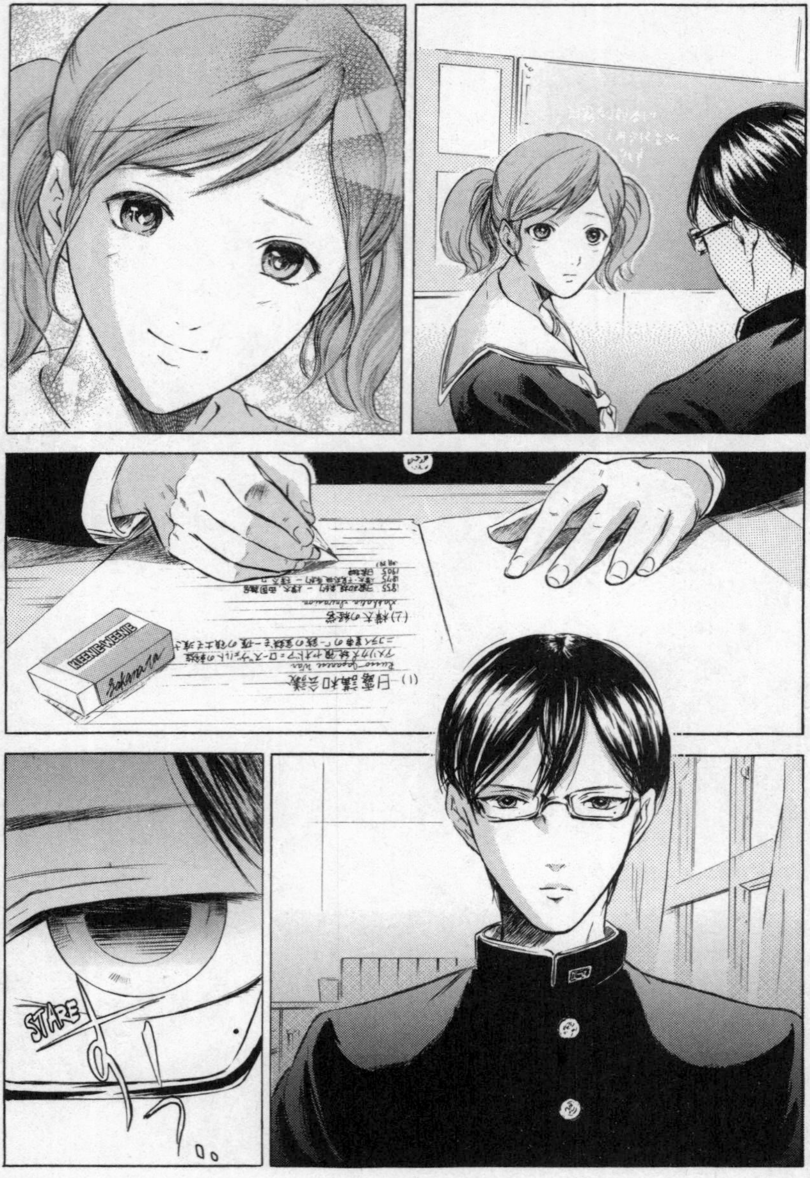
KEENIE-WEENIE
STARE

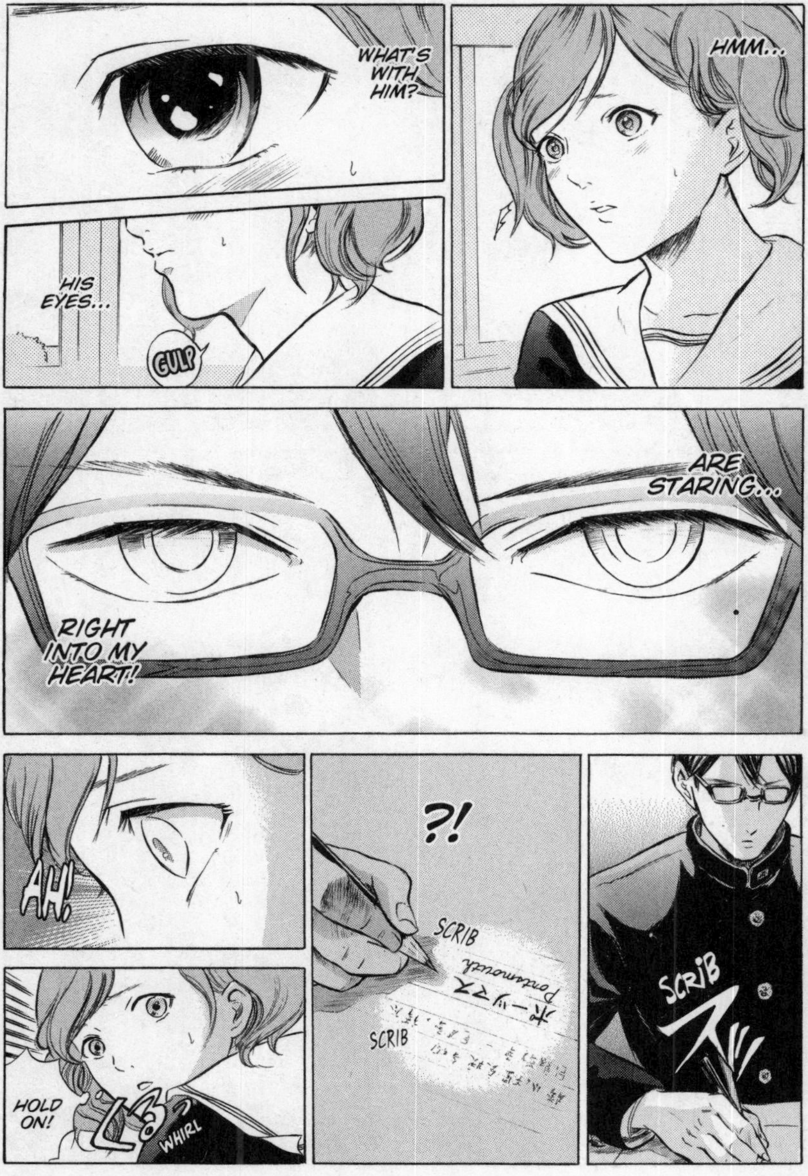
HMM...
WHAT'S WITH HIM?
HIS EYES...
GULP
ARE STARING...
RIGHT INTO MY HEART!
SCRIB
スッ
?!
SCRIB
ポーツマス
Portsmouth
SCRIB
AH!
HOLD ON!
くるっ
WHIRL

ポーツマス条約
The Treaty of Portsmouth

SWSH

WHAT?!

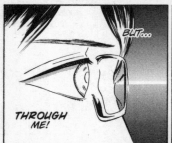

BUT...

THROUGH ME!

HE DIDN'T LOOK AT ME!

WEIRD!

Ahem!

KURO-NUMA!

HMM

EYES UP FRONT!

SCRIB
SCRIB
SCRIB

HE CAN SEE...

THE CHALK-BOARD?!

The Treaty of Portsmouth

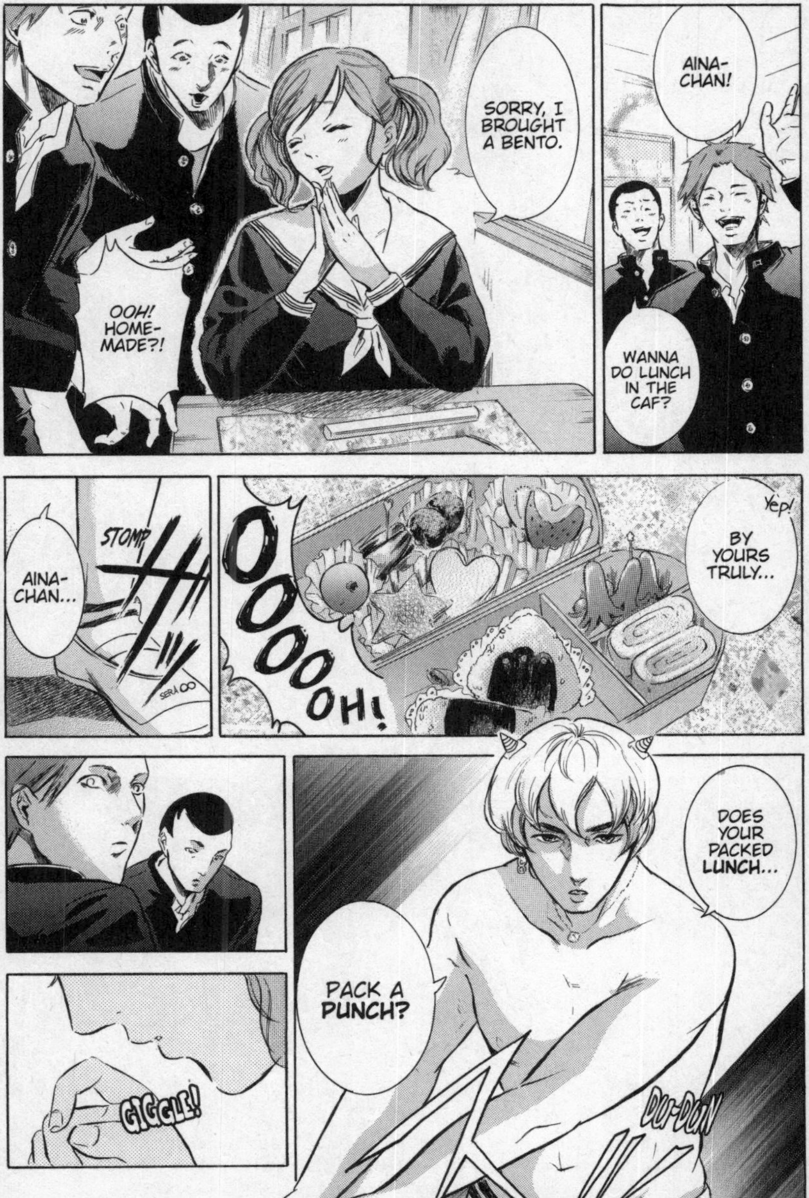
AINA-CHAN!
WANNA DO LUNCH IN THE CAF?
SORRY, I BROUGHT A BENTO.
OOH! HOME-MADE?!
Yep!
BY YOURS TRULY...
OOOOOOH!
STOMP
AINA-CHAN...
DOES YOUR PACKED LUNCH...
PACK A PUNCH?
DU-DON
GIGGLE!

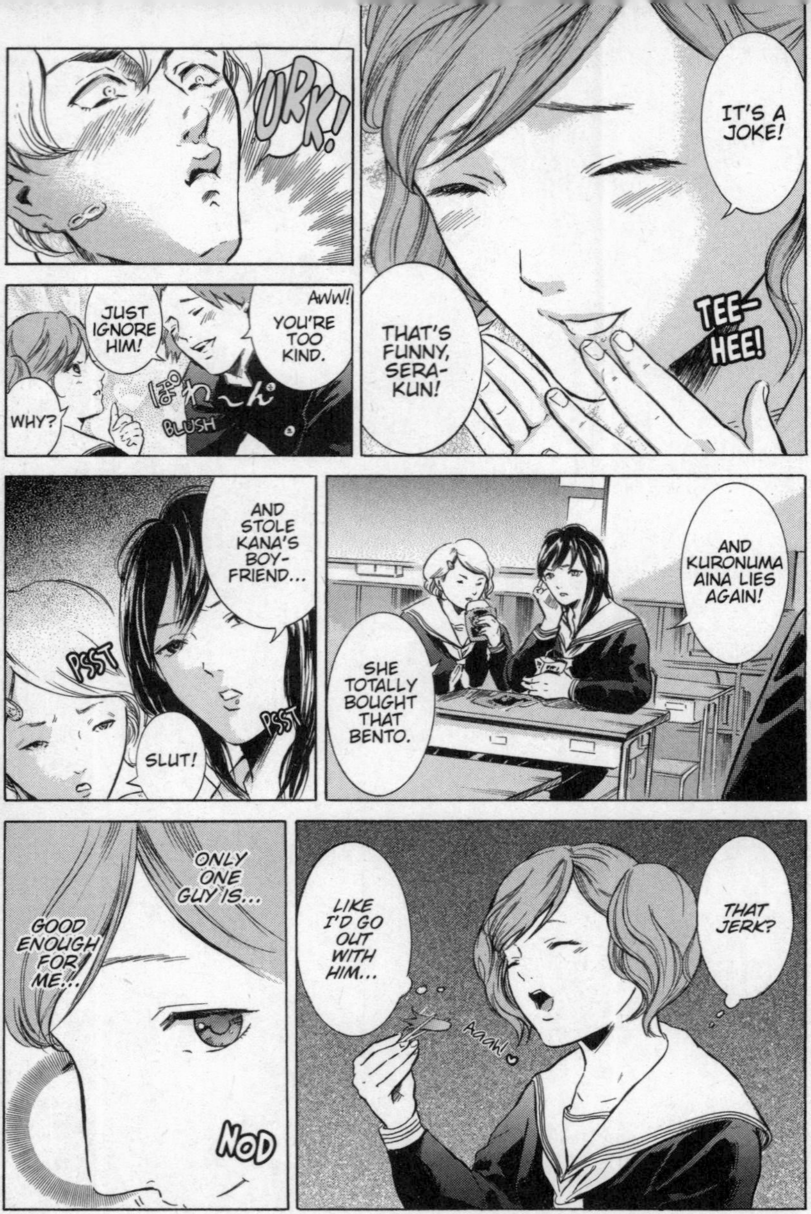
IT'S A JOKE!
TEE-HEE!
THAT'S FUNNY, SERA-KUN!
URK!
AWW! YOU'RE TOO KIND.
JUST IGNORE HIM!
ぽわ〜ん
BLUSH
WHY?
AND KURONUMA AINA LIES AGAIN!
SHE TOTALLY BOUGHT THAT BENTO.
AND STOLE KANA'S BOY-FRIEND...
PSST
PSST
SLUT!
THAT JERK?
LIKE I'D GO OUT WITH HIM...
Aaah!
ONLY ONE GUY IS...
GOOD ENOUGH FOR ME...
NOD

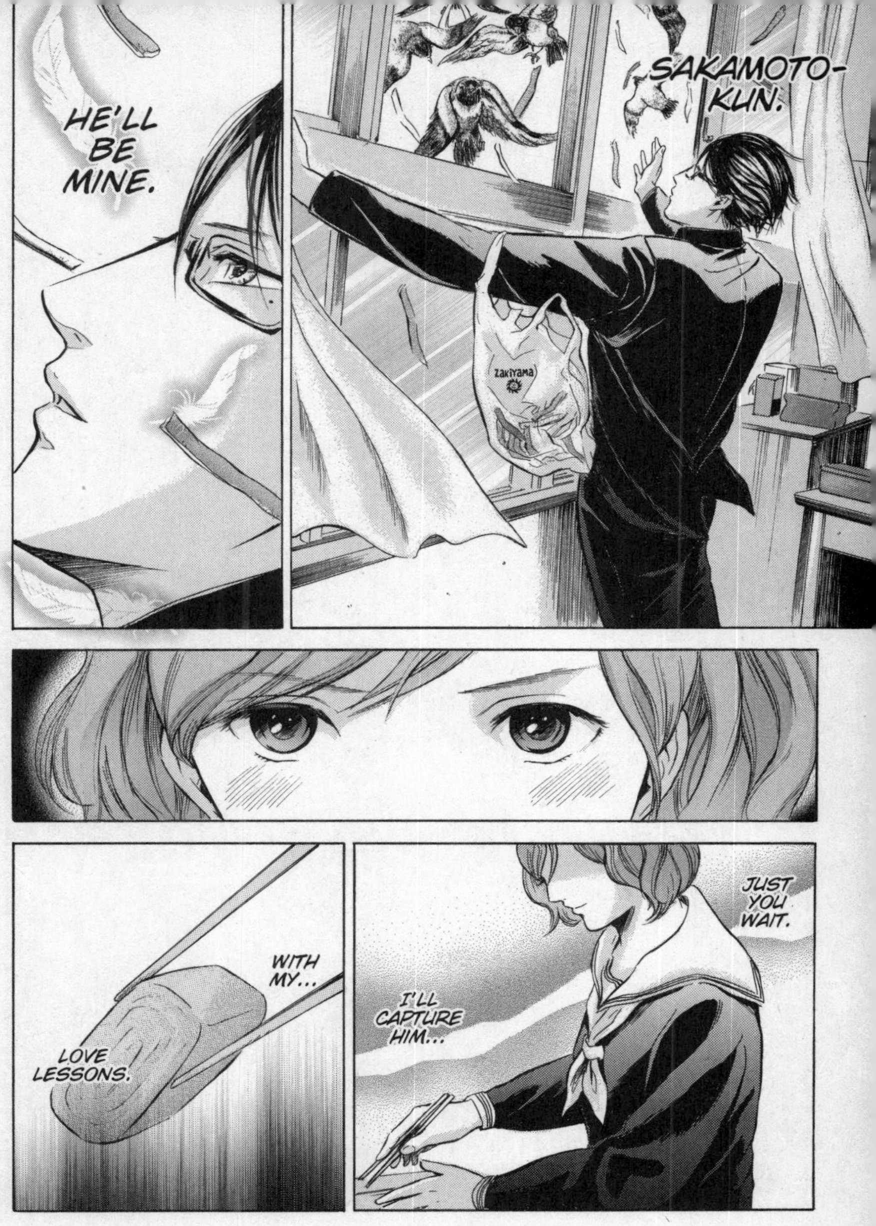

SAKAMOTO-KUN.
zakiyama
HE'LL BE MINE.
JUST YOU WAIT.
I'LL CAPTURE HIM...
WITH MY...
LOVE LESSONS.

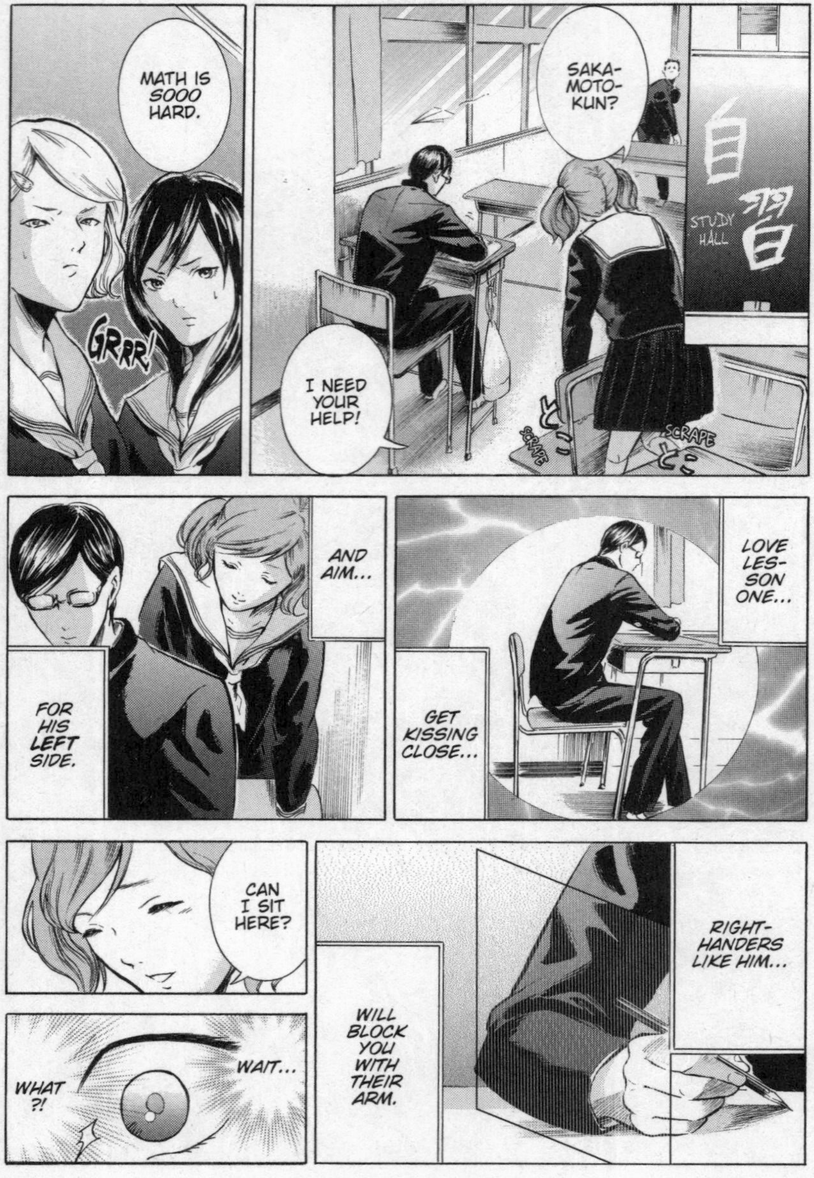
SAKA-MOTO-KUN?
STUDY HALL
SCRAPE
SCRAPE
I NEED YOUR HELP!
MATH IS SOOO HARD.
GRRR!
LOVE LES-SON ONE...
GET KISSING CLOSE...
AND AIM...
FOR HIS LEFT SIDE.
RIGHT-HANDERS LIKE HIM...
WILL BLOCK YOU WITH THEIR ARM.
CAN I SIT HERE?
WAIT...
WHAT ?!

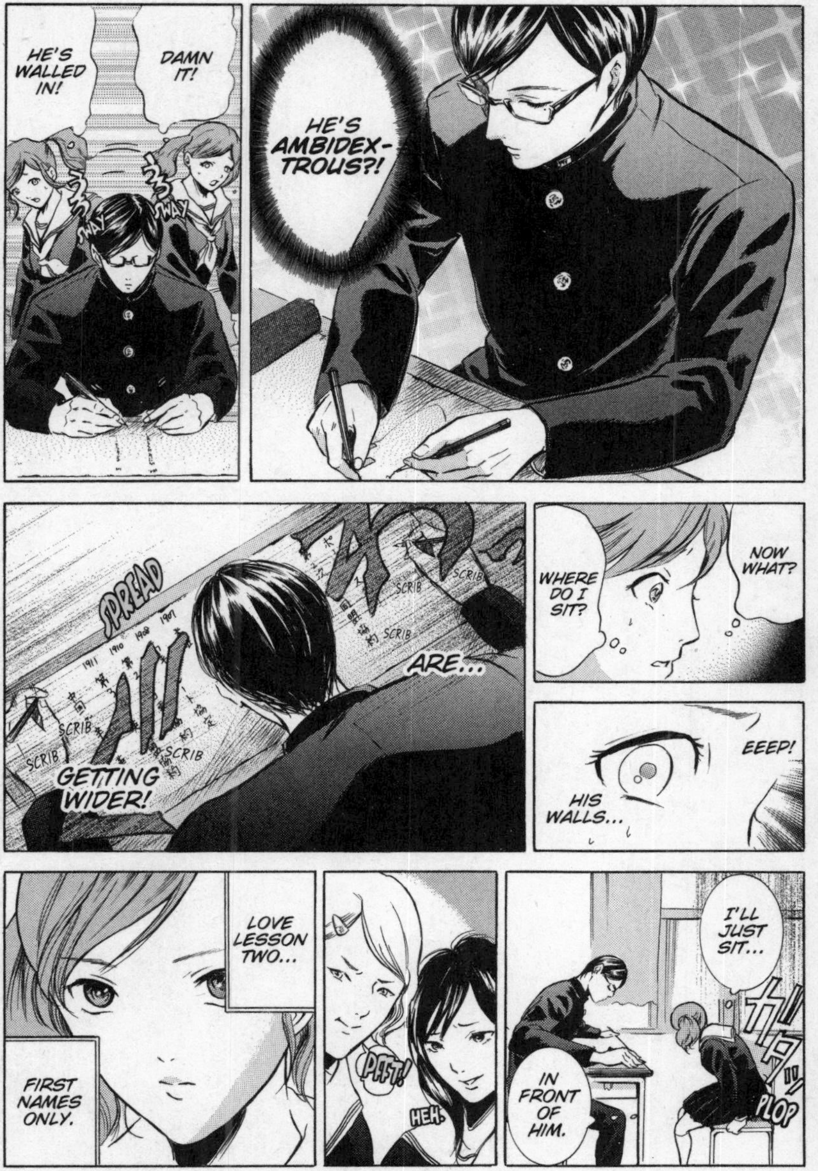
HE'S AMBIDEX-TROUS?!
DAMN IT!
HE'S WALLED IN!
SWAY
SWAY
NOW WHAT?
WHERE DO I SIT?
EEEP!
HIS WALLS...
ARE...
SCRIB
SCRIB
SCRIB
SPREAD
SCRIB
SCRIB
SCRIB
GETTING WIDER!
I'LL JUST SIT...
IN FRONT OF HIM.
PLOP
LOVE LESSON TWO...
PFFT!
HEH.
FIRST NAMES ONLY.

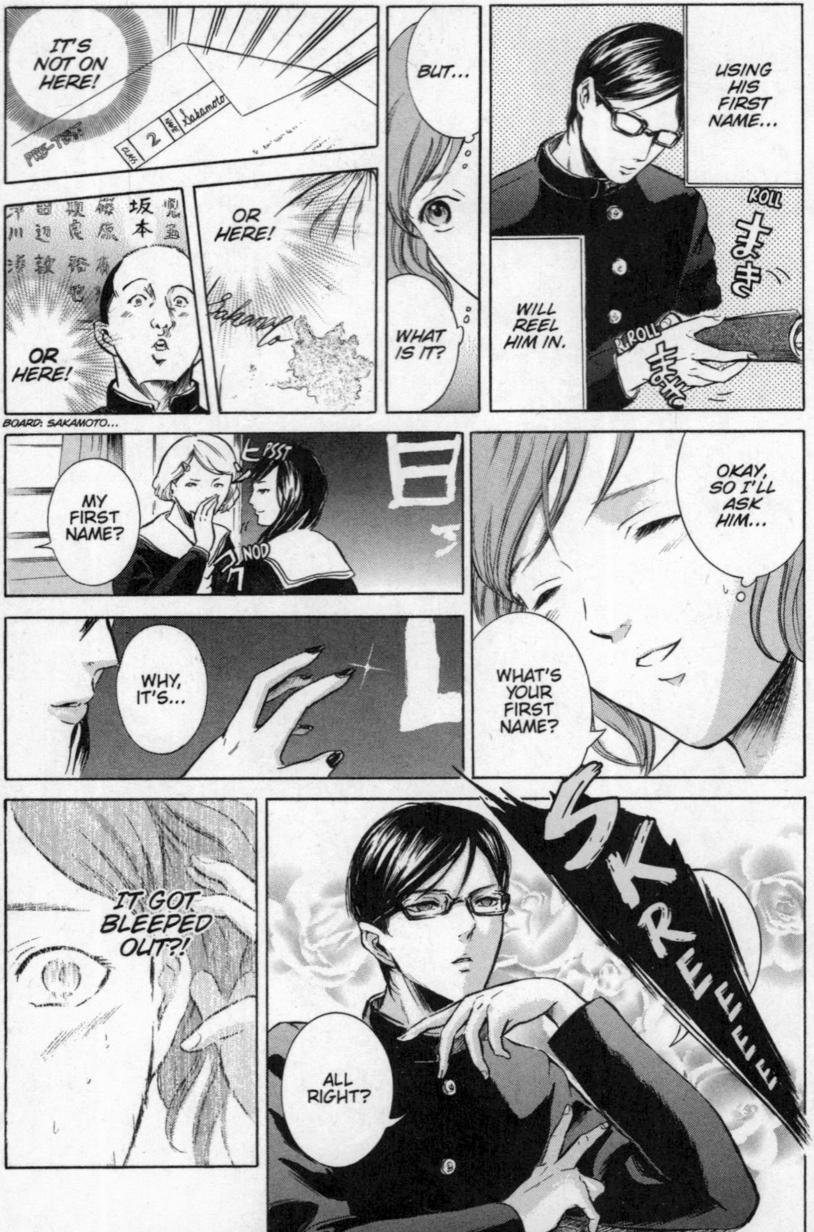
USING HIS FIRST NAME...
ROLL
WILL REEL HIM IN.
ROLL
BUT...
WHAT IS IT?
IT'S NOT ON HERE!
PRE-TEST
CLASS 2 NAME Sakamoto
OR HERE!
Sakamoto
OR HERE!
BOARD: SAKAMOTO...
OKAY, SO I'LL ASK HIM...
WHAT'S YOUR FIRST NAME?
PSST
MY FIRST NAME?
NOD
WHY, IT'S...
SKREEEEE
ALL RIGHT?
IT GOT BLEEPED OUT?!

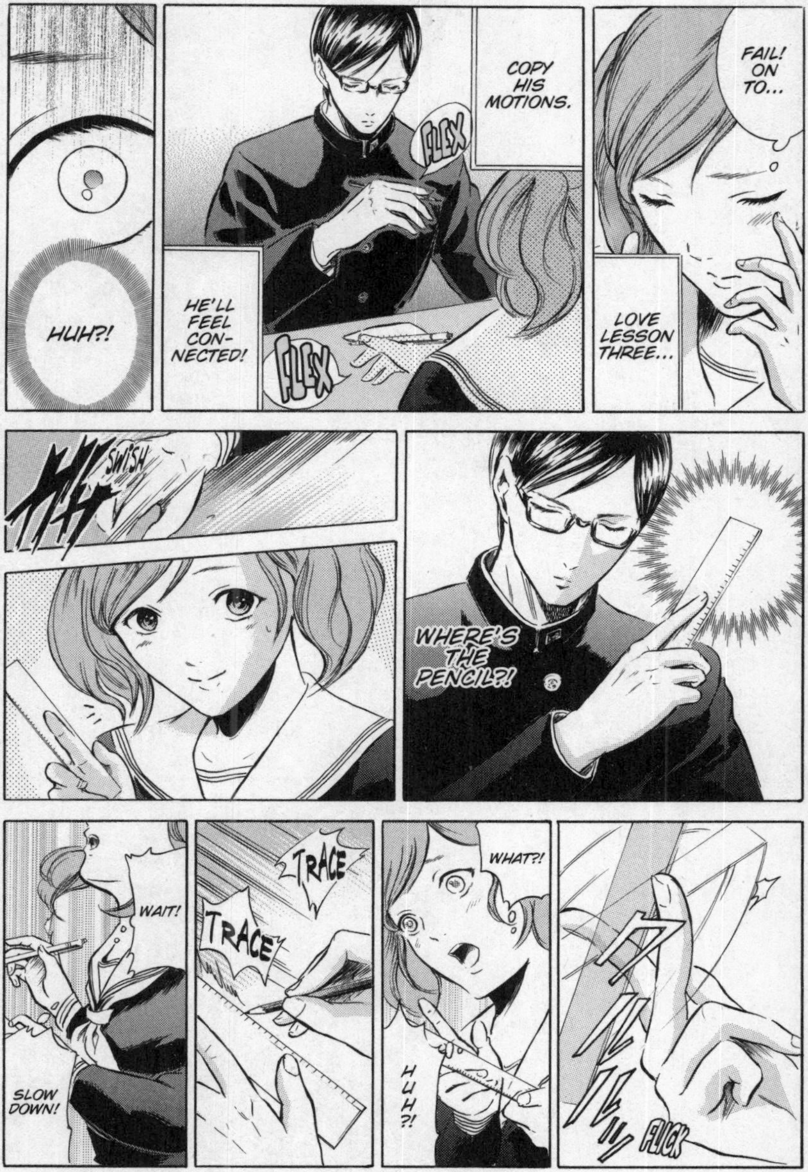
FAIL! ON TO...
LOVE LESSON THREE...
COPY HIS MOTIONS.
FLEX
HE'LL FEEL CON-NECTED!
FLEX
HUH?!
WHERE'S THE PENCIL?!
SWISH
FLICK
WHAT?!
HUH?!
TRACE
TRACE
WAIT!
SLOW DOWN!

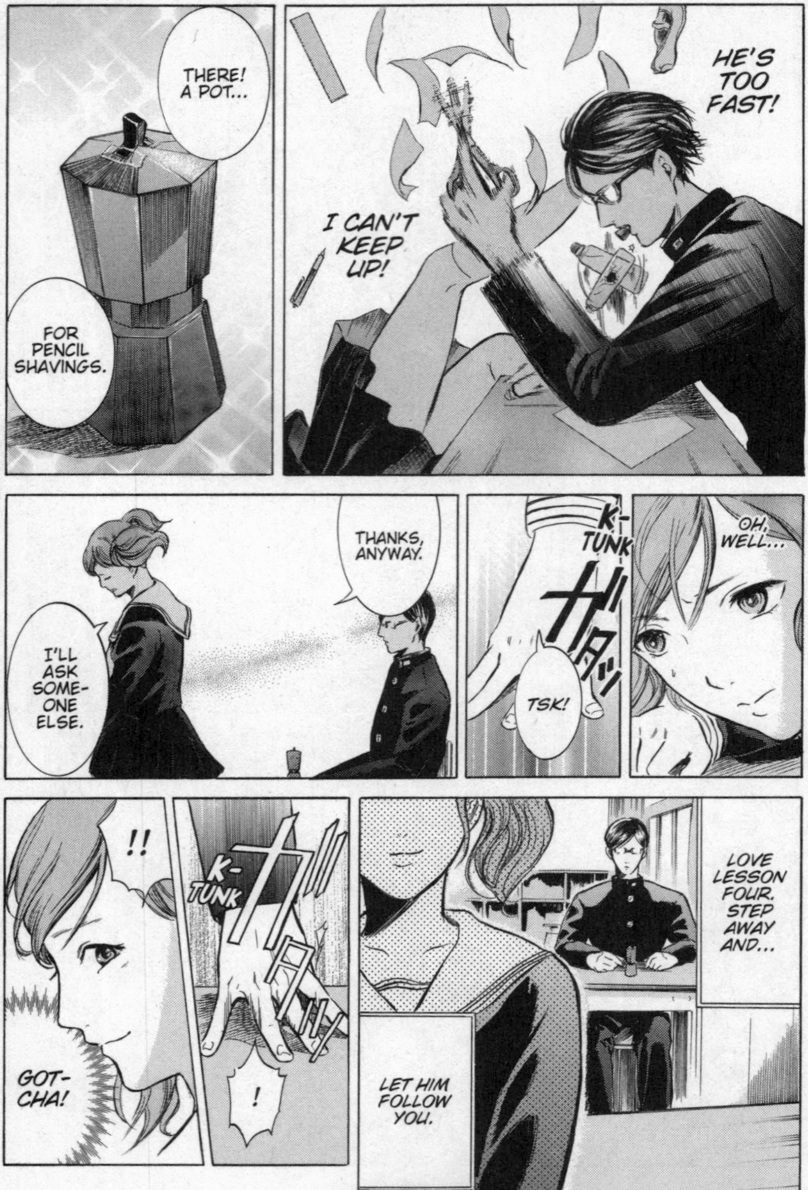
HE'S TOO FAST!
I CAN'T KEEP UP!
THERE! A POT...
FOR PENCIL SHAVINGS.
OH, WELL...
K-TUNK
TSK!
THANKS, ANYWAY.
I'LL ASK SOME-ONE ELSE.
LOVE LESSON FOUR. STEP AWAY AND...
LET HIM FOLLOW YOU.
K-TUNK
!
!!
GOT-CHA!

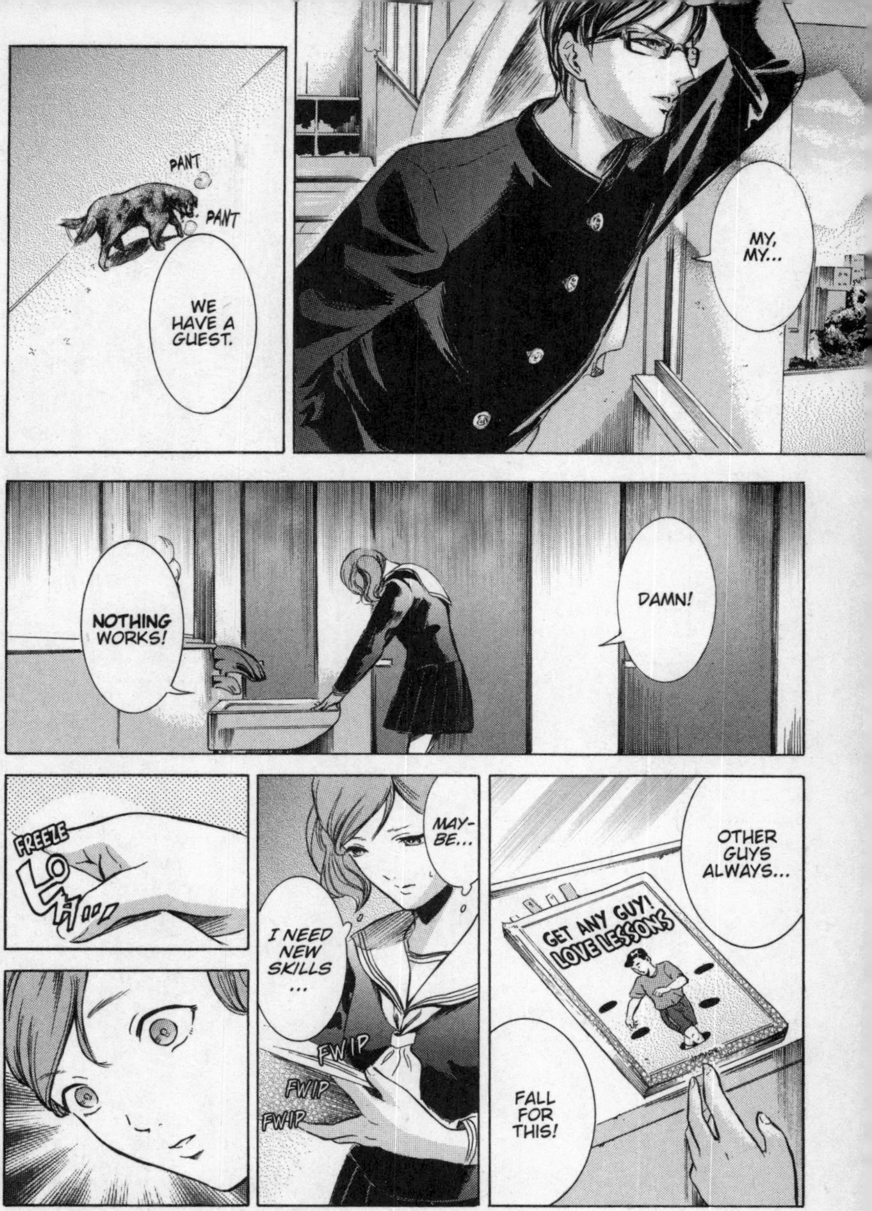
MY, MY...
PANT
PANT
WE HAVE A GUEST.
DAMN!
NOTHING WORKS!
OTHER GUYS ALWAYS...
GET ANY GUY! LOVE LESSONS
FALL FOR THIS!
MAY-BE...
I NEED NEW SKILLS ...
FWIP
FWIP
FWIP
FREEZE

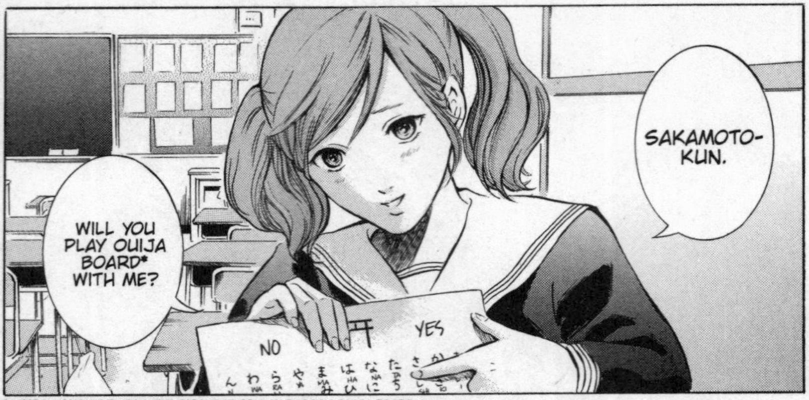
SAKAMOTO-KUN.
WILL YOU PLAY OUIJA BOARD* WITH ME?
NO
YES

*LITERALLY KOKKURI-SAN, THE JAPANESE EQUIVALENT OF A OUIJA BOARD.

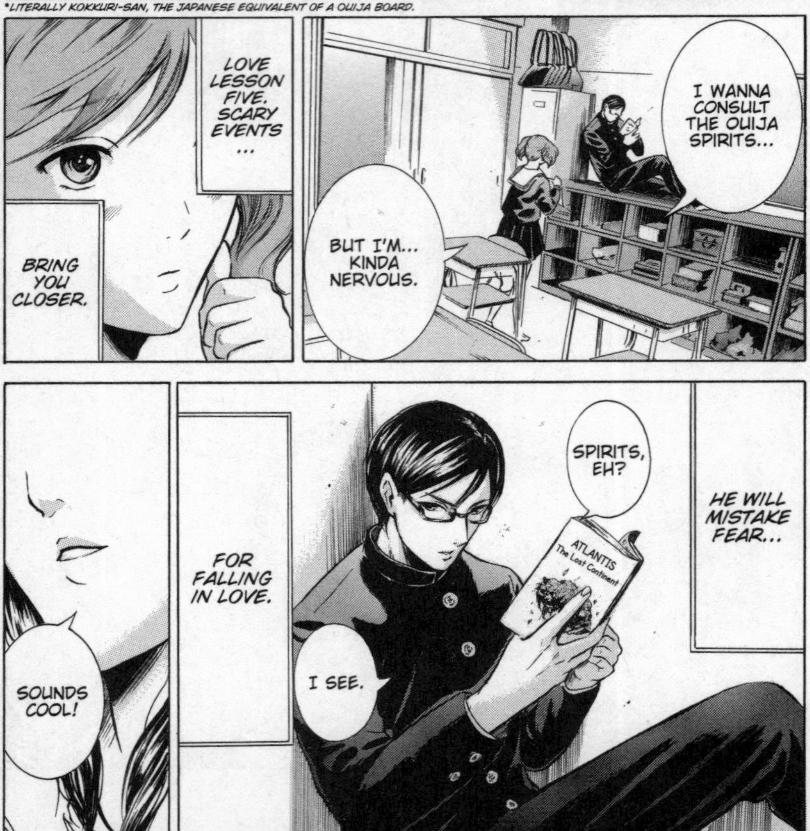
I WANNA CONSULT THE OUIJA SPIRITS...
BUT I'M... KINDA NERVOUS.
LOVE LESSON FIVE. SCARY EVENTS ...
BRING YOU CLOSER.
HE WILL MISTAKE FEAR...
SPIRITS, EH?
ATLANTIS The Lost Continent
FOR FALLING IN LOVE.
I SEE.
SOUNDS COOL!

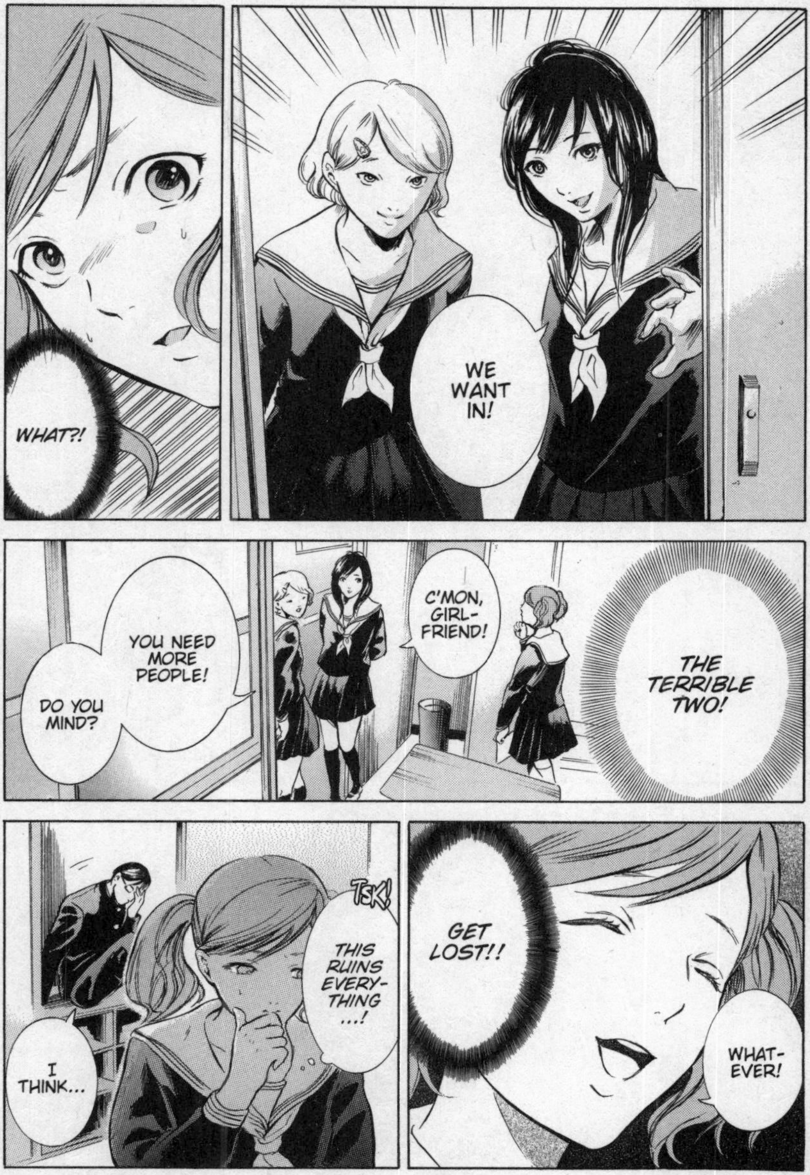
WE WANT IN!
WHAT?!
THE TERRIBLE TWO!
C'MON, GIRL-FRIEND!
YOU NEED MORE PEOPLE!
DO YOU MIND?
GET LOST!!
WHAT-EVER!
TSK!
THIS RUINS EVERY-THING ...!
I THINK...

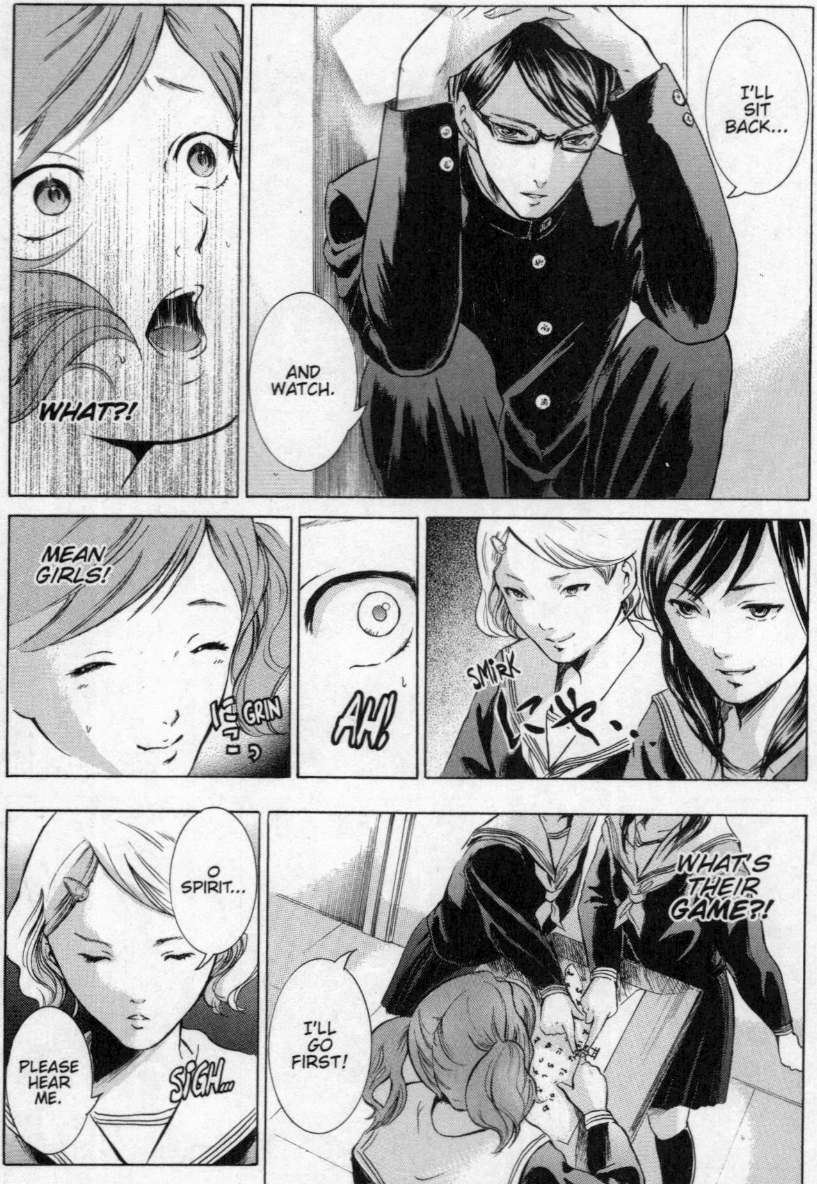
I'LL SIT BACK...
AND WATCH.
WHAT?!
SMIRK
AH!
MEAN GIRLS!
GRIN
WHAT'S THEIR GAME?!
I'LL GO FIRST!
O SPIRIT...
PLEASE HEAR ME.
SIGH...

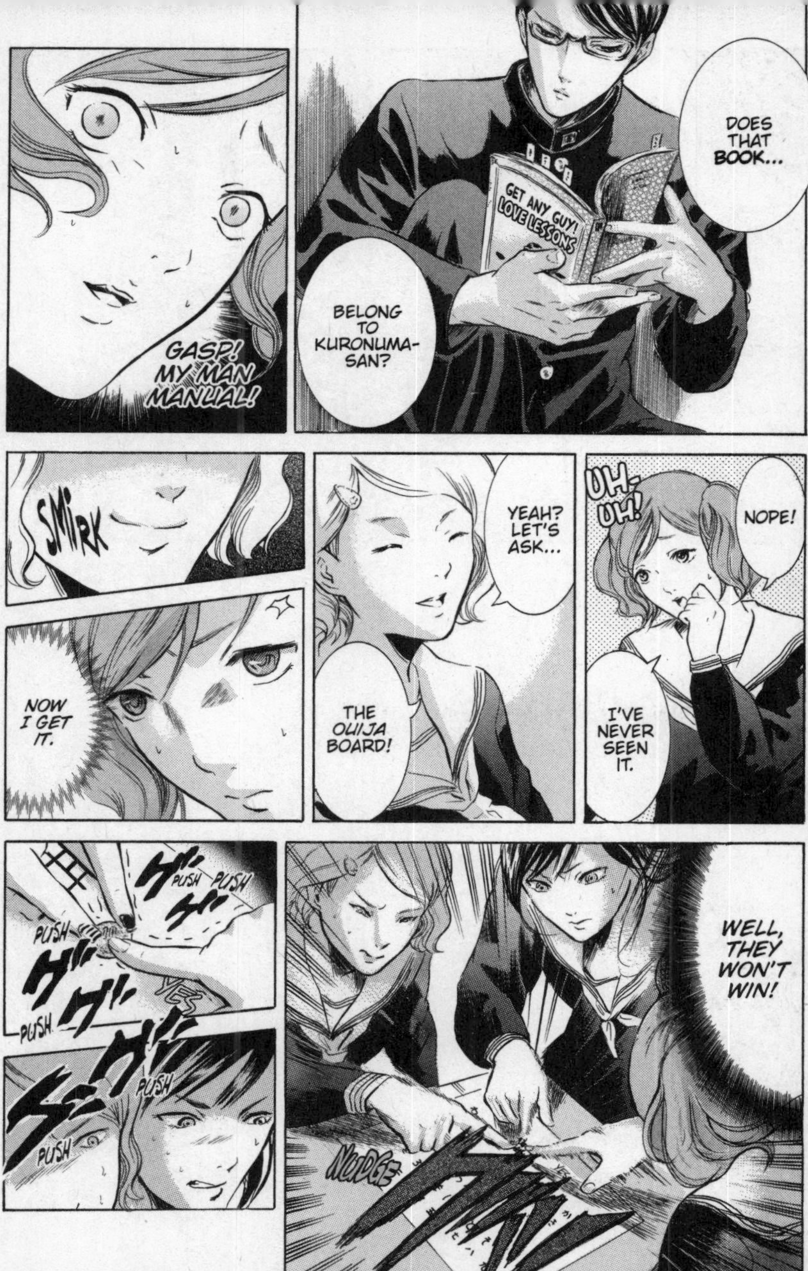
DOES THAT BOOK...
GET ANY GUY! LOVE LESSONS
BELONG TO KURONUMA-SAN?
GASP! MY MAN MANUAL!
UH-UH!
NOPE!
I'VE NEVER SEEN IT.
YEAH? LET'S ASK...
THE OUIJA BOARD!
SMIRK
NOW I GET IT.
WELL, THEY WON'T WIN!
NUDGE
PUSH PUSH
PUSH
YES
PUSH
PUSH
PUSH

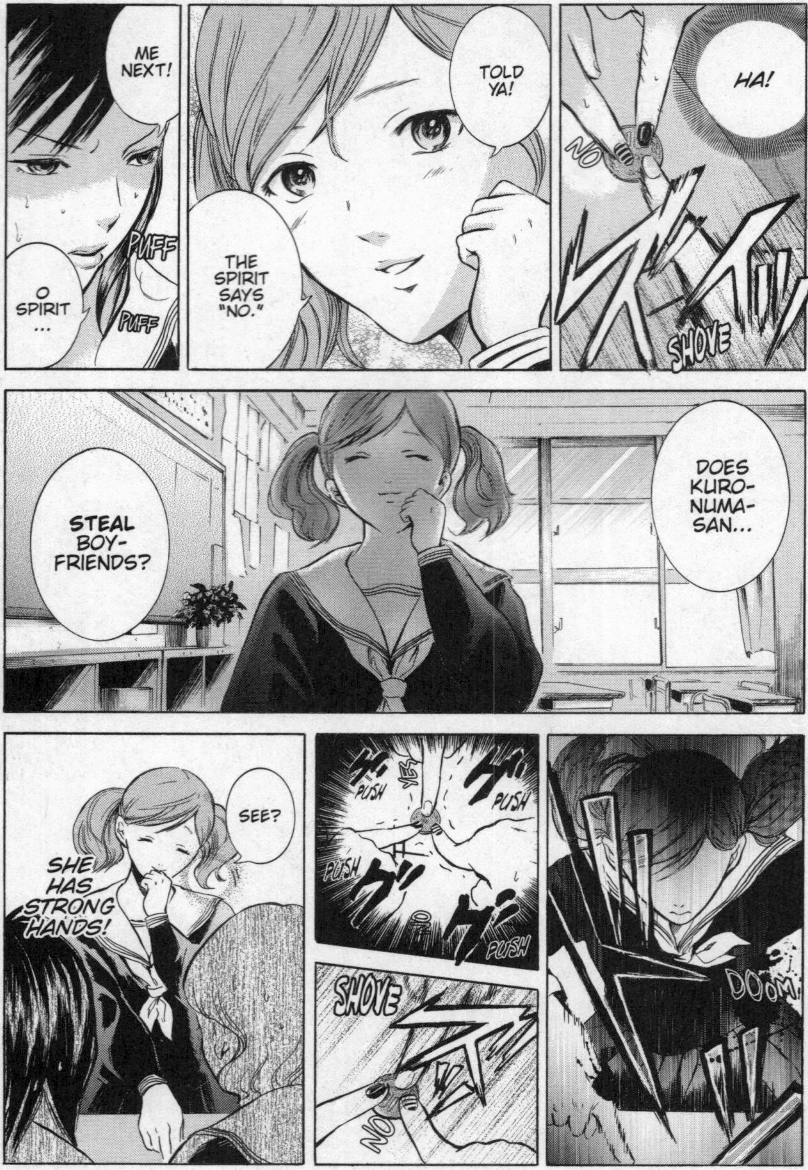
HA!
NO
SHOVE
TOLD YA!
THE SPIRIT SAYS "NO."
ME NEXT!
PUFF
O SPIRIT ...
PUFF
DOES KURO-NUMA-SAN...
STEAL BOY-FRIENDS?
DOOM
YES
PUSH
PUSH
PUSH
PUSH
SHOVE
NO
SEE?
SHE HAS STRONG HANDS!

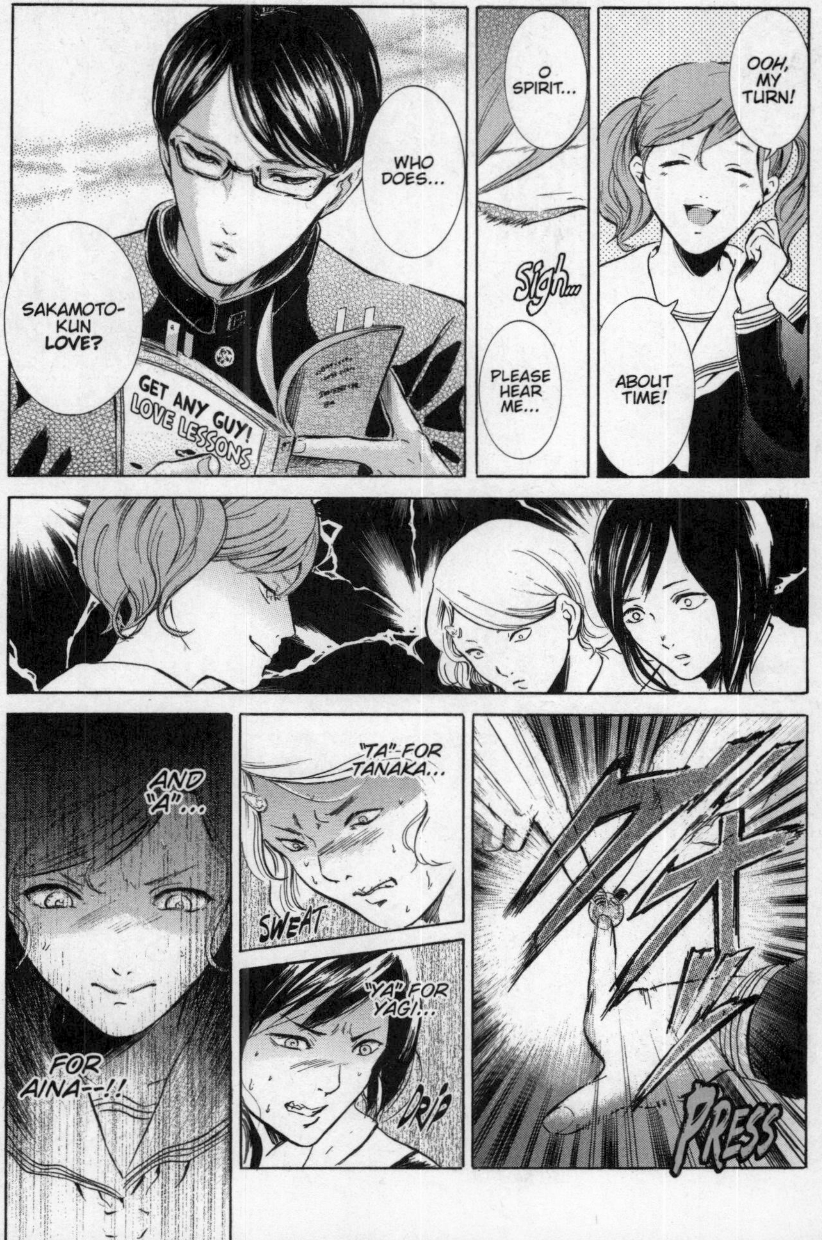
OOH, MY TURN!
ABOUT TIME!
O SPIRIT...
Sigh...
PLEASE HEAR ME...
WHO DOES...
SAKAMOTO-KUN LOVE?
GET ANY GUY! LOVE LESSONS
PRESS
"TA" FOR TANAKA...
SWEAT
"YA" FOR YAGI...
DRIP
AND "A"...
FOR AINA--!!

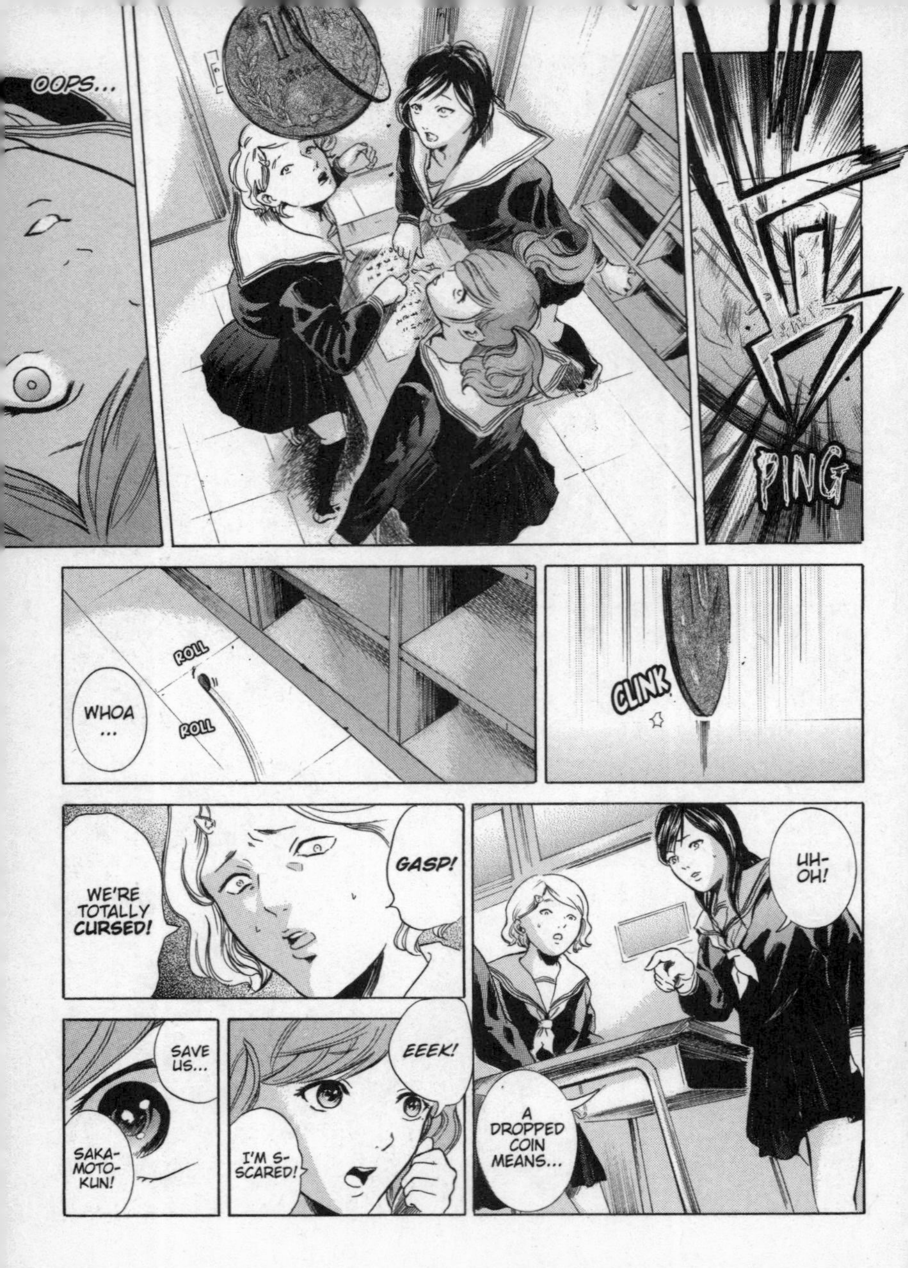
PING
OOPS...
CLINK
ROLL
ROLL
WHOA ...
UH-OH!
A DROPPED COIN MEANS...
GASP!
WE'RE TOTALLY CURSED!
EEEK!
I'M S-SCARED!
SAVE US...
SAKAMOTO-KUN!

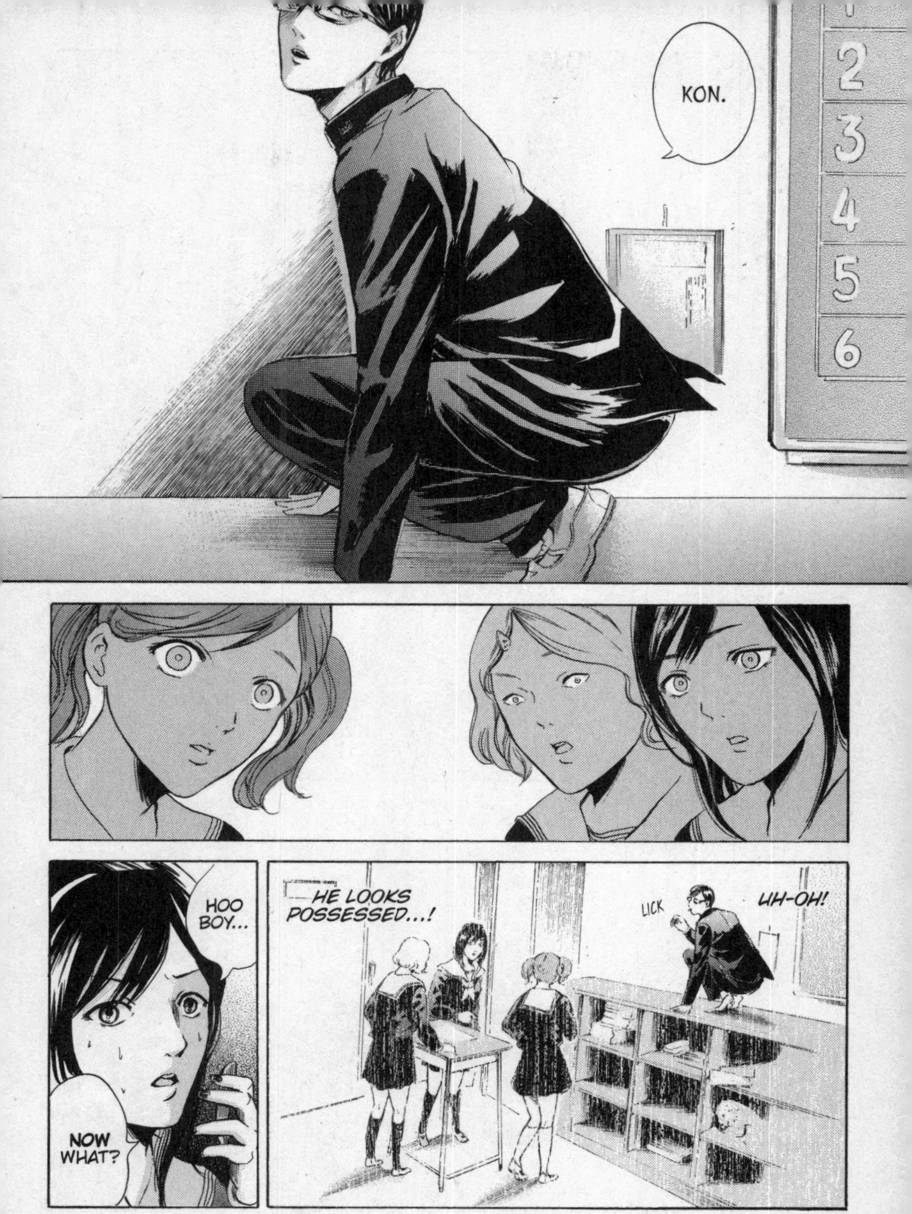
KON.
UH-OH!
LICK
HE LOOKS POSSESSED...!
HOO BOY...
NOW WHAT?

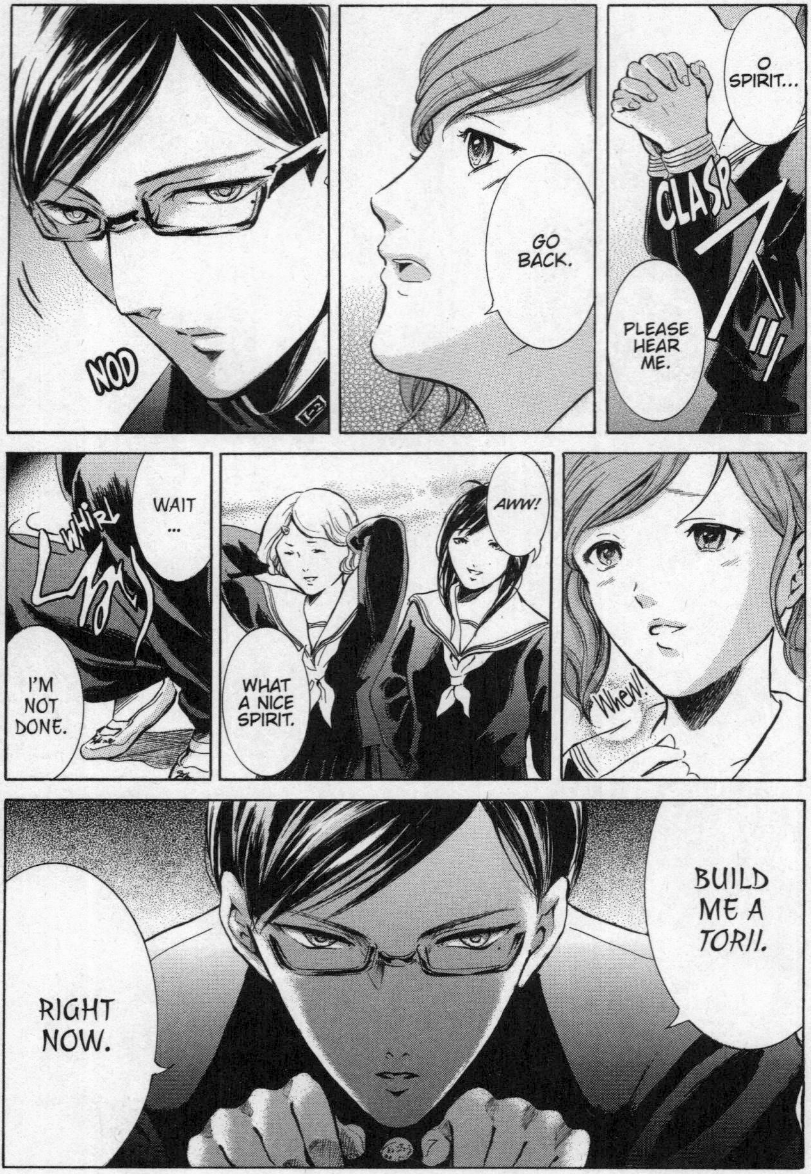
O SPIRIT...
CLASP
PLEASE HEAR ME.
GO BACK.
NOD
Whew!
AWW!
WHAT A NICE SPIRIT.
WAIT ...
WHIRL
I'M NOT DONE.
BUILD ME A TORII.
RIGHT NOW.

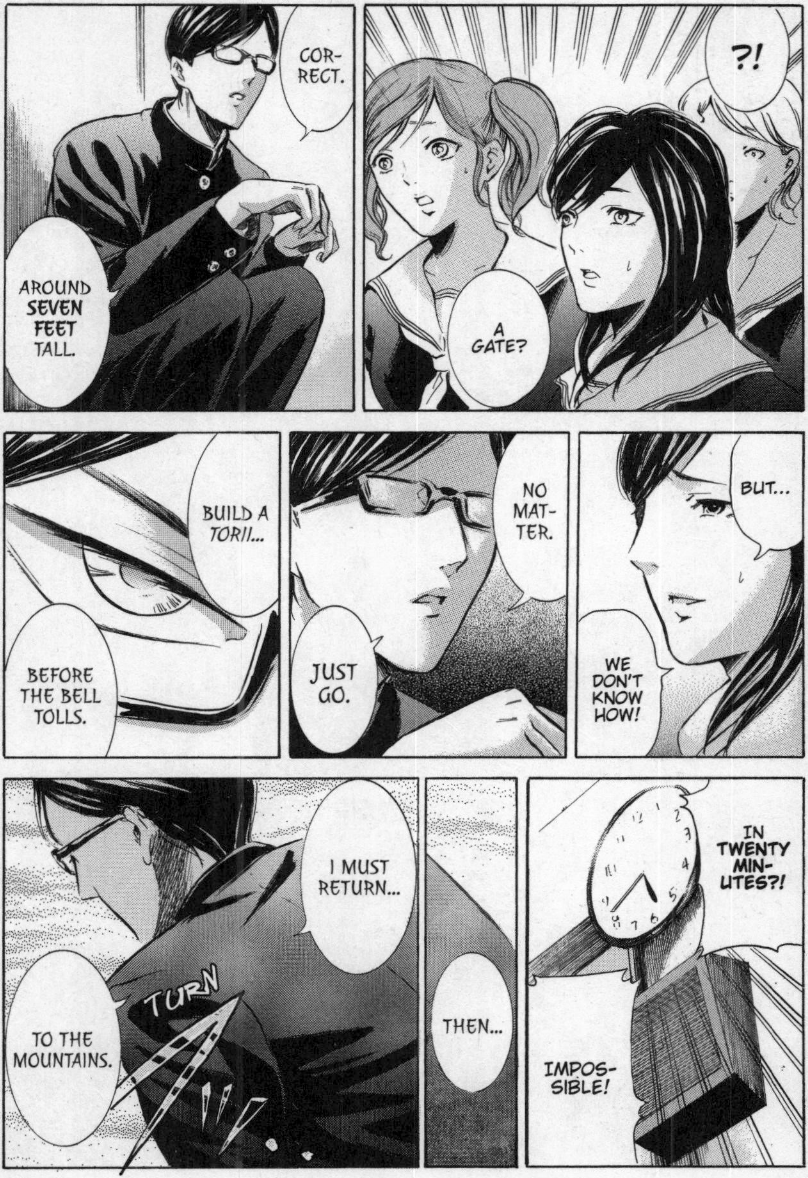
?!
A GATE?
CORRECT.
AROUND SEVEN FEET TALL.
BUT...
WE DON'T KNOW HOW!
NO MATTER.
JUST GO.
BUILD A *TORII*...
BEFORE THE BELL TOLLS.
IN TWENTY MINUTES?!
IMPOSSIBLE!
THEN...
I MUST RETURN...
TURN
TO THE MOUNTAINS.

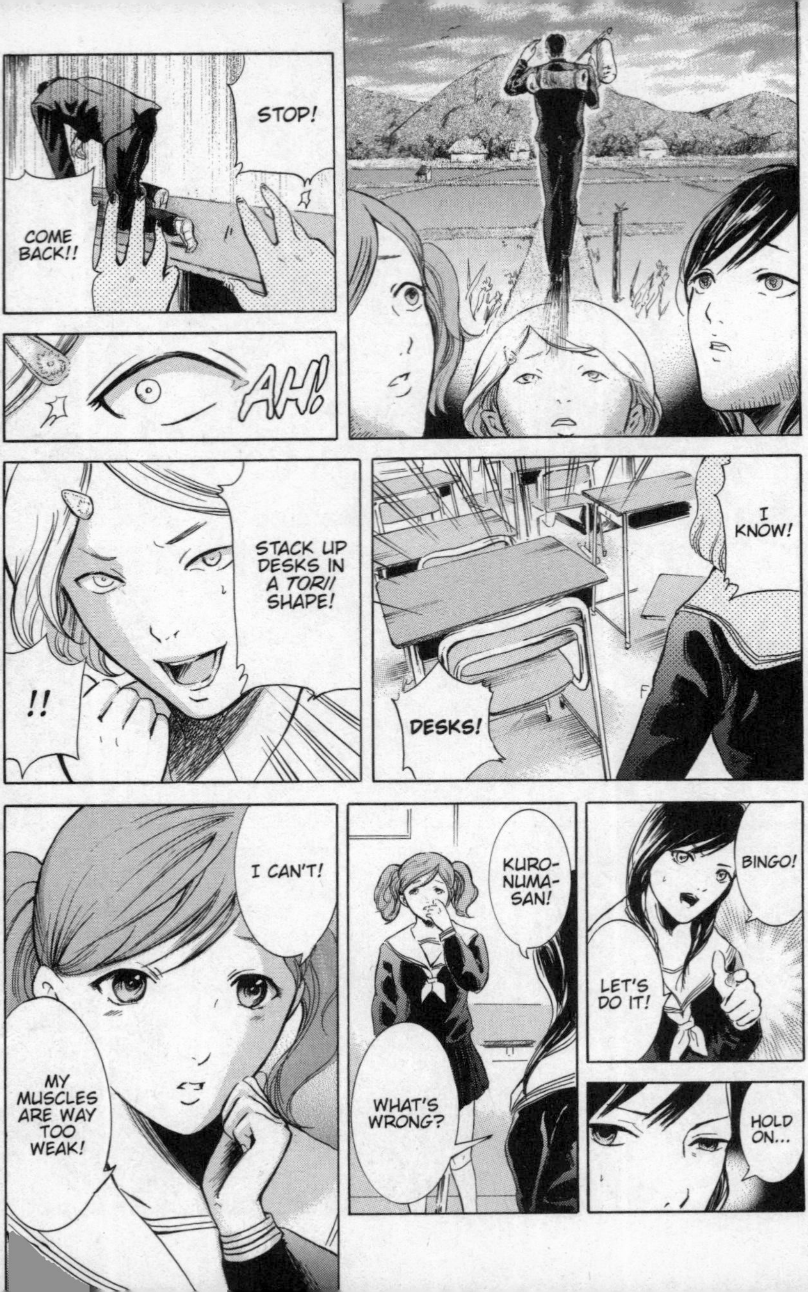
STOP!
COME BACK!!
AH!
I KNOW!
DESKS!
STACK UP DESKS IN A TORII SHAPE!
!!
BINGO!
LET'S DO IT!
HOLD ON...
KURO-NUMA-SAN!
WHAT'S WRONG?
I CAN'T!
MY MUSCLES ARE WAY TOO WEAK!

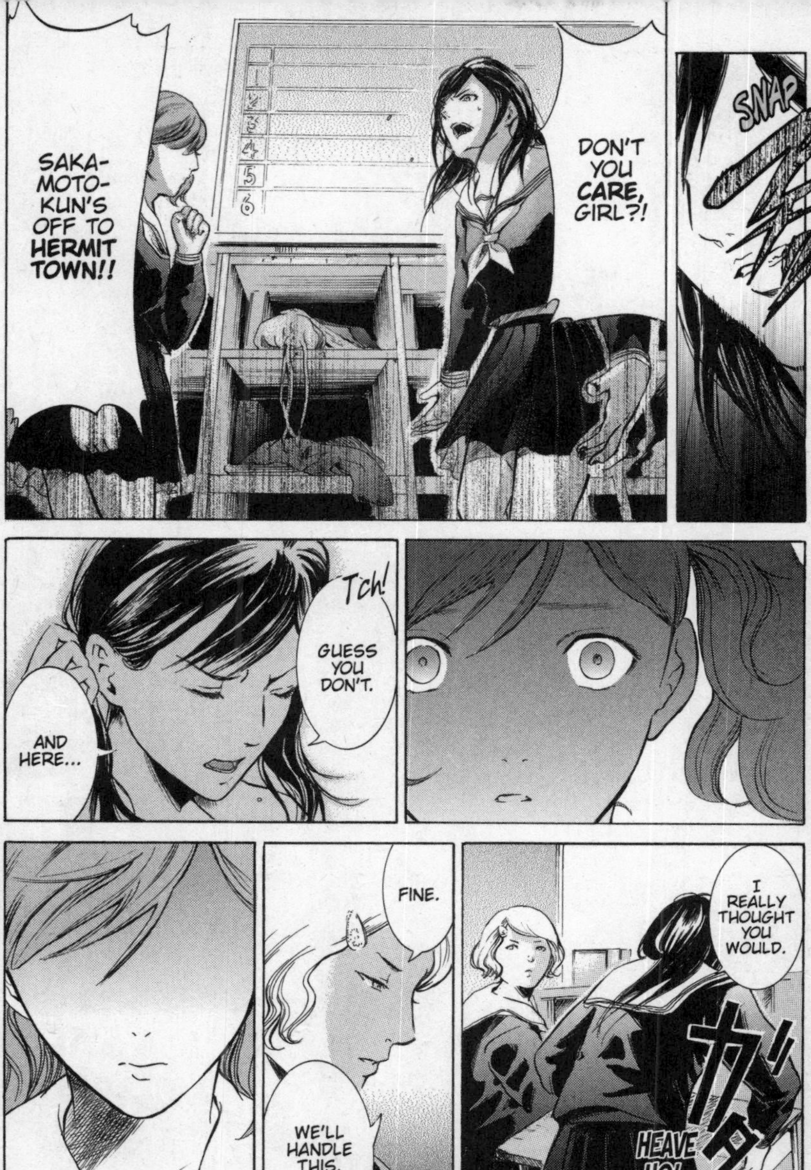
SNAP
DON'T YOU CARE, GIRL?!
SAKA-MOTO-KUN'S OFF TO HERMIT TOWN!!
Tch!
GUESS YOU DON'T.
AND HERE...
I REALLY THOUGHT YOU WOULD.
カタ
HEAVE HO!
FINE.
WE'LL HANDLE THIS.

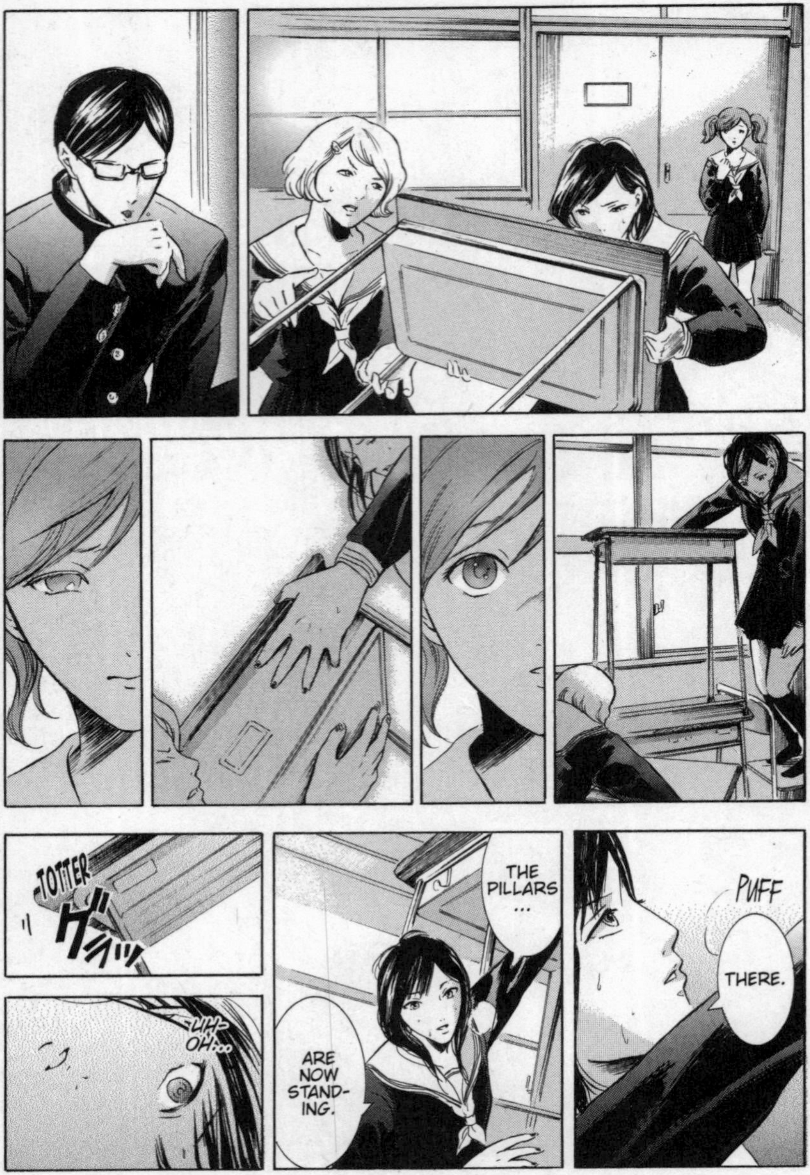
PUFF
THERE.
THE PILLARS...
ARE NOW STANDING.
TOTTER
UH-OH...

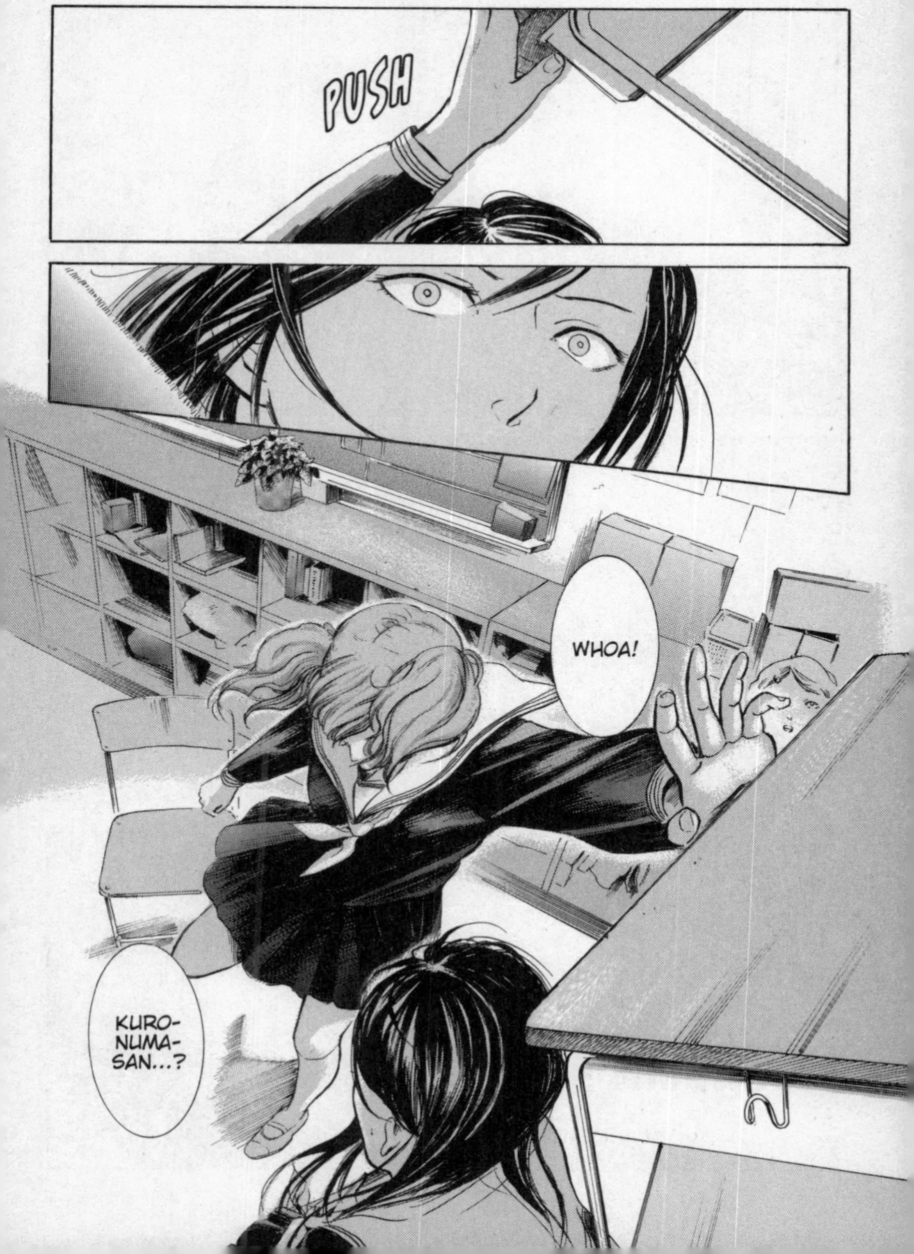
PUSH
WHOA!
KURO-NUMA-SAN...?

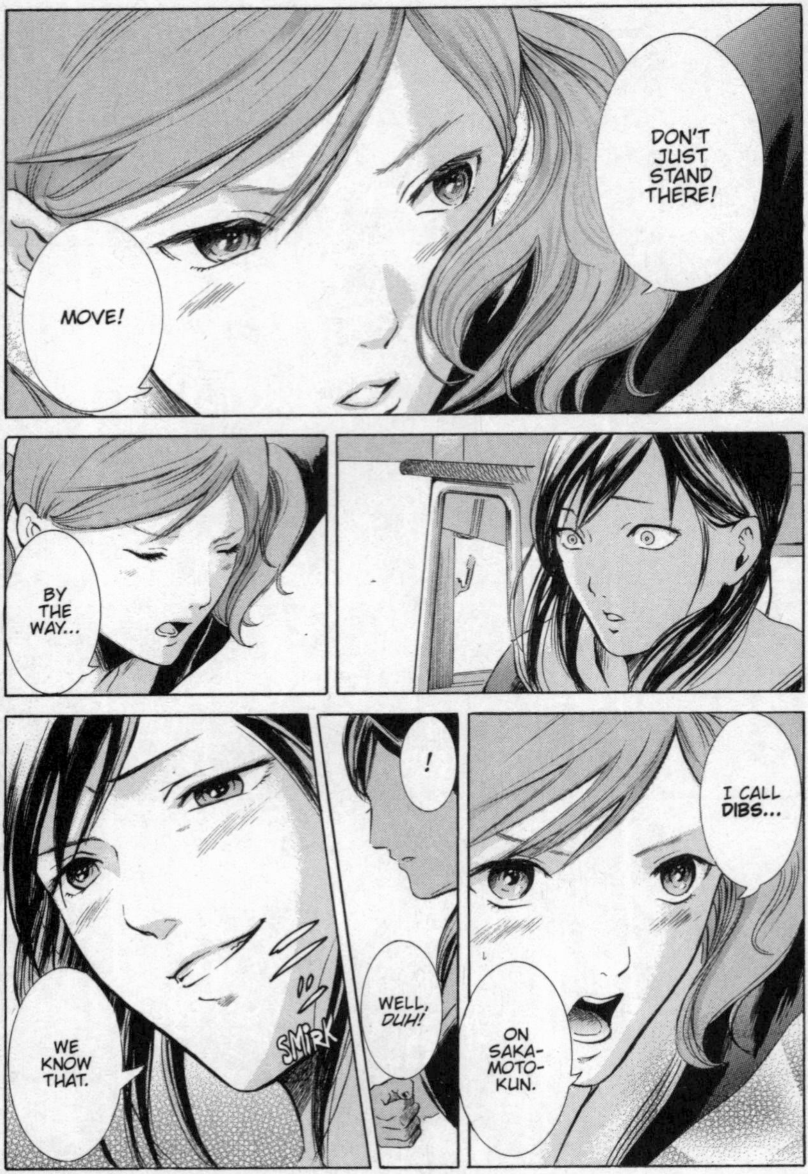
DON'T JUST STAND THERE!
MOVE!
BY THE WAY...
I CALL DIBS...
ON SAKA-MOTO-KUN.
!
WELL, DUH!
WE KNOW THAT.
SMIRK

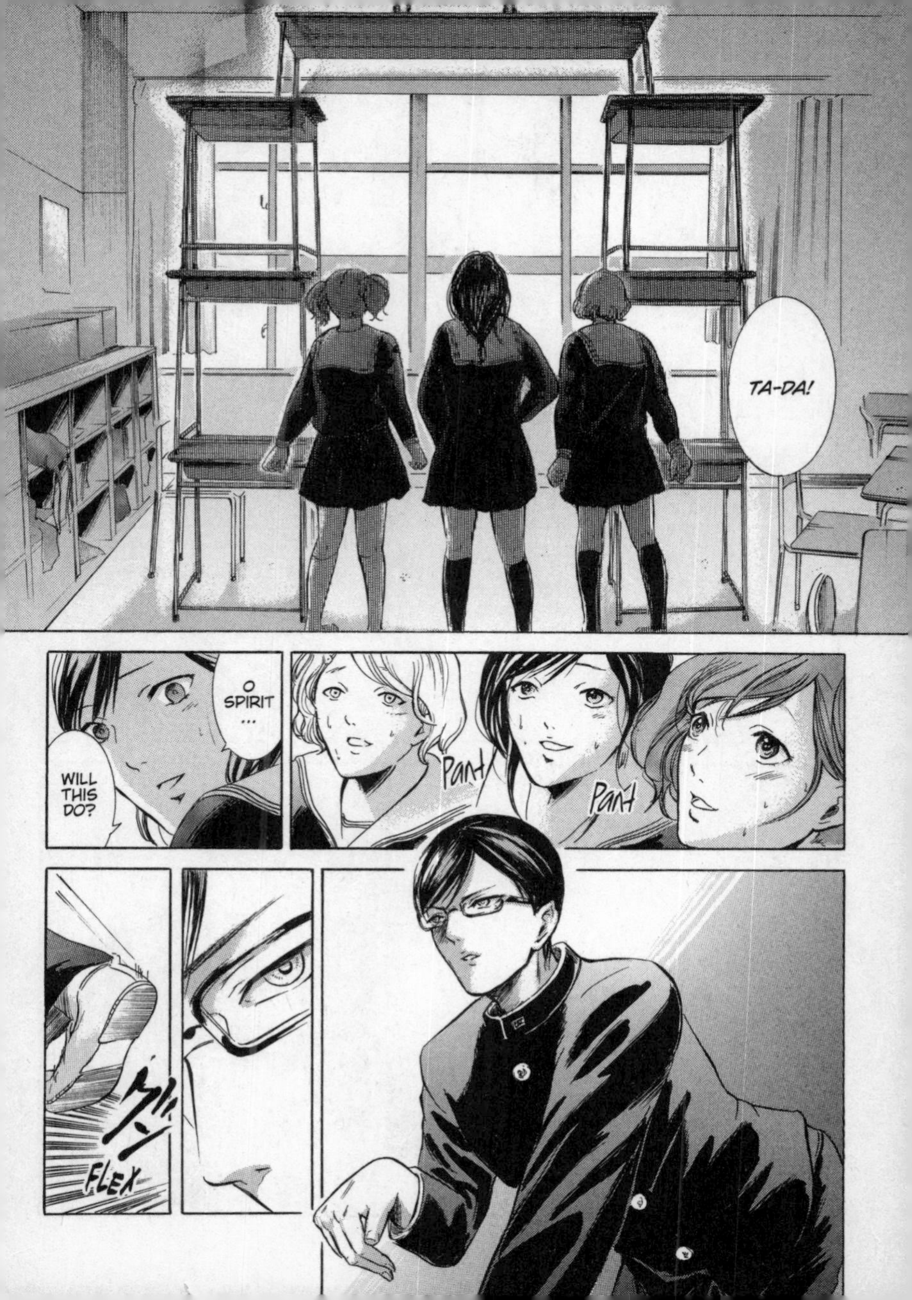
TA-DA!
Pant
Pant
O SPIRIT ...
WILL THIS DO?
FLEX

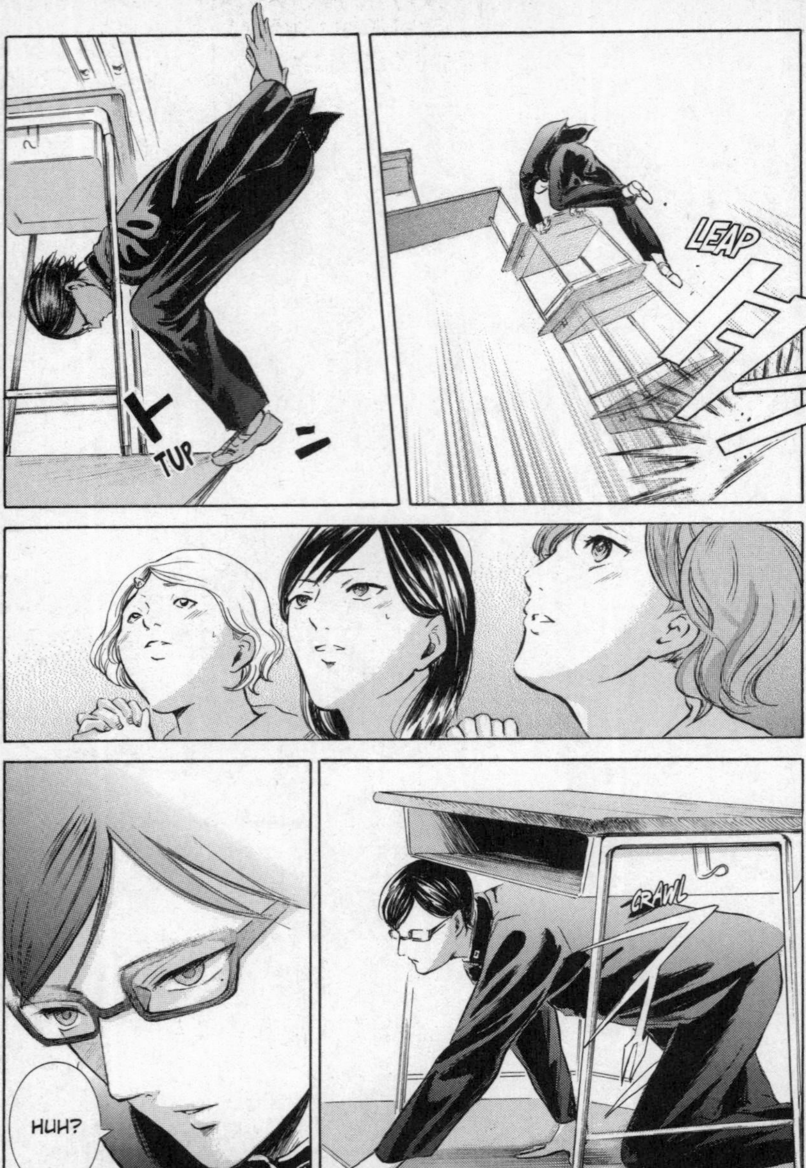
LEAP
TUP
CRAWL
HUH?

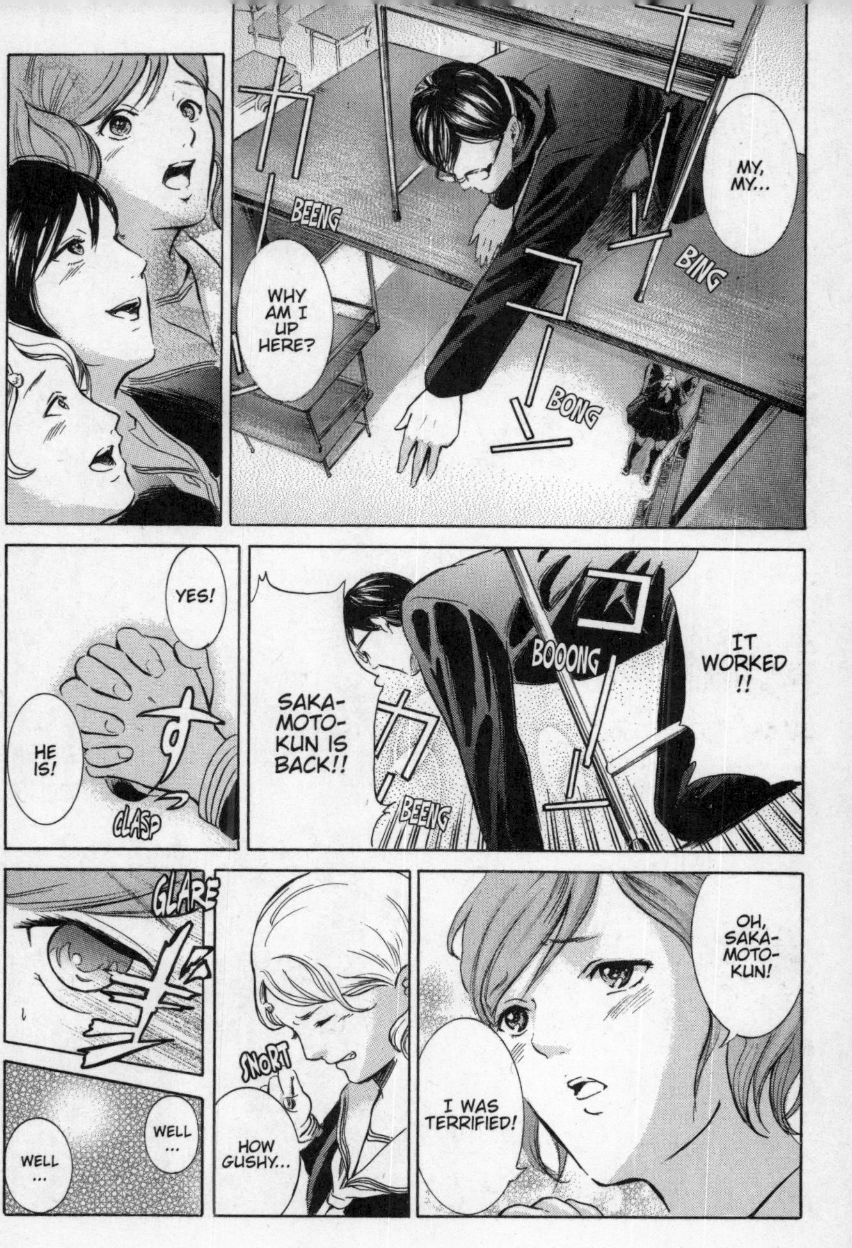
MY, MY...
BING
BEENG
WHY AM I UP HERE?
BONG
IT WORKED!!
BOOONG
SAKA-MOTO-KUN IS BACK!!
BEENG
YES!
HE IS!
CLASP
OH, SAKA-MOTO-KUN!
I WAS TERRIFIED!
SNORT
HOW GUSHY...
GLARE
WELL ...
WELL ...

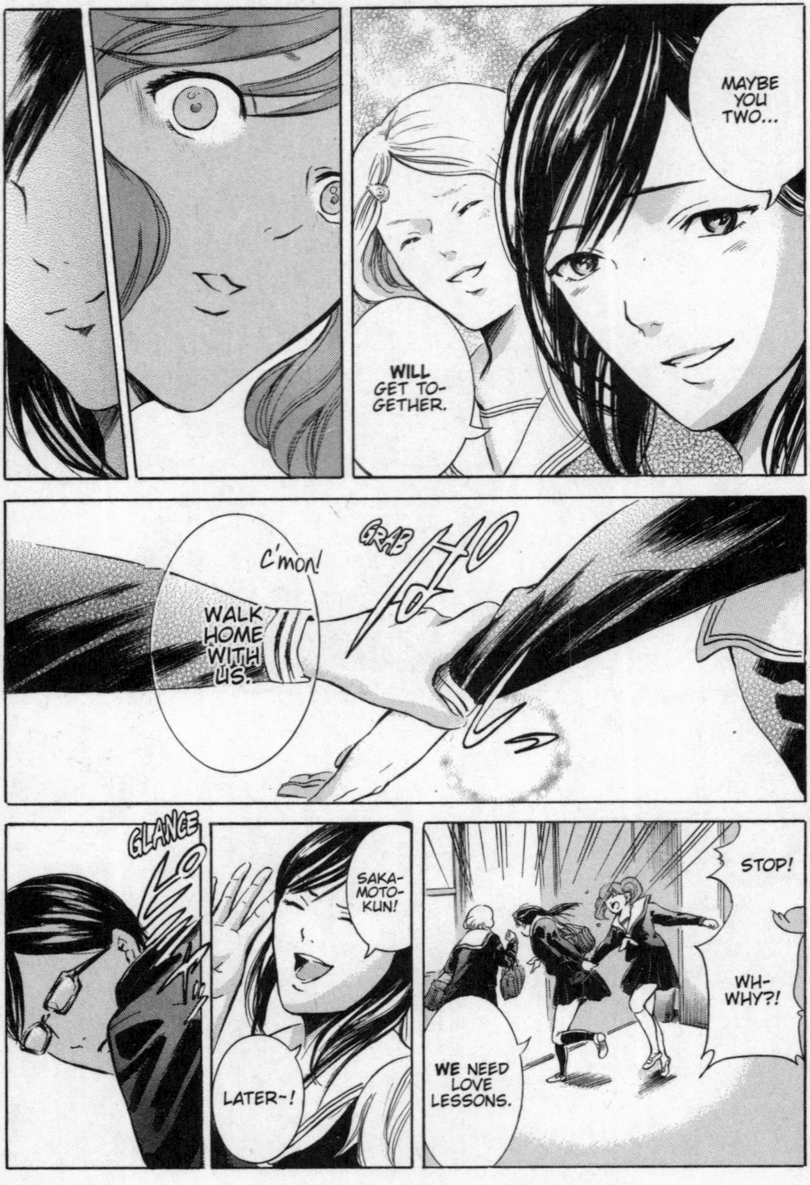
MAYBE YOU TWO...
WILL GET TO-GETHER.
GRAB
C'mon!
WALK HOME WITH US.
STOP!
WH-WHY?!
WE NEED LOVE LESSONS.
SAKA-MOTO-KUN!
LATER~!
GLANCE

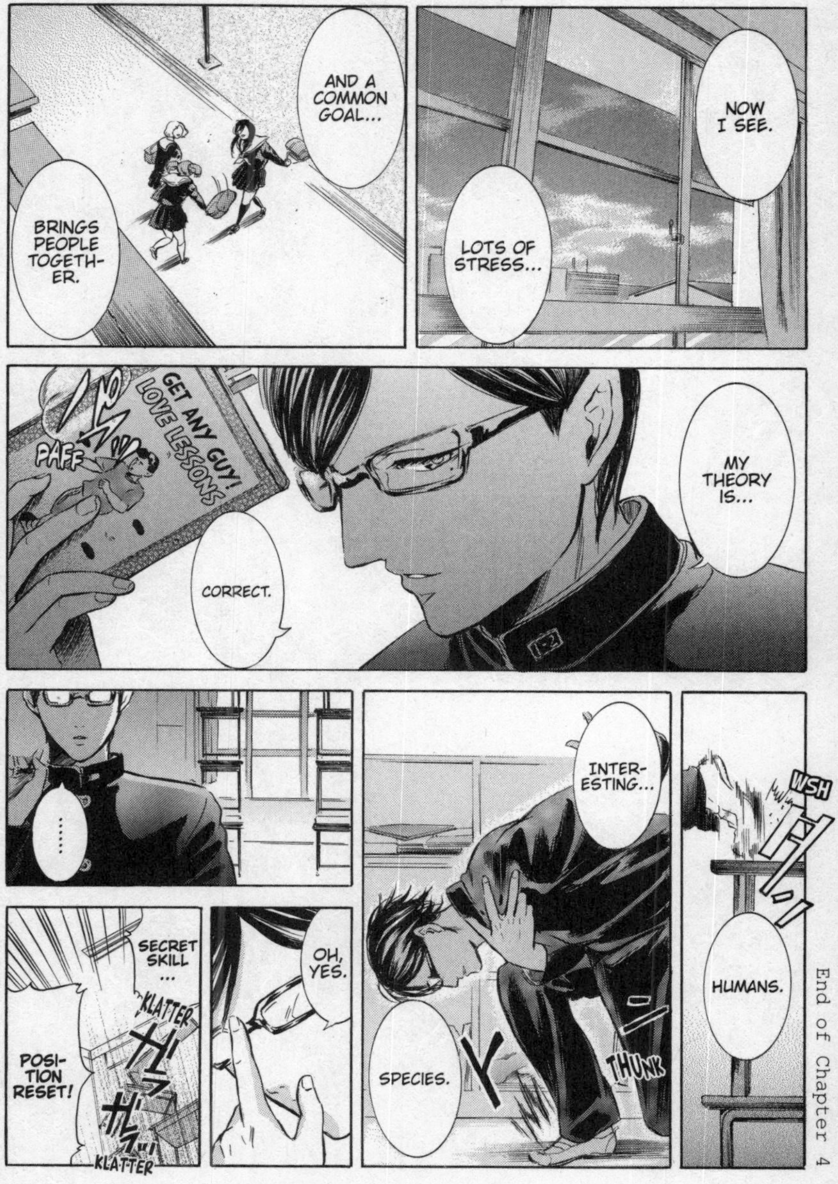
NOW I SEE.
LOTS OF STRESS...
AND A COMMON GOAL...
BRINGS PEOPLE TOGETH-ER.
MY THEORY IS...
GET ANY GUY! LOVE LESSONS
PAFF
CORRECT.
WSH
HUMANS.
INTER-ESTING...
THUNK
SPECIES.
......
OH, YES.
SECRET SKILL ...
KLATTER
POSI-TION RESET!
KLA-T-TER

End of Chapter 4

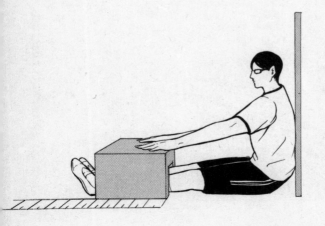

P.E. Test #4:
Seated
Forward
Stretch

LUNGE
BOOF

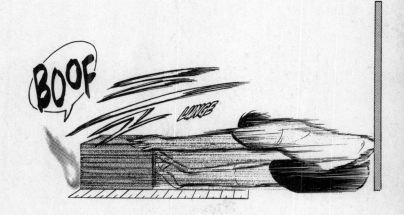

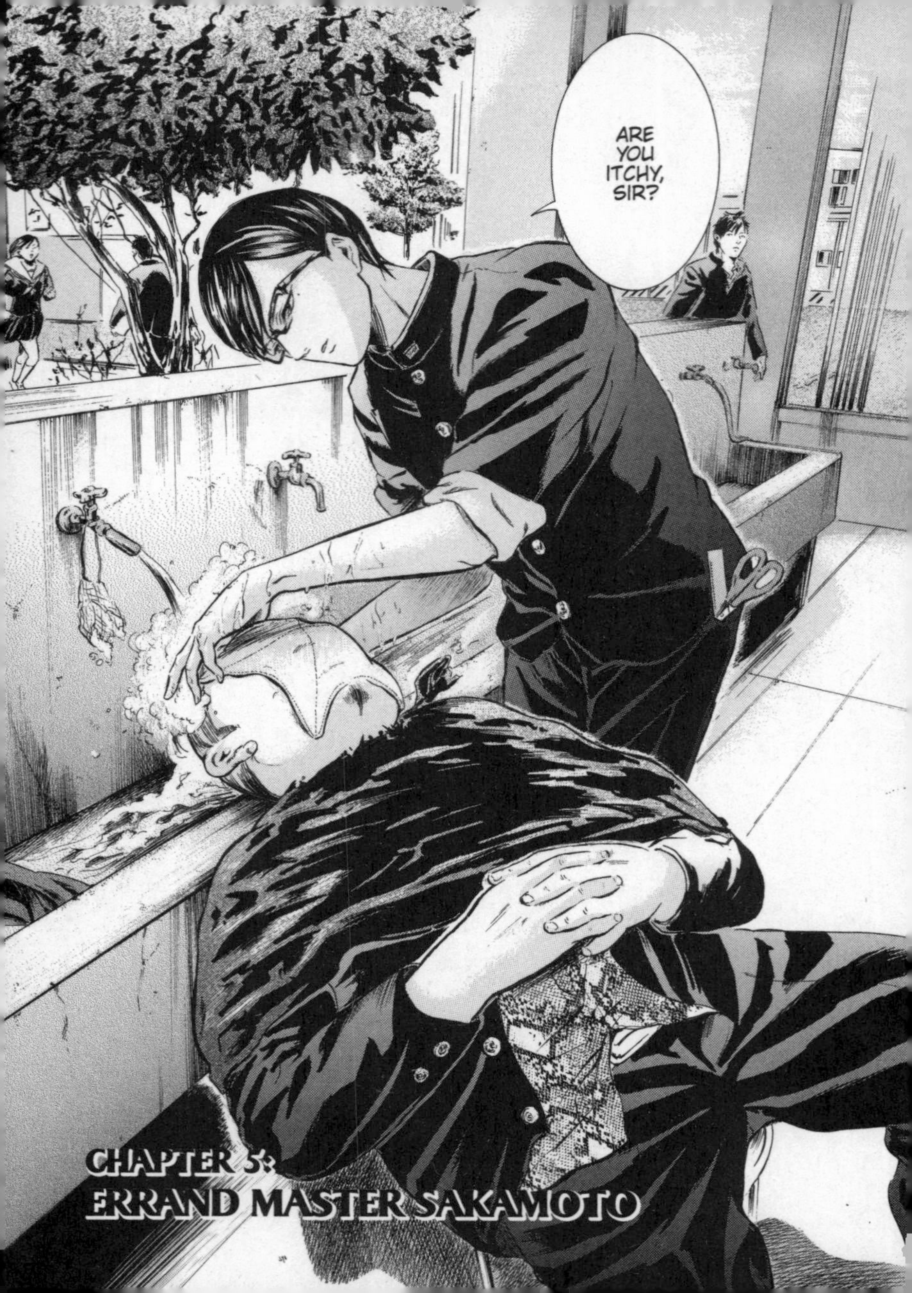
ARE YOU ITCHY, SIR?
CHAPTER 5:
ERRAND MASTER SAKAMOTO

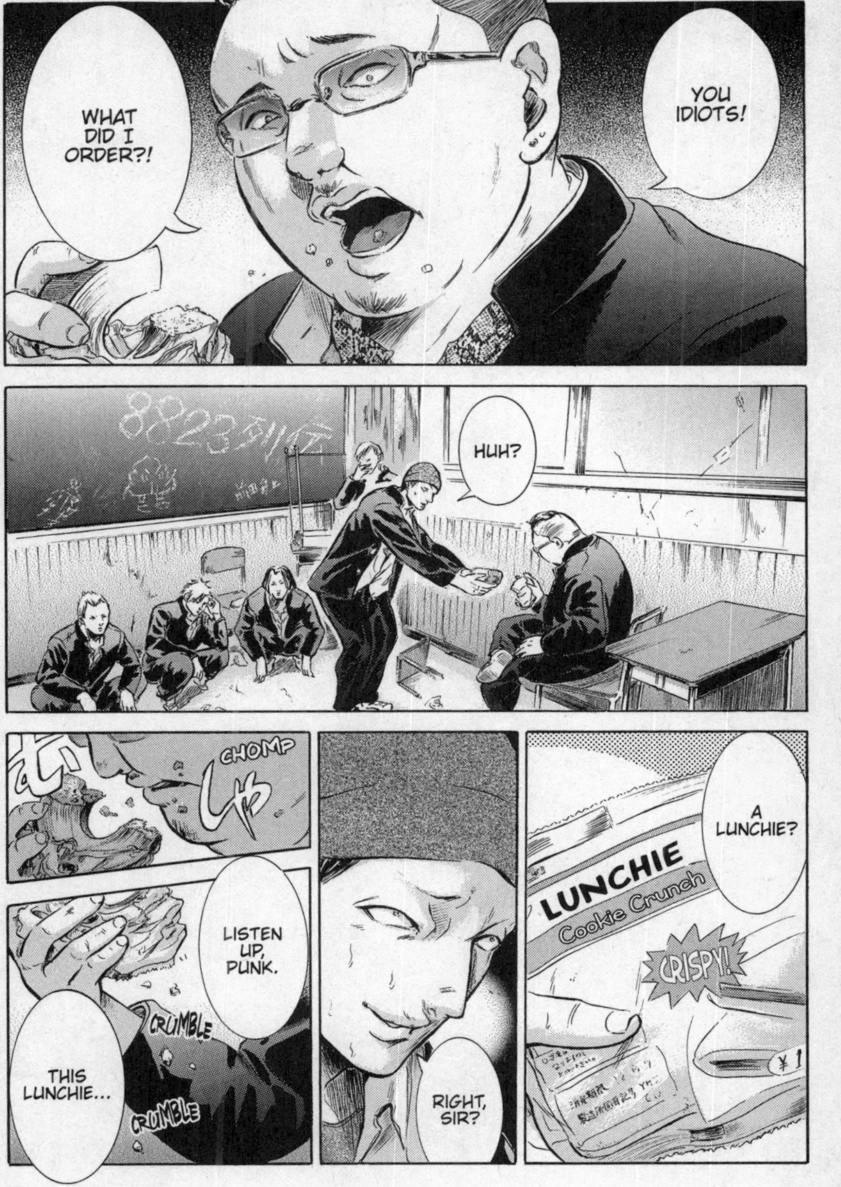
YOU IDIOTS!
WHAT DID I ORDER?!
HUH?
A LUNCHIE?
LUNCHIE
Cookie Crunch
CRISPY!
RIGHT, SIR?
CHOMP
むしゃ
LISTEN UP, PUNK.
CRUMBLE
THIS LUNCHIE...
CRUMBLE

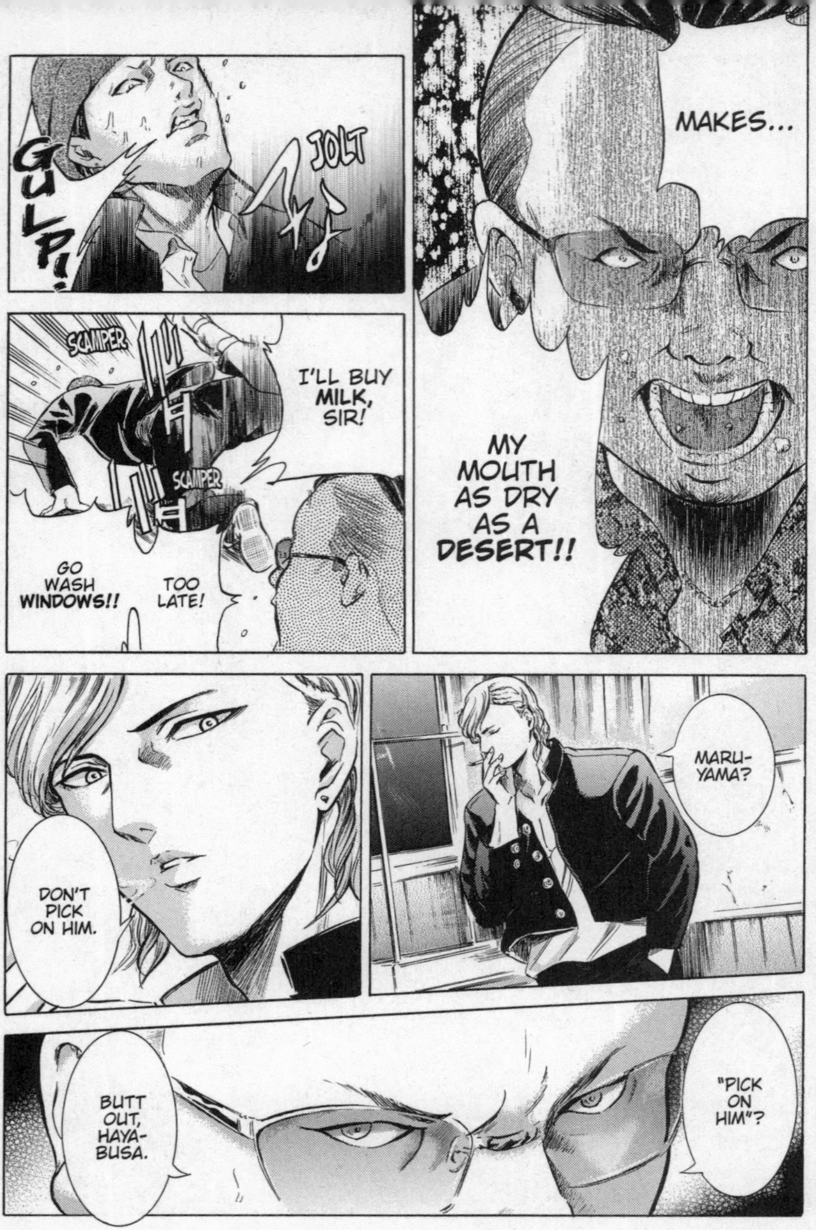
MAKES...
MY MOUTH AS DRY AS A DESERT!!
JOLT
GULP!
I'LL BUY MILK, SIR!
SCAMPER
SCAMPER
TOO LATE!
GO WASH WINDOWS!!
MARU-YAMA?
DON'T PICK ON HIM.
"PICK ON HIM"?
BUTT OUT, HAYA-BUSA.

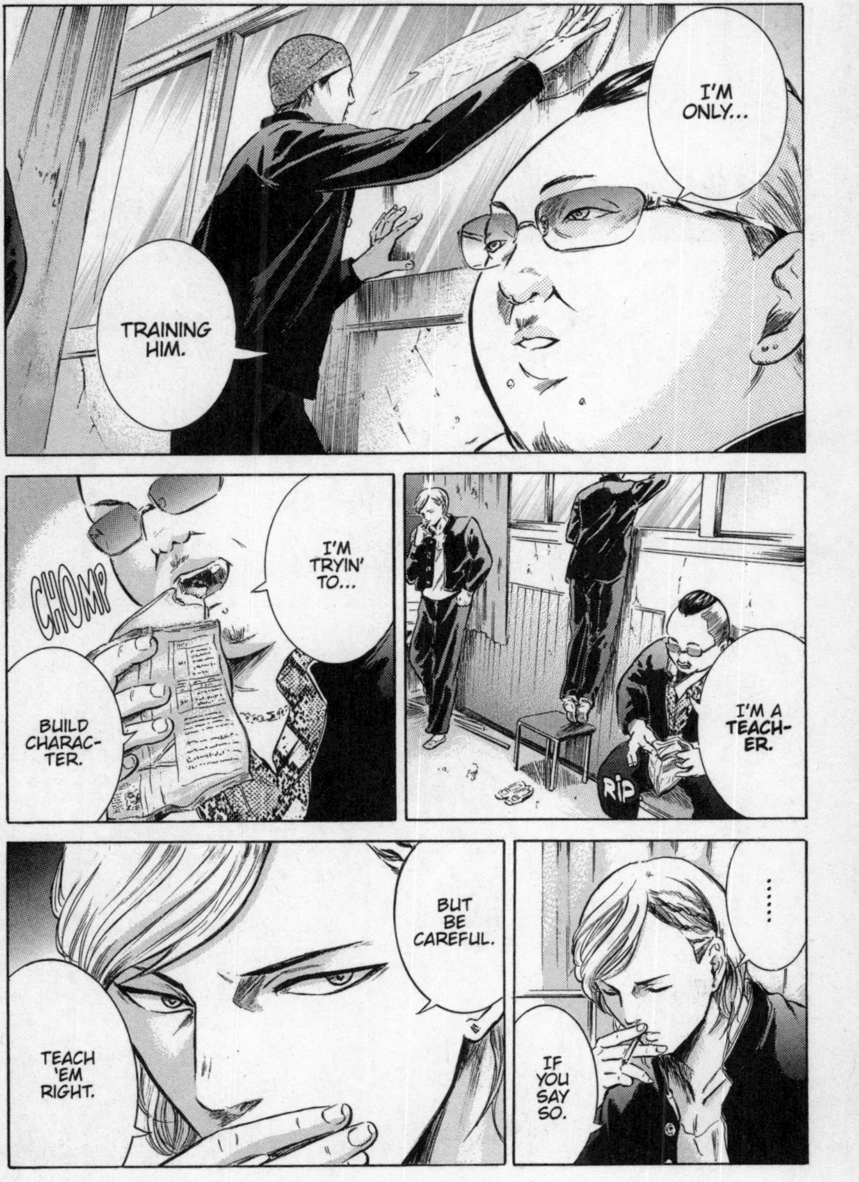
I'M ONLY...
TRAINING HIM.
RIP
I'M A TEACHER.
I'M TRYIN' TO...
CHOMP
BUILD CHARACTER.
......
IF YOU SAY SO.
BUT BE CAREFUL.
TEACH 'EM RIGHT.

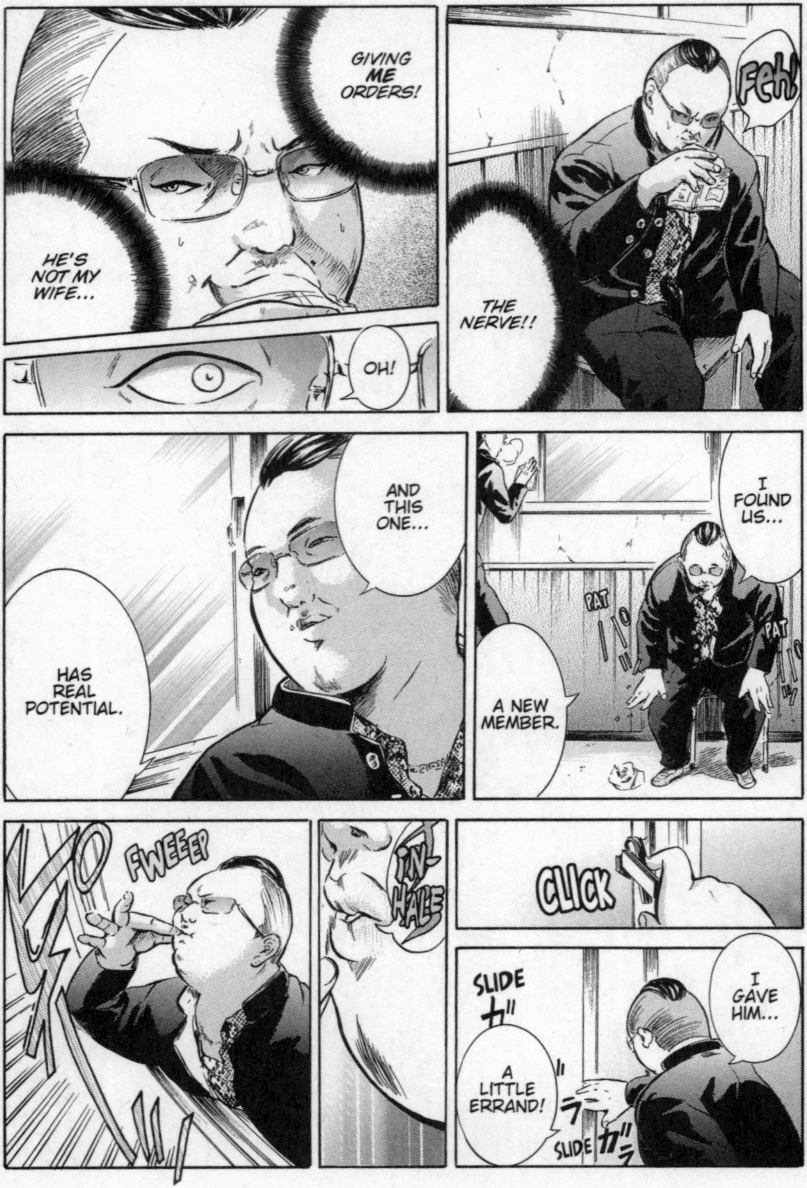
Feh!
THE NERVE!!
GIVING ME ORDERS!
HE'S NOT MY WIFE...
OH!
I FOUND US...
PAT
PAT
A NEW MEMBER.
AND THIS ONE...
HAS REAL POTENTIAL.
CLICK
I GAVE HIM...
SLIDE
A LITTLE ERRAND!
SLIDE
INHALE
FWEEEP

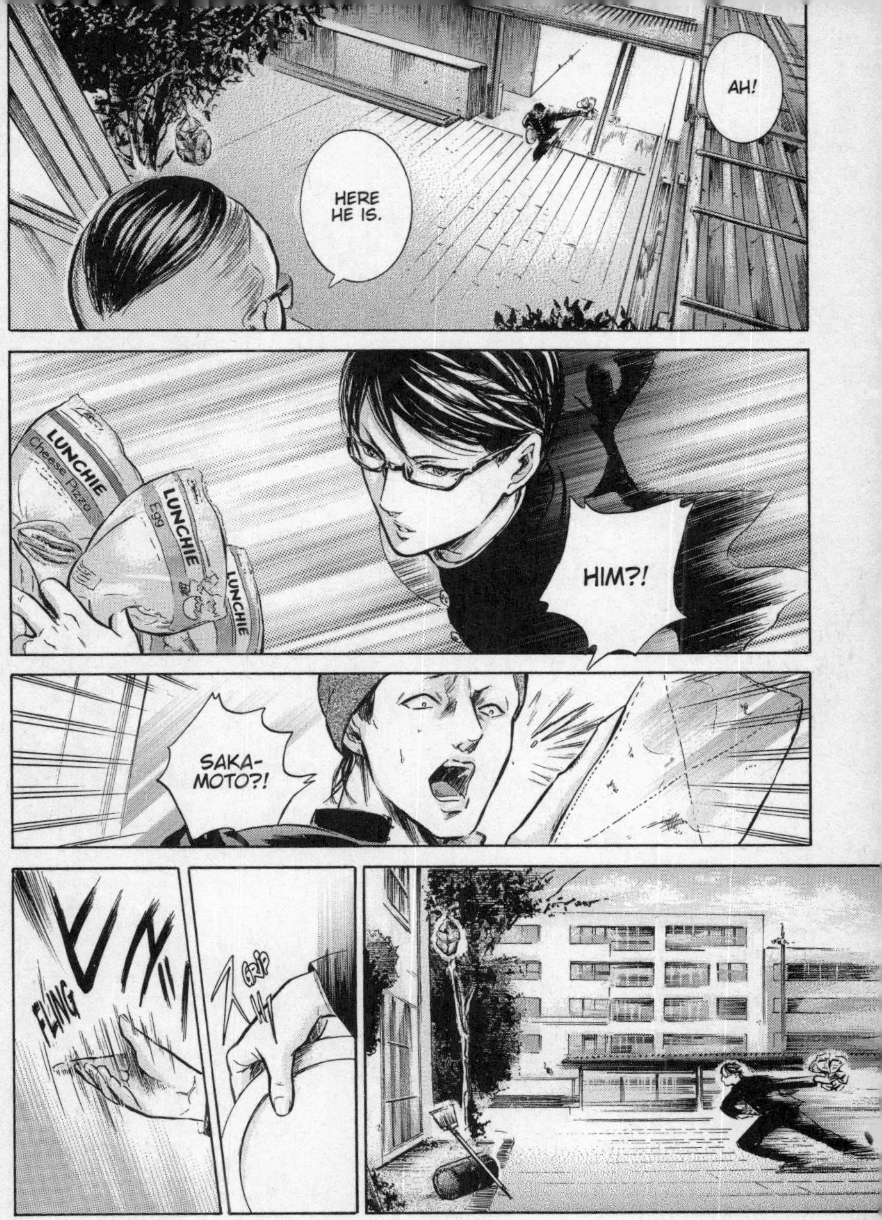
AH!
HERE HE IS.
LUNCHIE
Cheese Pizza
LUNCHIE
Egg
LUNCHIE
LUNCHIE
HIM?!
SAKA-MOTO?!
GRIP
FLING

SNAP

BOUND

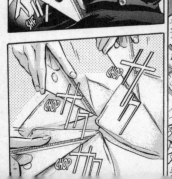

SHF

CHOP

CHOP

CHOP

RIP

LUNCHIE

RIP

RIP

WHOOSH

THUNK

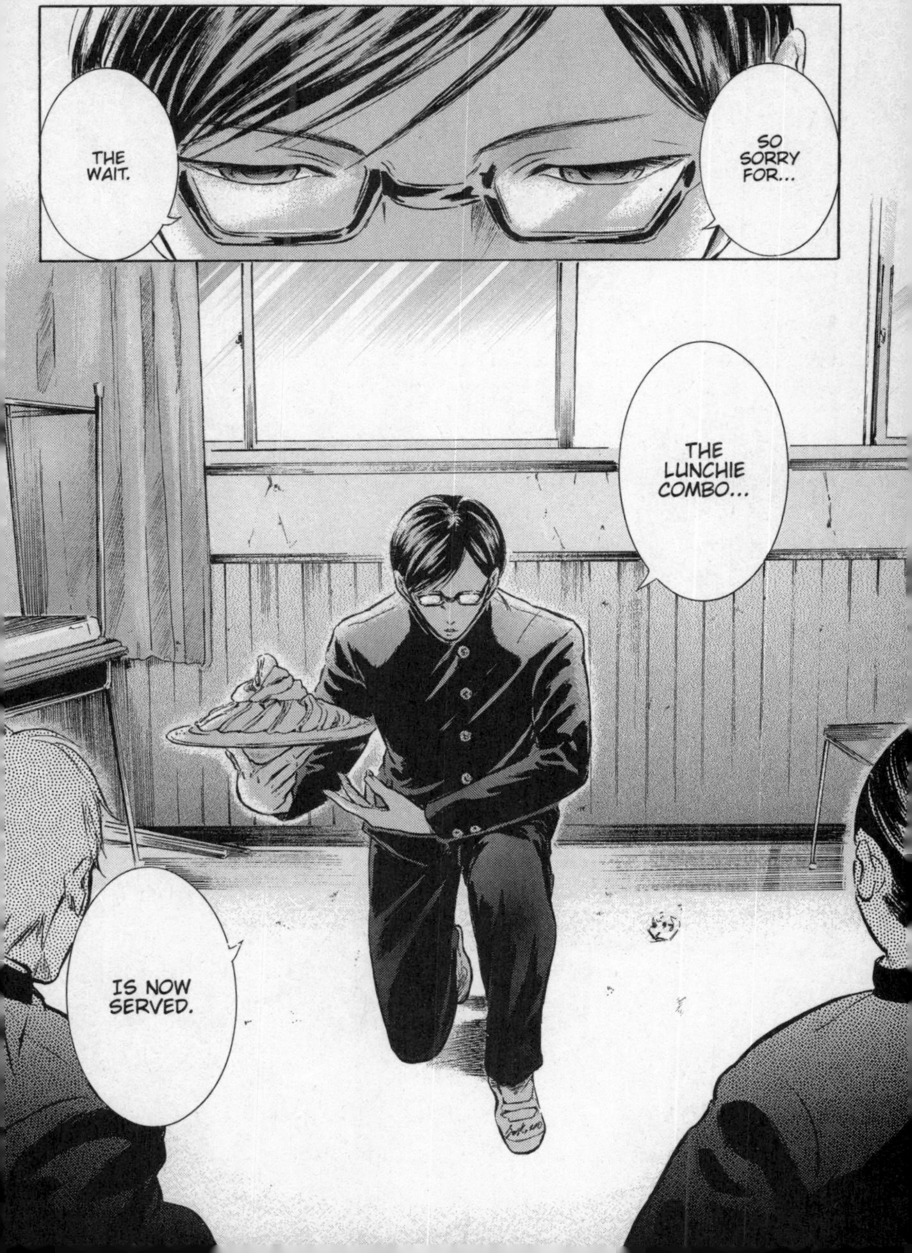
SO SORRY FOR...
THE WAIT.
THE LUNCHIE COMBO...
IS NOW SERVED.

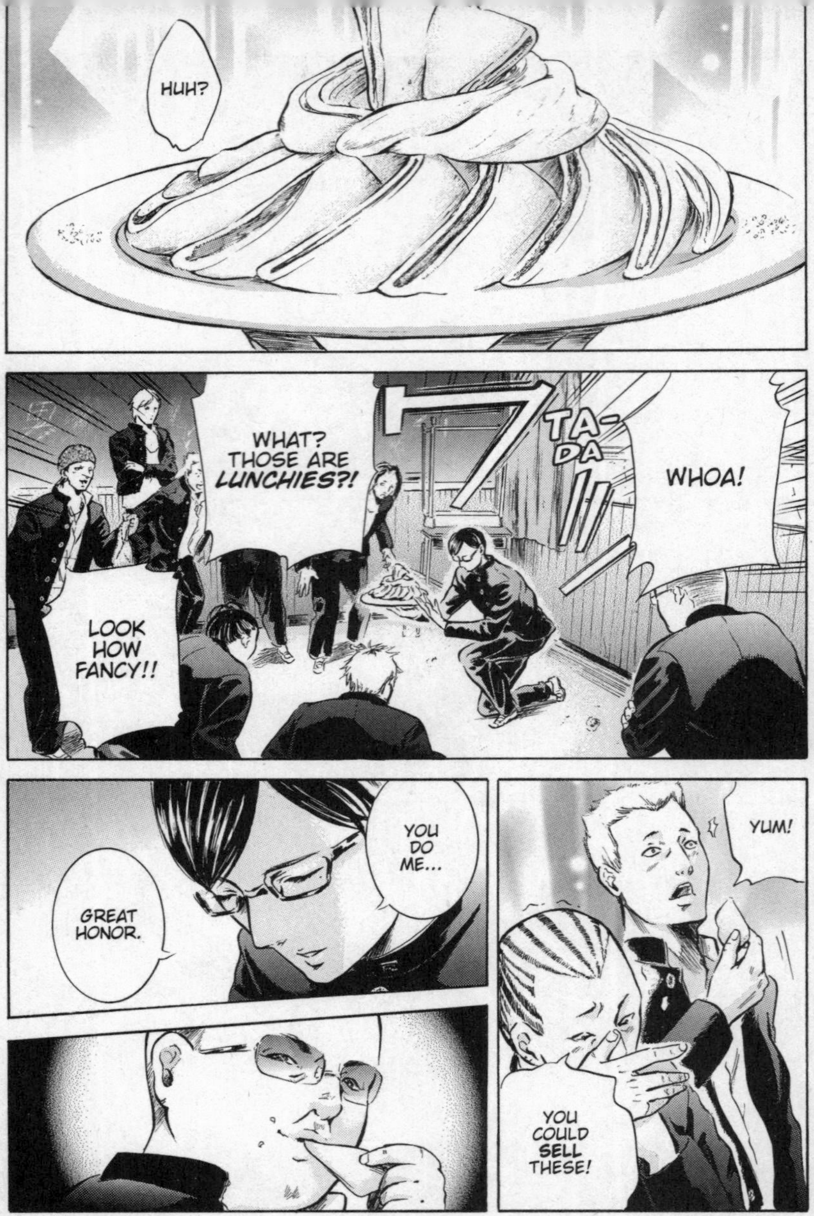
HUH?
WHOA!
TA-DA
WHAT? THOSE ARE *LUNCHIES*?!
LOOK HOW FANCY!!
YUM!
YOU COULD **SELL** THESE!
YOU DO ME...
GREAT HONOR.

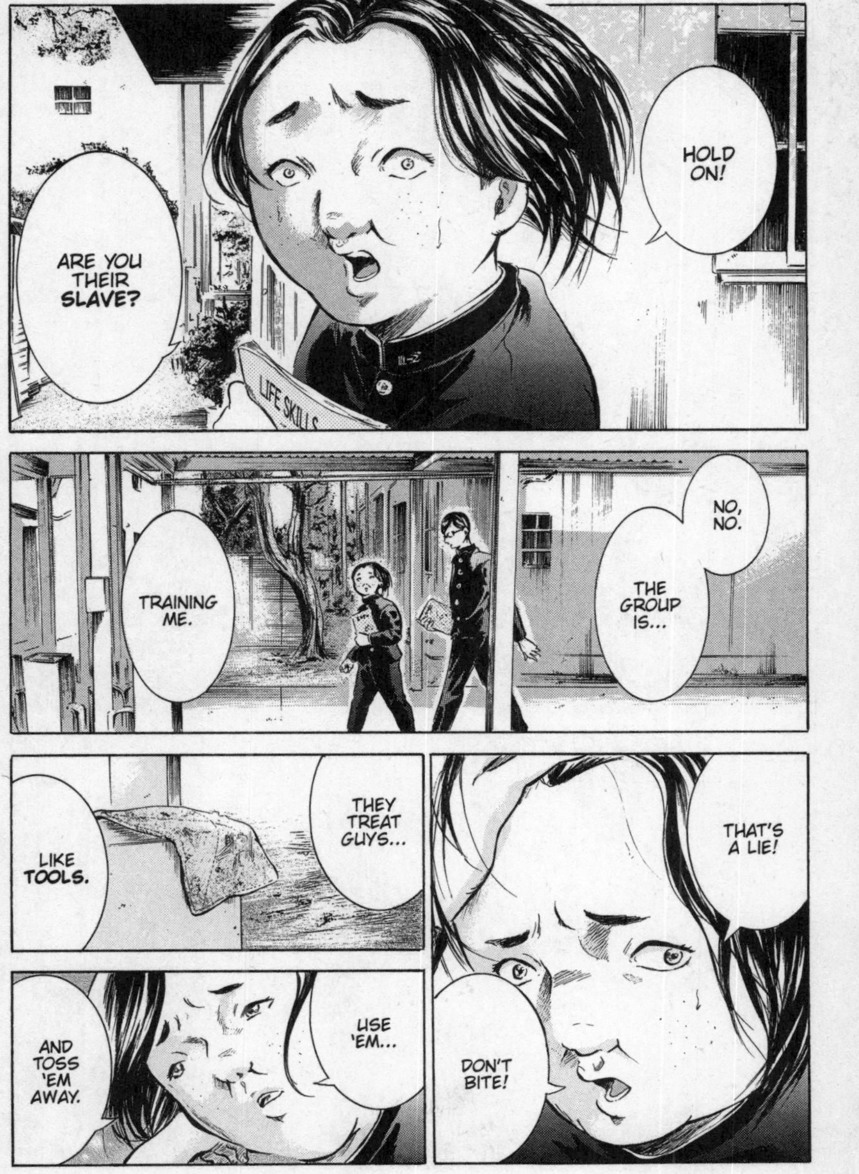
HOLD ON!
ARE YOU THEIR SLAVE?
LIFE SKILLS
NO, NO.
THE GROUP IS...
TRAINING ME.
THAT'S A LIE!
DON'T BITE!
THEY TREAT GUYS...
LIKE TOOLS.
USE 'EM...
AND TOSS 'EM AWAY.

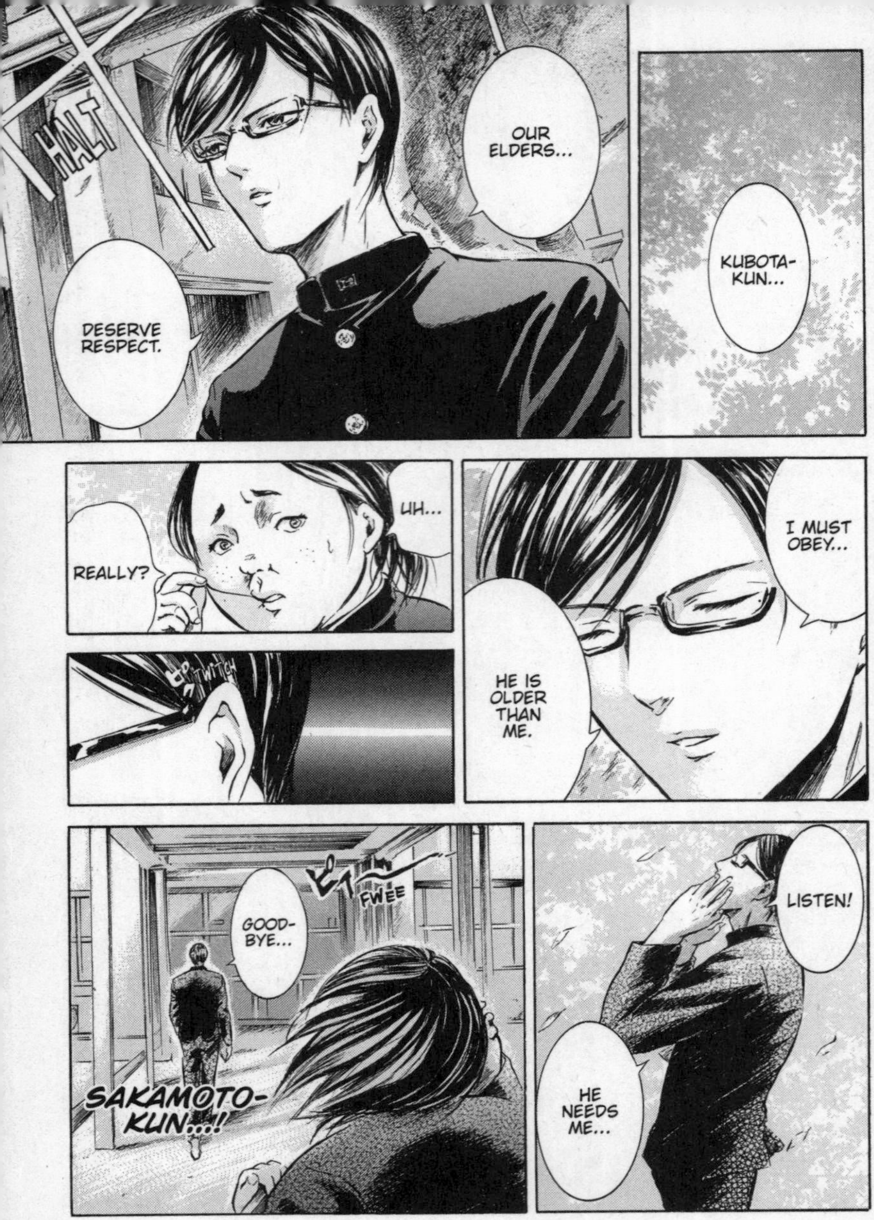
KUBOTA-KUN...
OUR ELDERS...
HALT
DESERVE RESPECT.
I MUST OBEY...
HE IS OLDER THAN ME.
UH...
REALLY?
TWITCH
LISTEN!
HE NEEDS ME...
FWEE
GOOD-BYE...
SAKAMOTO-KUN...!

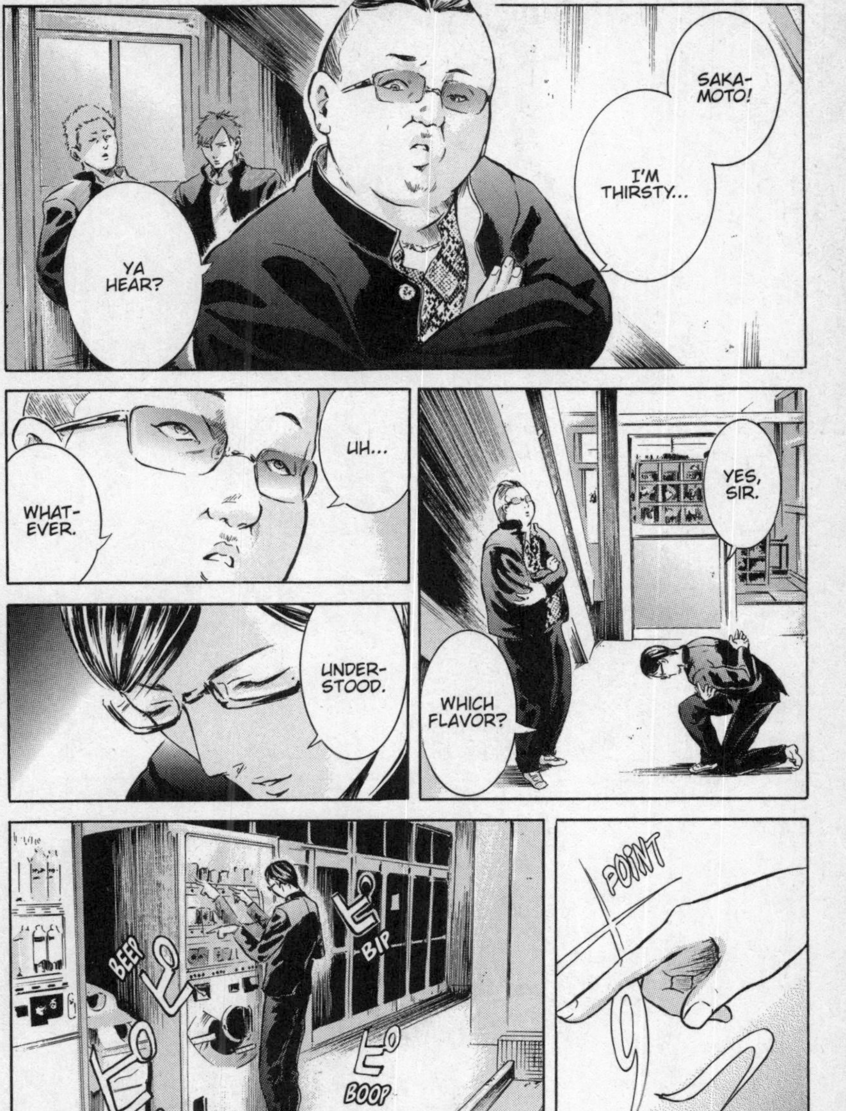
SAKA-MOTO!
I'M THIRSTY...
YA HEAR?
YES, SIR.
WHICH FLAVOR?
UH...
WHAT-EVER.
UNDER-STOOD.
POINT
BIP
BEEP
BOOP
BOOP

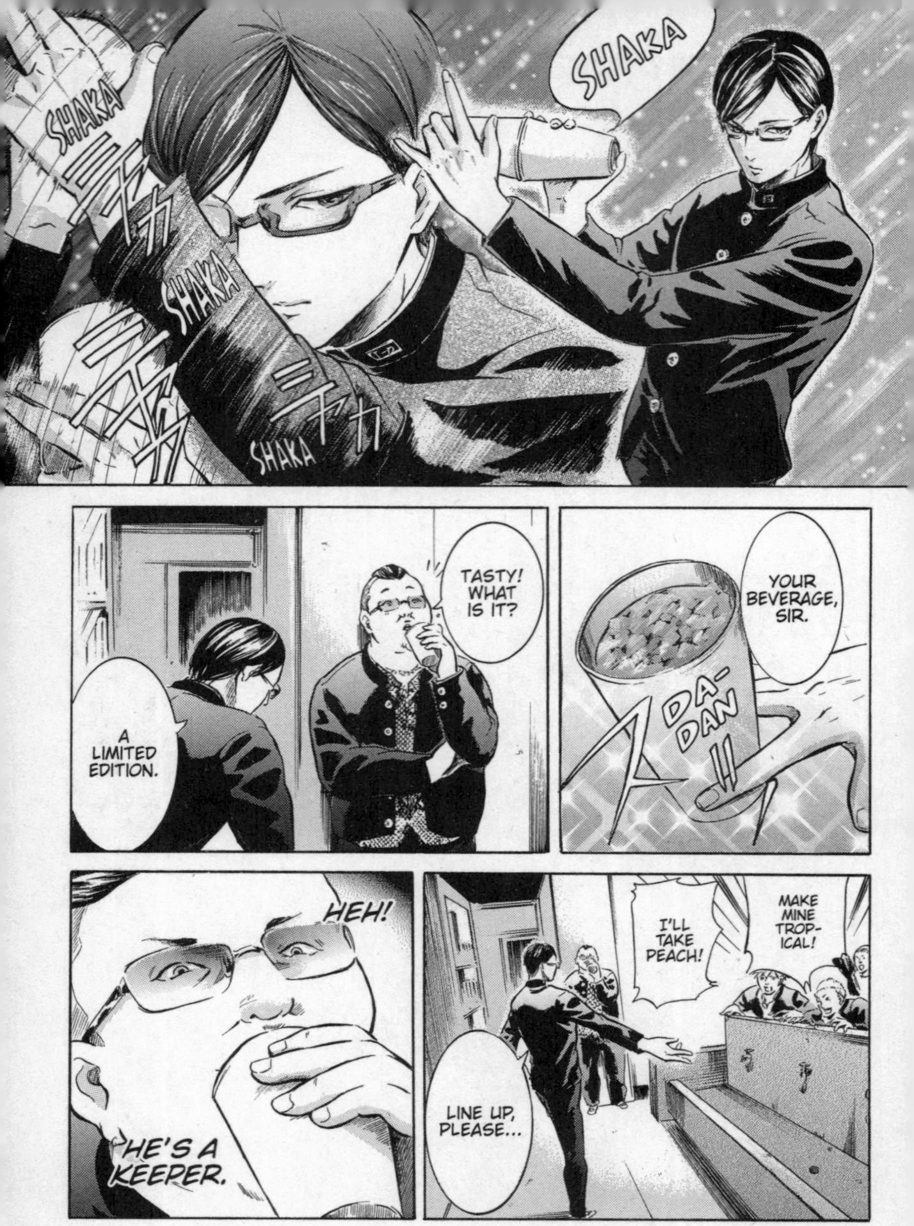
SHAKA
SHAKA
SHAKA
SHAKA
YOUR BEVERAGE, SIR.
DA-DAN!!
TASTY! WHAT IS IT?
A LIMITED EDITION.
MAKE MINE TROP-ICAL!
I'LL TAKE PEACH!
LINE UP, PLEASE...
HEH!
HE'S A KEEPER.

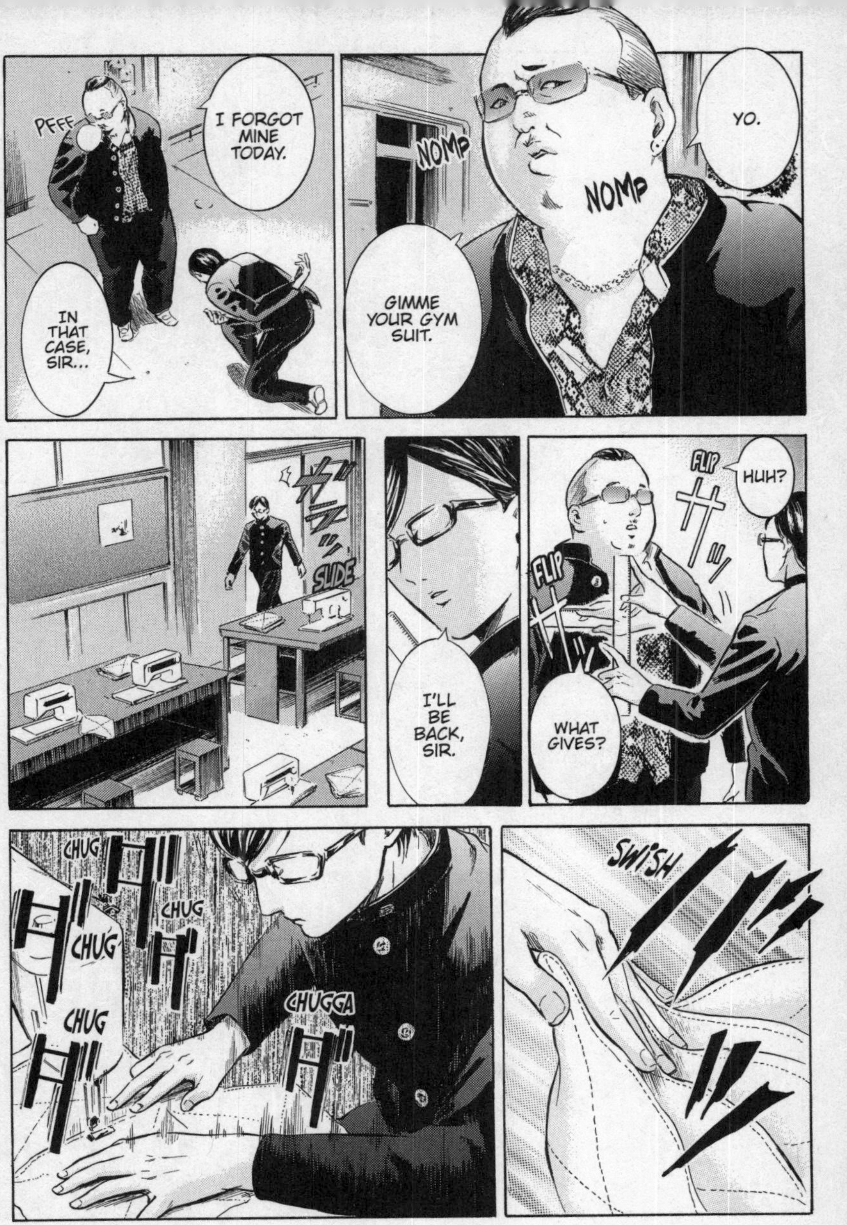
YO.
NOMP
NOMP
GIMME YOUR GYM SUIT.
PFFF
I FORGOT MINE TODAY.
IN THAT CASE, SIR...
FLIP
HUH?
FLIP
WHAT GIVES?
I'LL BE BACK, SIR.
SLIDE
SWISH
CHUG
CHUG
CHUG
CHUG
CHUGGA

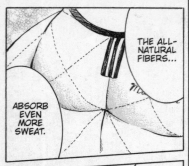

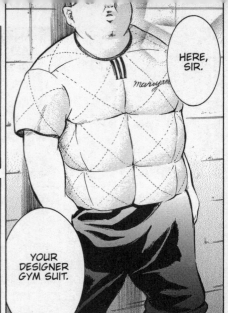

HERE, SIR.
YOUR DESIGNER GYM SUIT.
THE ALL-NATURAL FIBERS...
ABSORB EVEN MORE SWEAT.
SORRY YOUR NAME...
CAME OUT CROOKED.
WHOA! COOL GYM SUIT!!
CLAMOR
WHERE'D YOU GET THAT, MARUYAMA?!
Heh!
SORRY! I AIN'T TELLIN'!

SWP
SWP
SWP
SWP
SWP

SAKA-MOTO!

FAH-WHUMP

SHOE SHINE!

WHEE!

GLIIIDE

TAKE NOTES FOR ME.

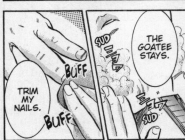

TRIM MY NAILS.

BUFF

BUFF

SUD

THE GOATEE STAYS.

SUD

ROLL   ROLL

NICE MAS-SAGE.

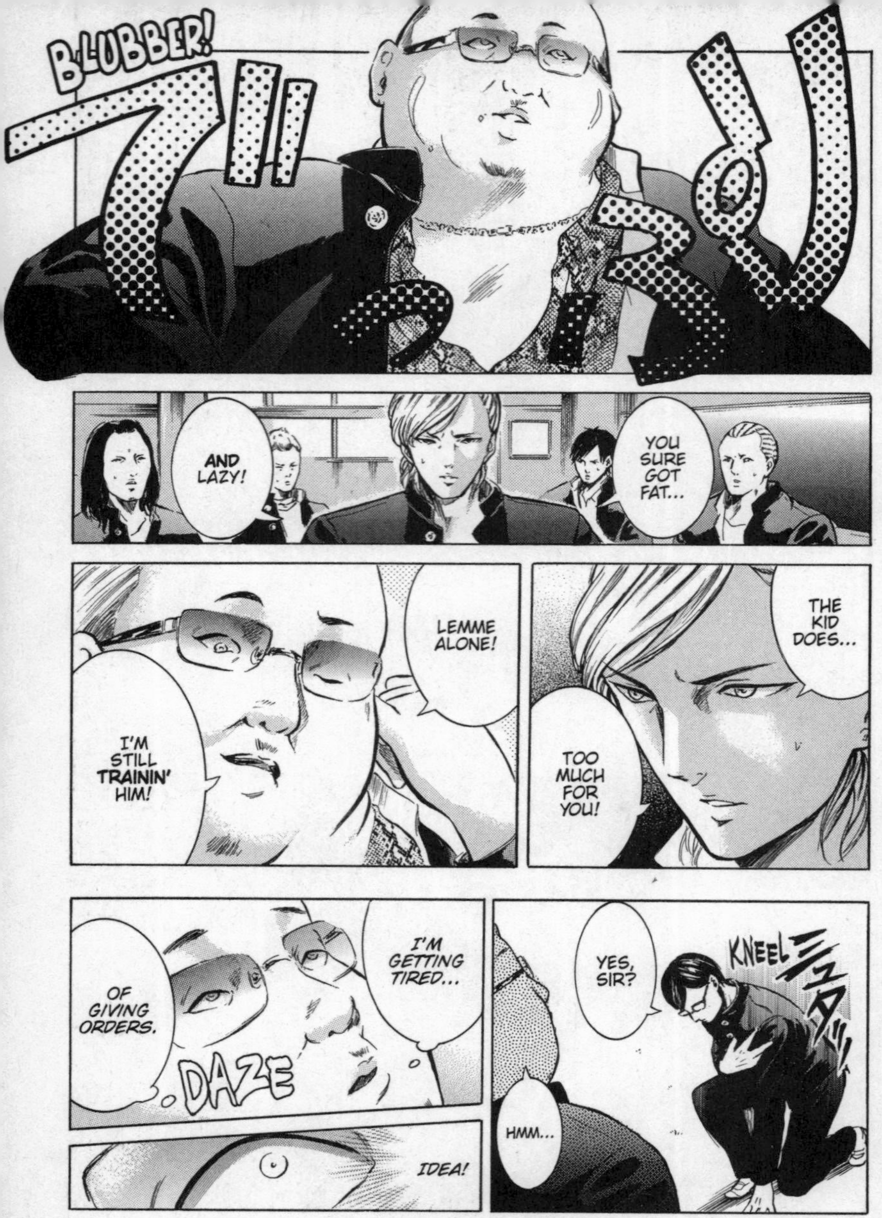
B-LUBBER!
YOU SURE GOT FAT...
AND LAZY!
THE KID DOES...
TOO MUCH FOR YOU!
LEMME ALONE!
I'M STILL TRAININ' HIM!
KNEEL
YES, SIR?
HMM...
I'M GETTING TIRED...
OF GIVING ORDERS.
DAZE
IDEA!

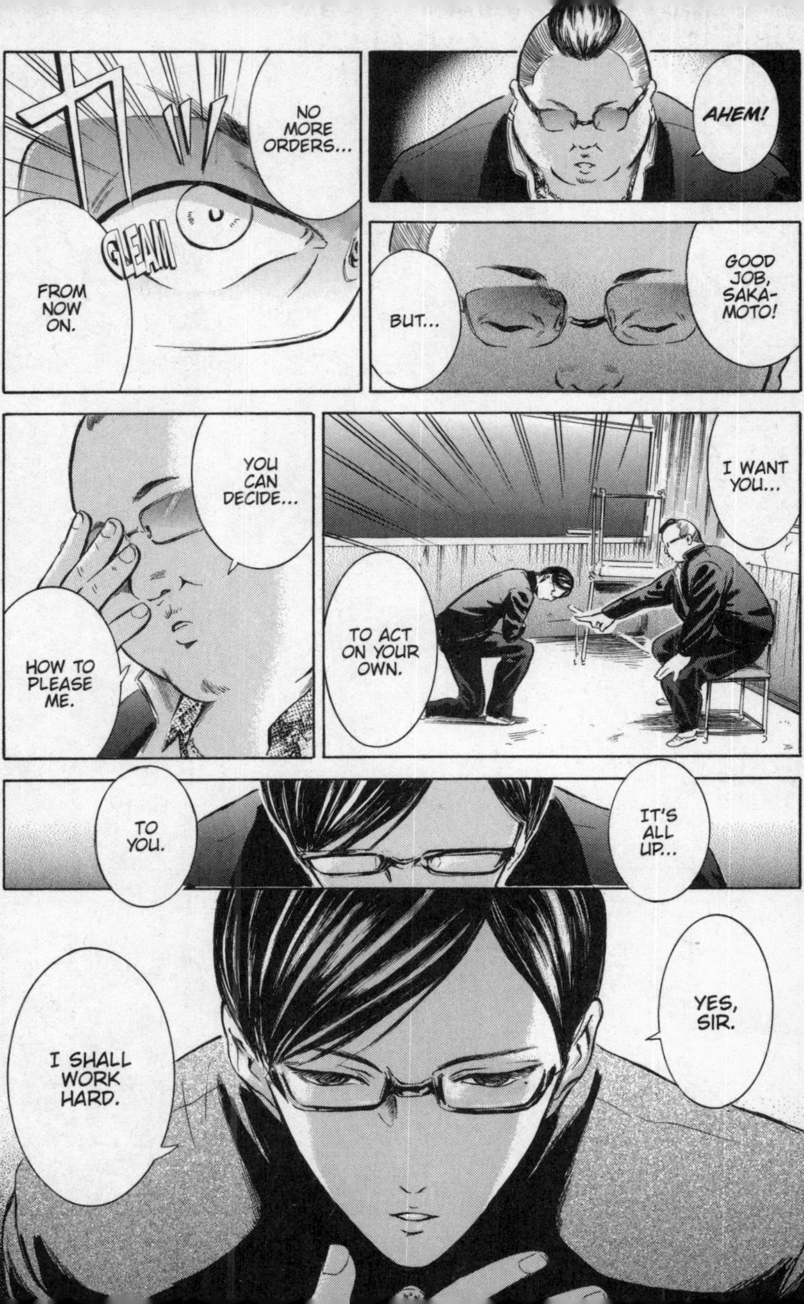
AHEM!
GOOD JOB, SAKAMOTO!
BUT...
NO MORE ORDERS...
GLEAM
FROM NOW ON.
I WANT YOU...
TO ACT ON YOUR OWN.
YOU CAN DECIDE...
HOW TO PLEASE ME.
IT'S ALL UP...
TO YOU.
YES, SIR.
I SHALL WORK HARD.

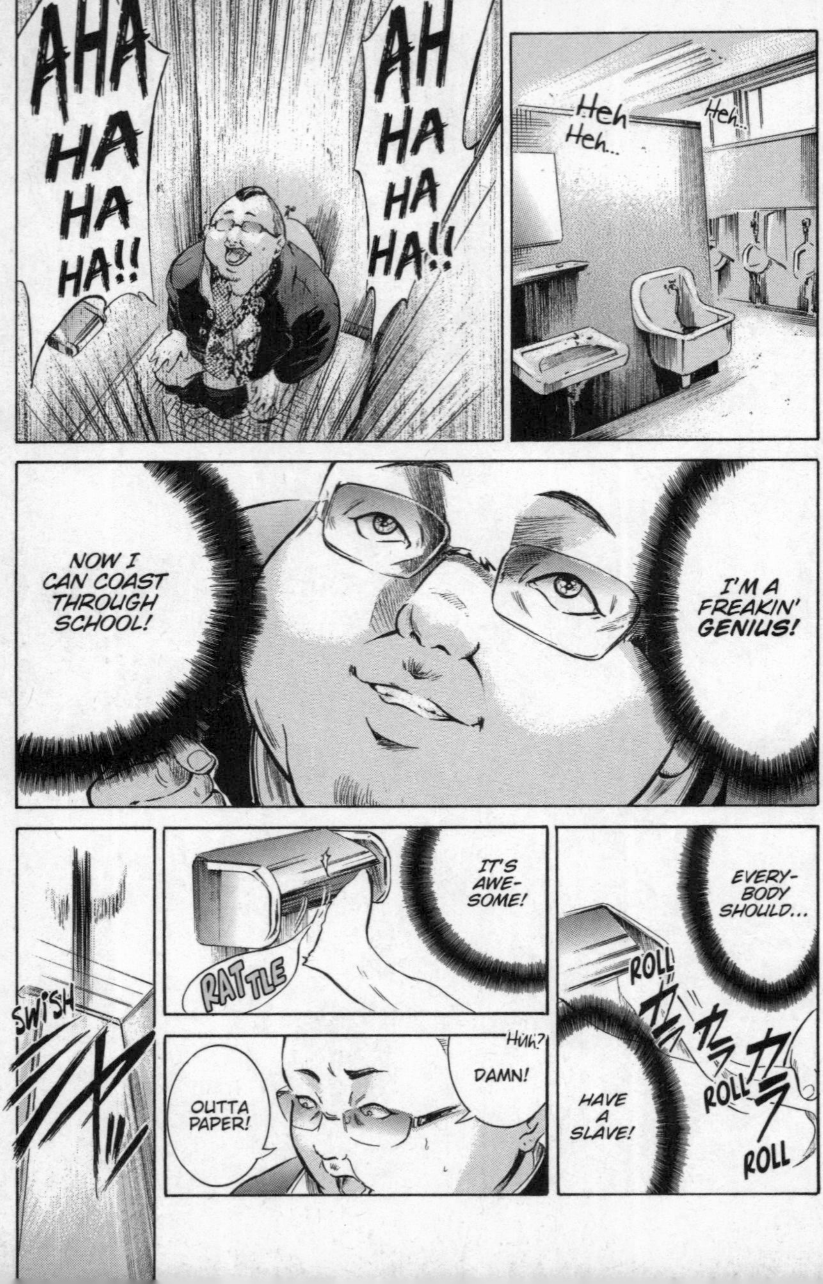
Heh...
Heh Heh...
AH HA HA HA!!
AHA HA HA HA!!
I'M A FREAKIN' GENIUS!
NOW I CAN COAST THROUGH SCHOOL!
EVERYBODY SHOULD...
ROLL
ROLL
ROLL
HAVE A SLAVE!
IT'S AWESOME!
RATTLE
Huh?
DAMN!
OUTTA PAPER!
SWISH

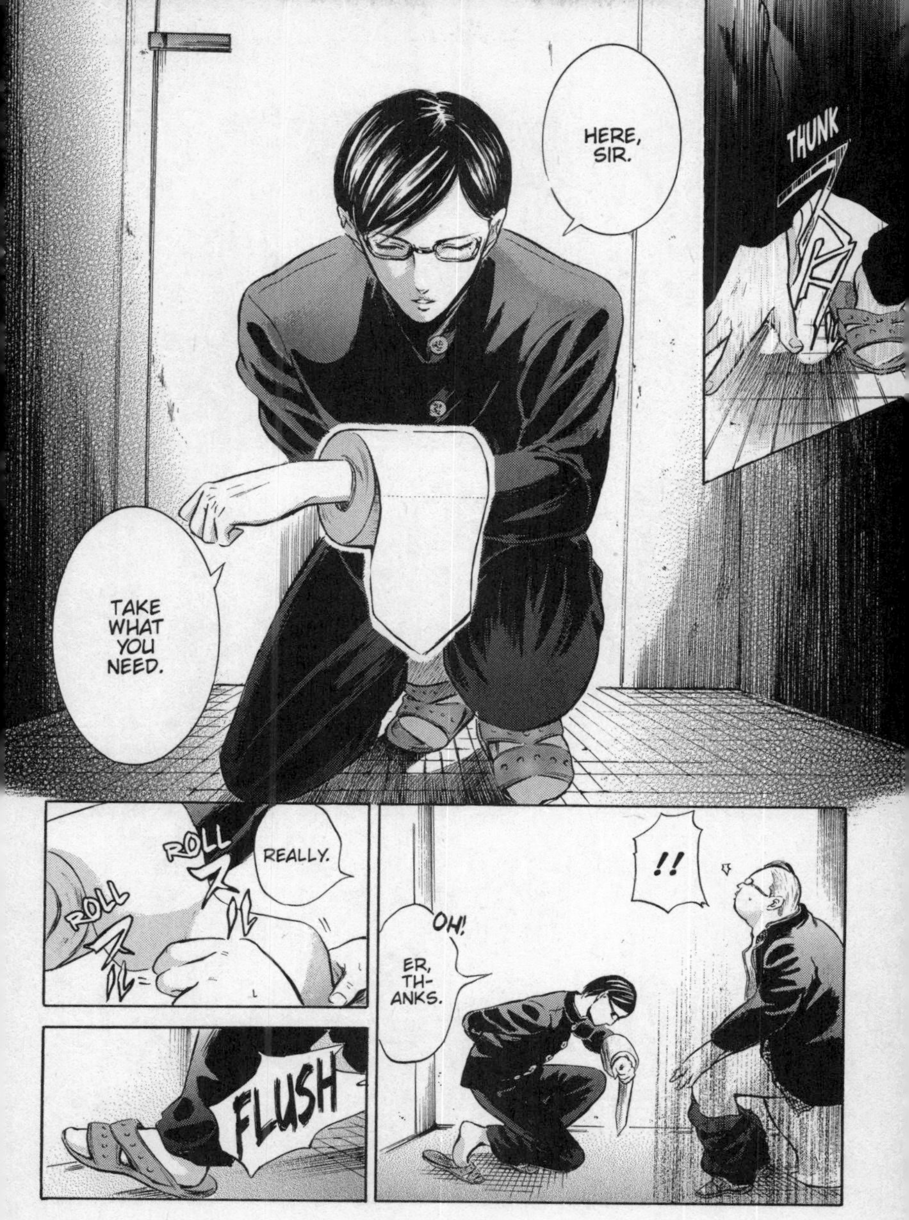
THUNK
HERE, SIR.
TAKE WHAT YOU NEED.
!!
OH!
ER, TH- ANKS.
REALLY.
ROLL
ROLL
FLUSH

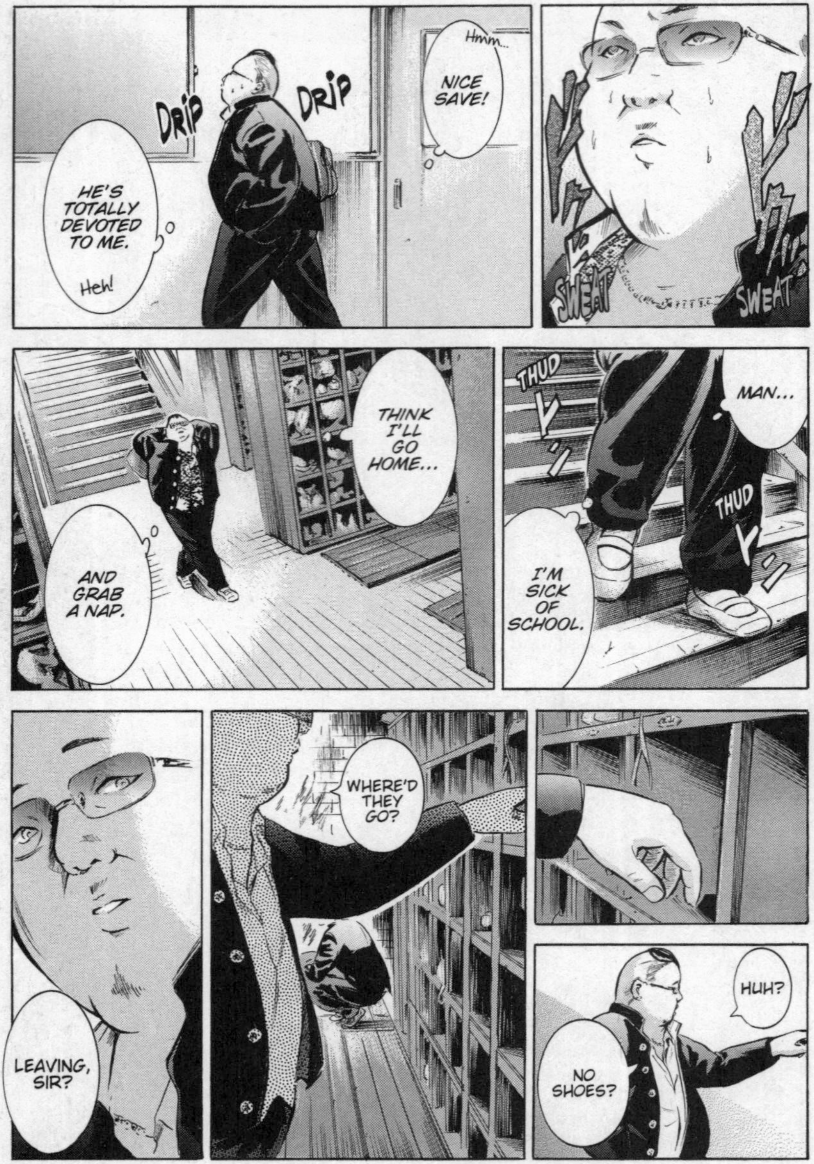
SWEAT
SWEAT
Hmm...
NICE SAVE!
DRIP
DRIP
HE'S TOTALLY DEVOTED TO ME.
Heh!
MAN...
THUD
THUD
I'M SICK OF SCHOOL.
THINK I'LL GO HOME...
AND GRAB A NAP.
HUH?
NO SHOES?
WHERE'D THEY GO?
LEAVING, SIR?

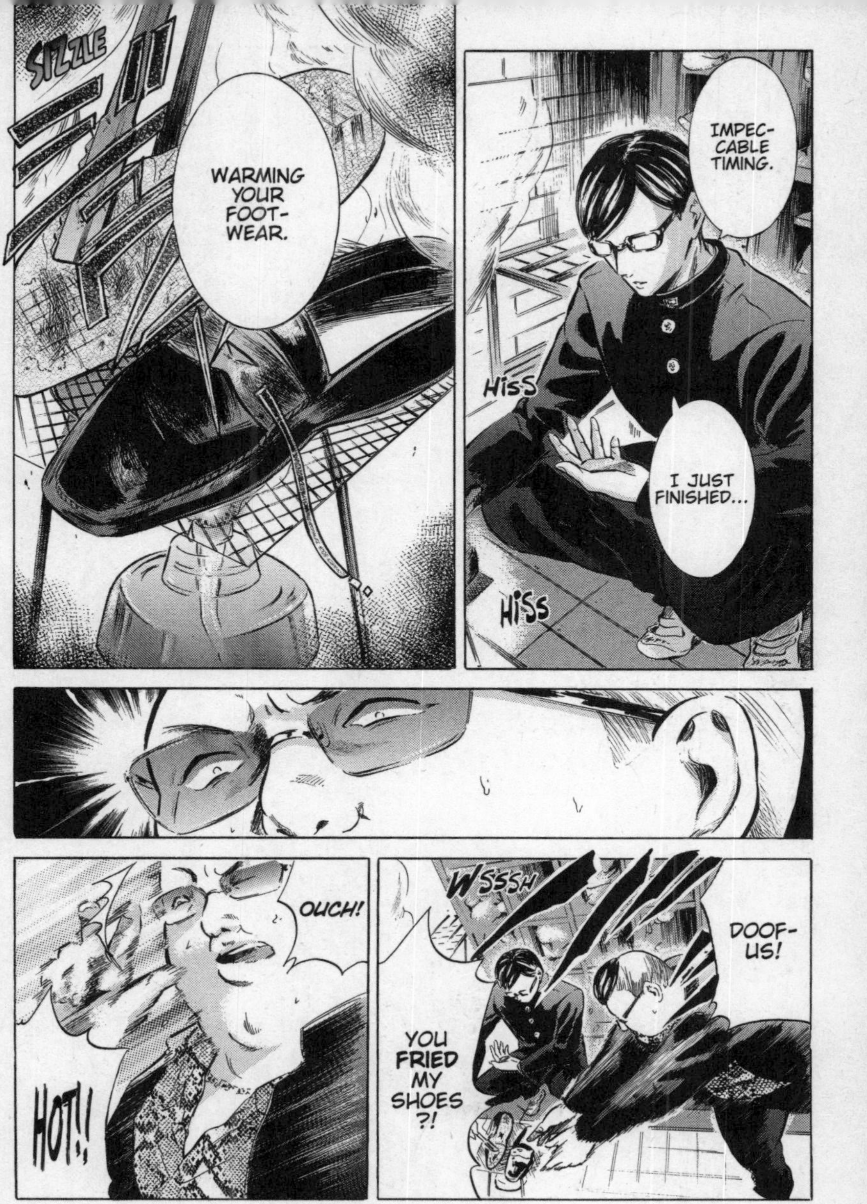
IMPECCABLE TIMING.
HISS
I JUST FINISHED...
HISS
SIZZLE
WARMING YOUR FOOTWEAR.
WSSSH
DOOFUS!
YOU FRIED MY SHOES?!
OUCH!
HOT!!

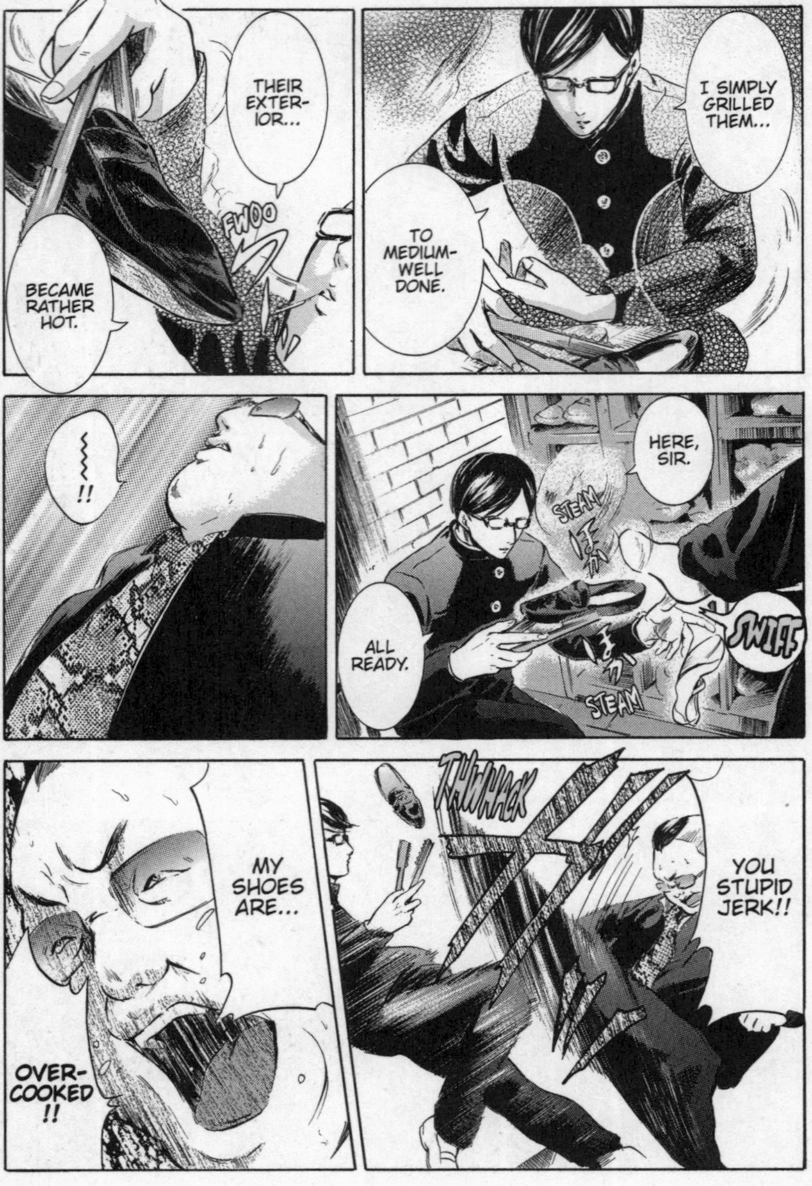
I SIMPLY GRILLED THEM...
TO MEDIUM-WELL DONE.
THEIR EXTERIOR...
FWOO
BECAME RATHER HOT.
HERE, SIR.
STEAM
ALL READY.
SWIFF
STEAM
...!!
THWHACK
YOU STUPID JERK!!
MY SHOES ARE...
OVER-COOKED!!

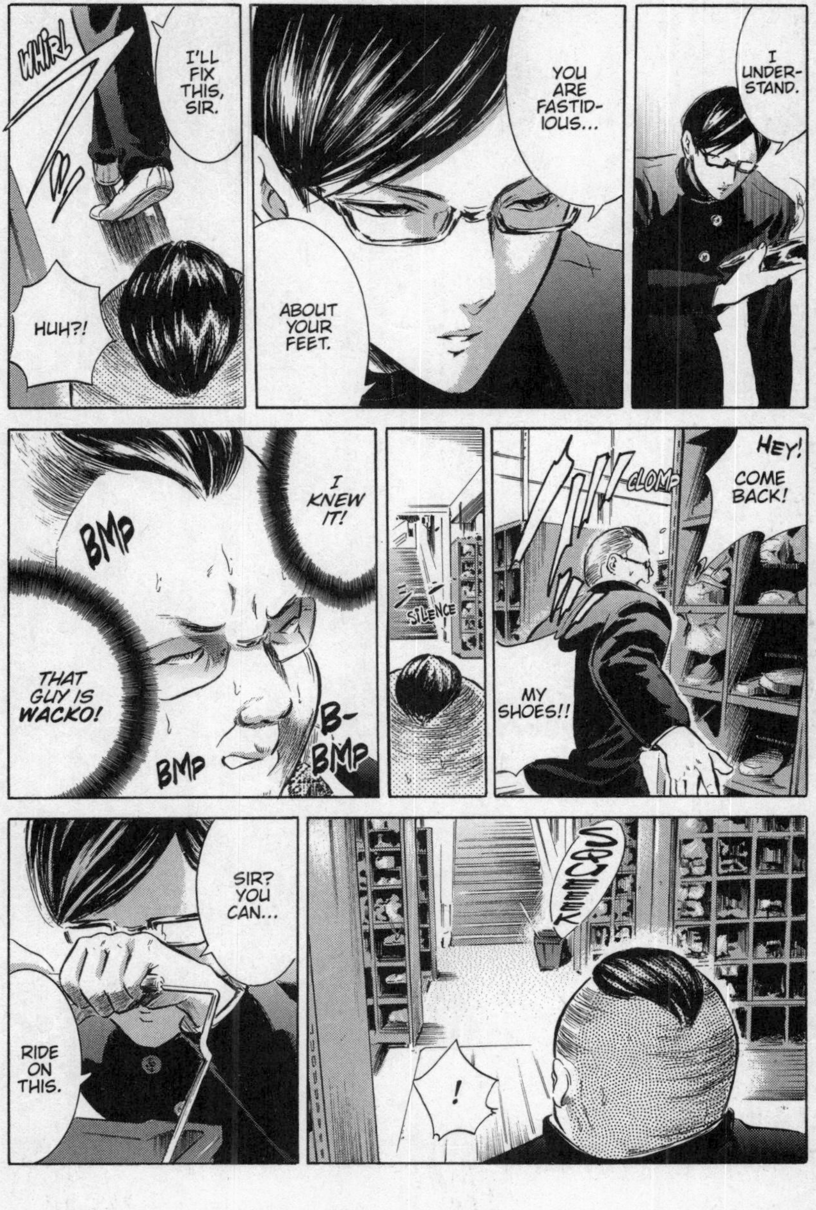
I UNDER-STAND.
YOU ARE FASTID-IOUS...
ABOUT YOUR FEET.
I'LL FIX THIS, SIR.
WHIRL
HUH?!
HEY!
COME BACK!
CLOMP
MY SHOES!!
SILENCE
I KNEW IT!
BMP
THAT GUY IS WACKO!
B-BMP
BMP
SQUEEEK
!
SIR? YOU CAN...
RIDE ON THIS.

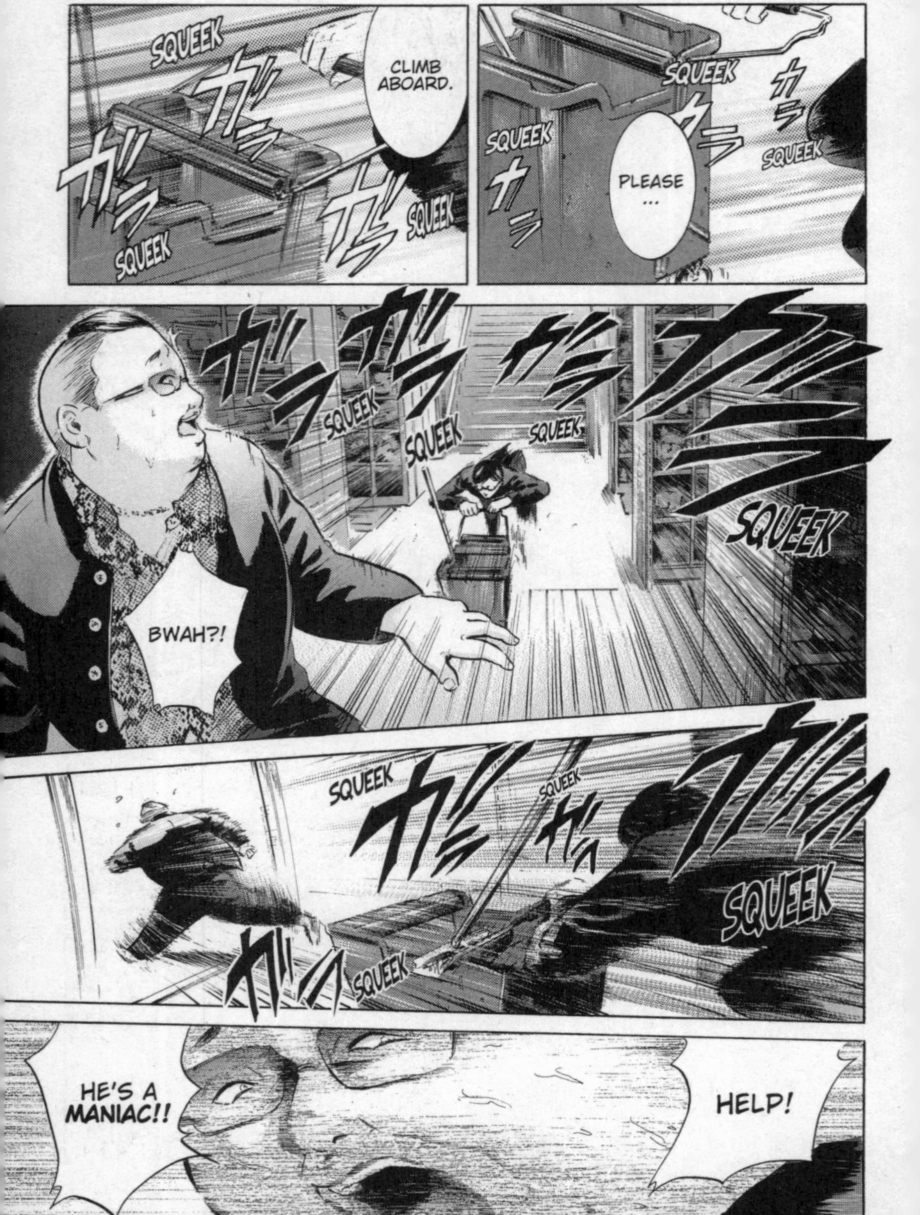
SQUEEK
SQUEEK
PLEASE ...
SQUEEK
SQUEEK
CLIMB ABOARD.
SQUEEK
SQUEEK
SQUEEK
SQUEEK
SQUEEK
SQUEEK
SQUEEK
BWAH?!
SQUEEK
SQUEEK
SQUEEK
SQUEEK
HELP!
HE'S A MANIAC!!

SQUEEK
SQUEEK
SQUEEK
SQUEEK

WHEW!

HUFF

HUFF

SQUEEK
SQUEEK
SQUEEK

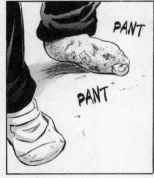

PANT

PANT

!

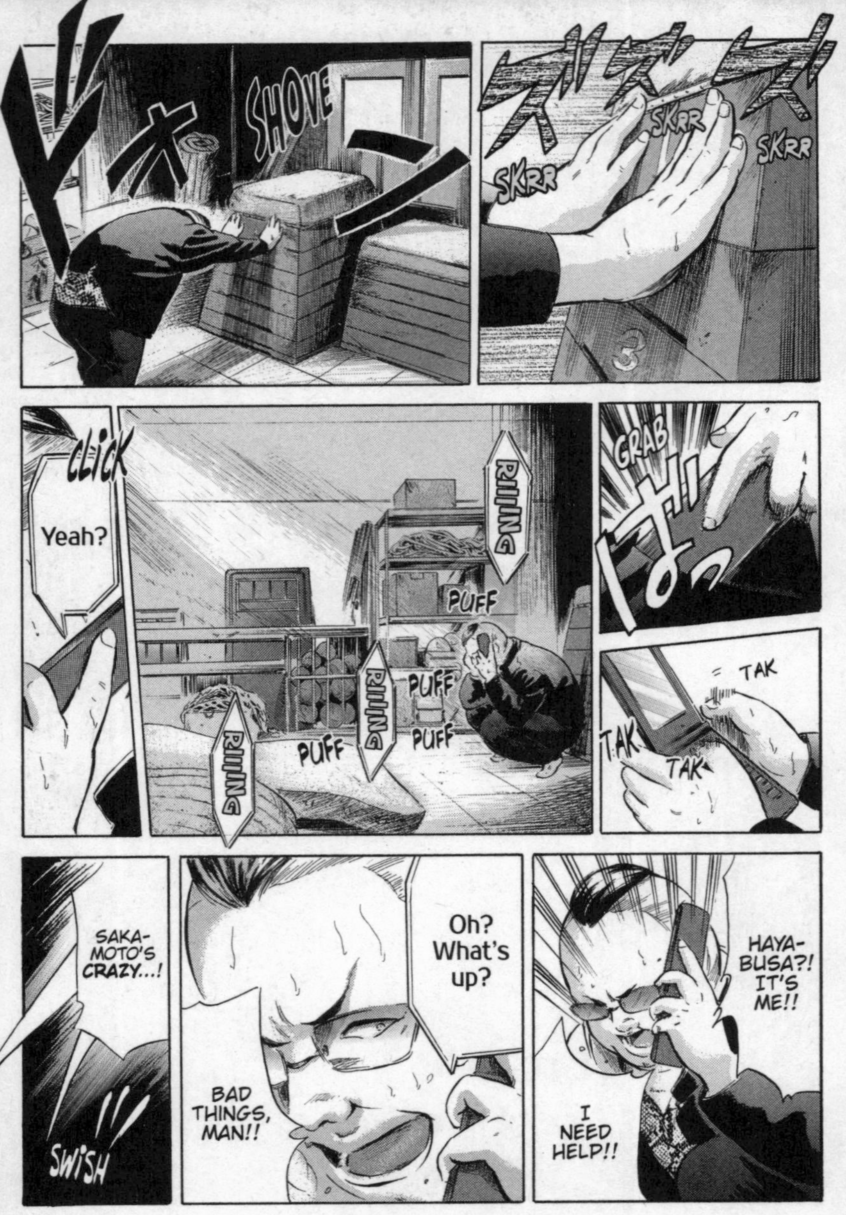
SKRR
SKRR
SKRR
SHOVE
GRAB
TAK
TAK
TAK
RIIING
RIIING
RIIING
PUFF
PUFF
PUFF
PUFF
CLICK
Yeah?
HAYA-BUSA?! IT'S ME!!
I NEED HELP!!
Oh? What's up?
BAD THINGS, MAN!!
SAKA-MOTO'S CRAZY...!
SWISH

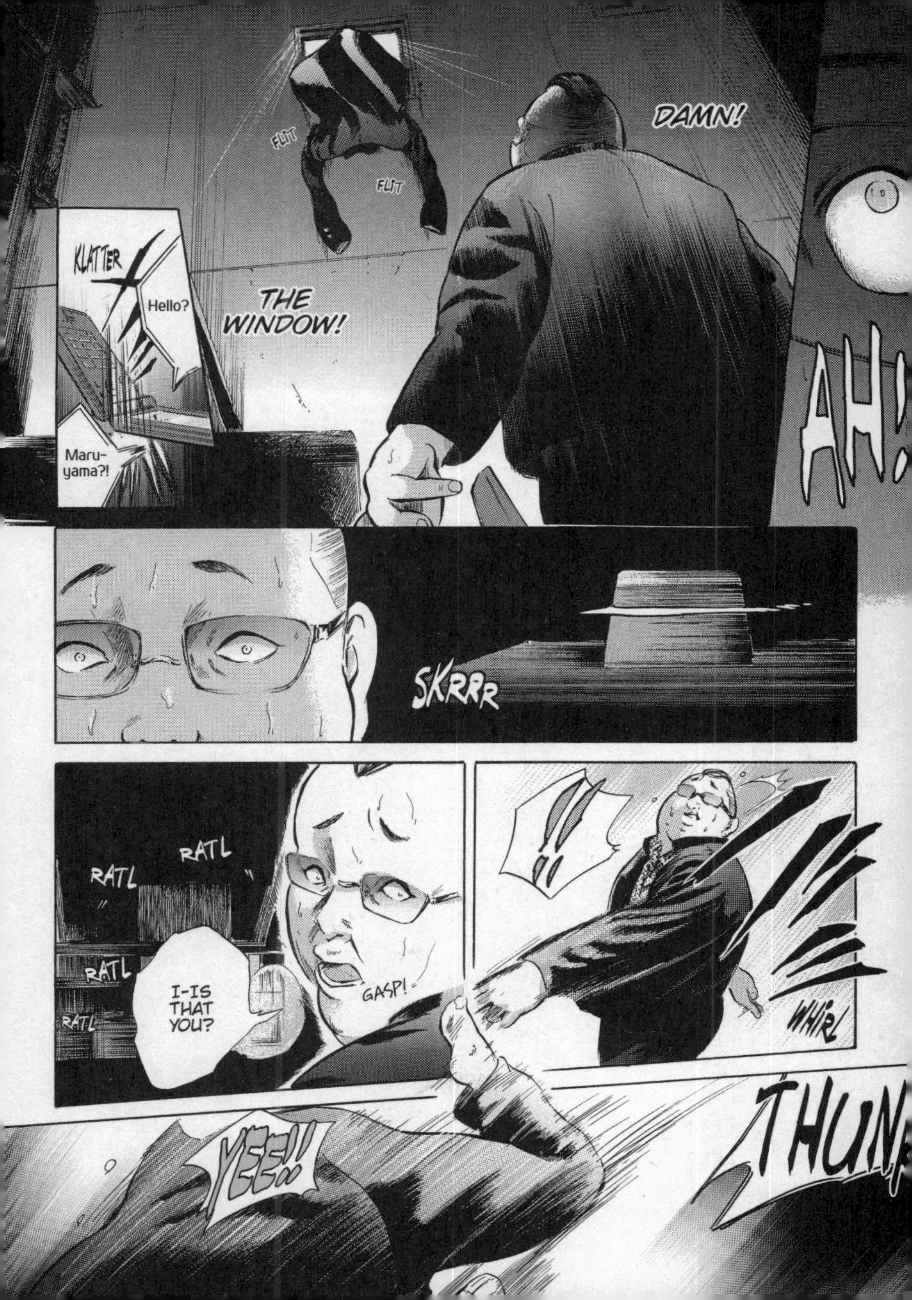
AH!
DAMN!
FLIT
FLIT
THE WINDOW!
KLATTER
Hello?
Maru-yama?!
SKRRR
WHIRL
RATL
RATL
GASP!
RATL
I-IS THAT YOU?
RATL
THUN
YEE!!

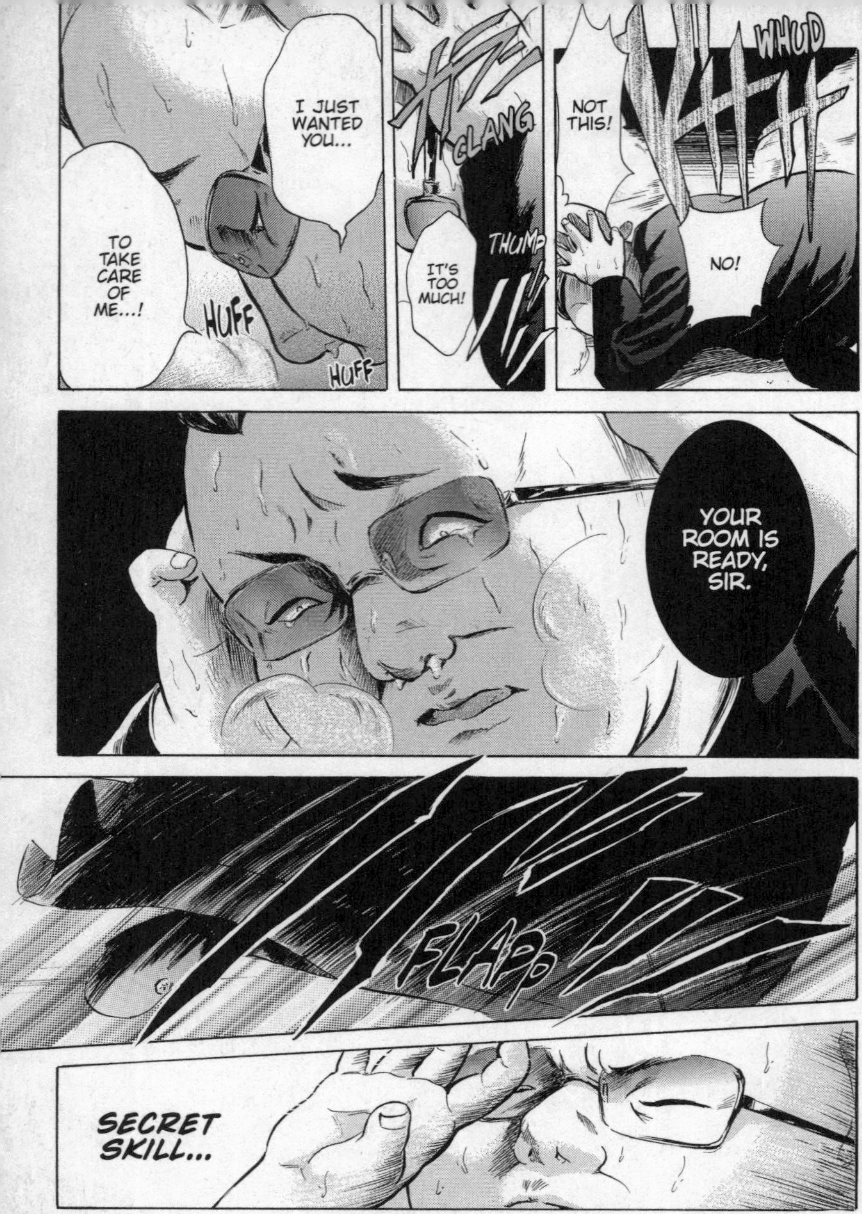
WHUD
NOT THIS!
NO!
CLANG
THUMP
IT'S TOO MUCH!
I JUST WANTED YOU...
TO TAKE CARE OF ME...!
HUFF
HUFF
YOUR ROOM IS READY, SIR.
FLAPP
SECRET SKILL...

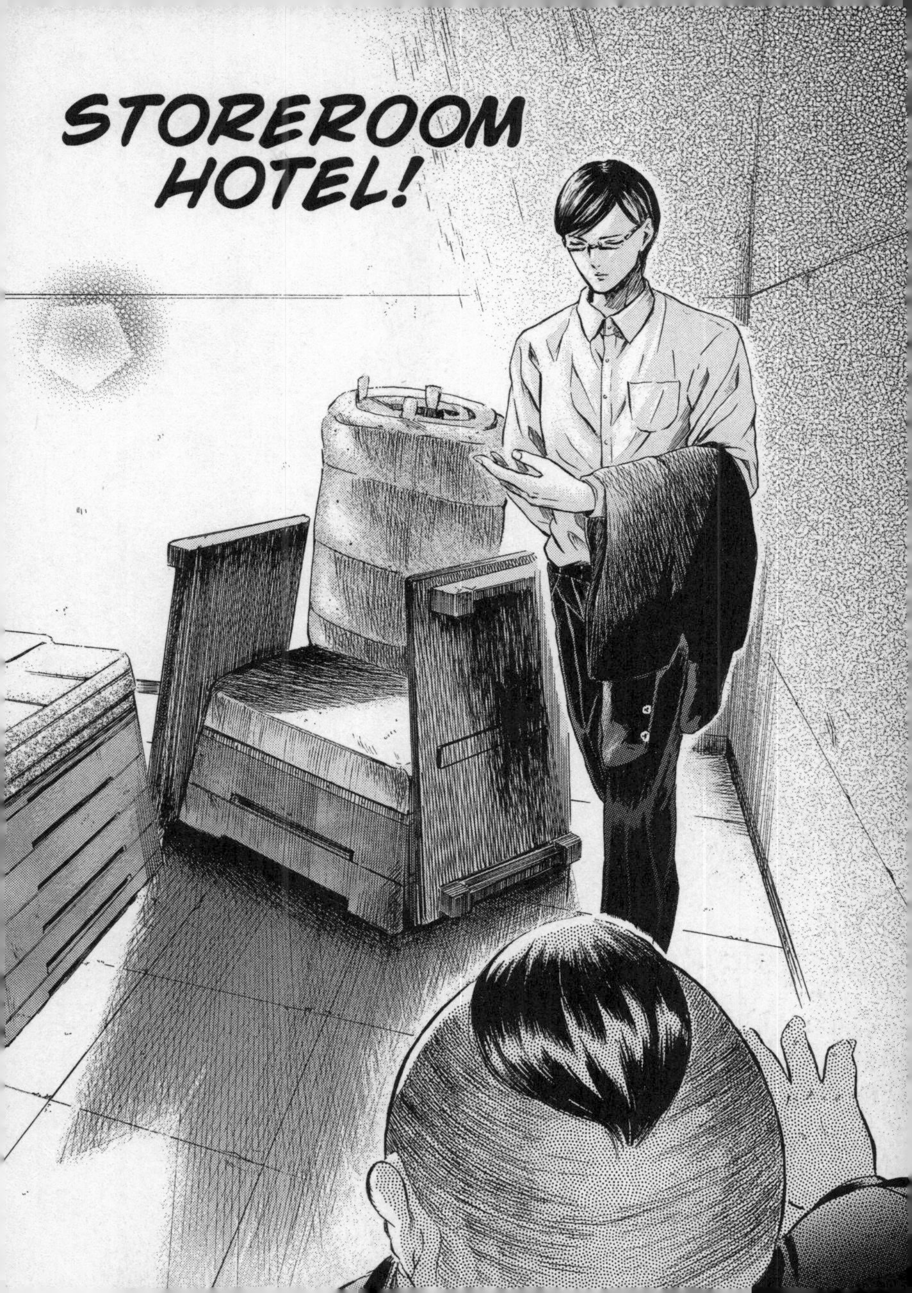
STOREROOM HOTEL!

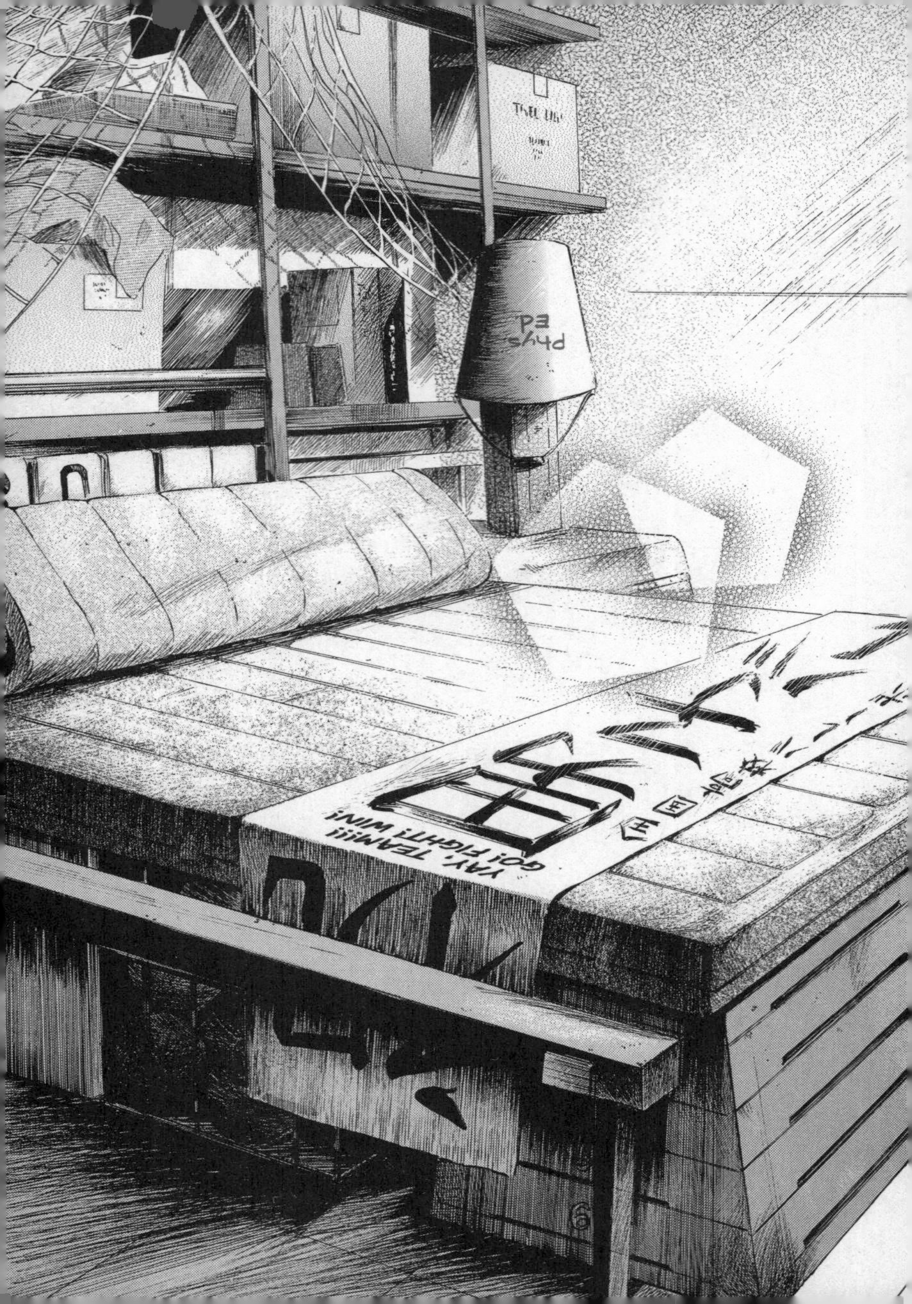
Phys Ed.
"YAY, TEAM!!!
GO! FIGHT! WIN!

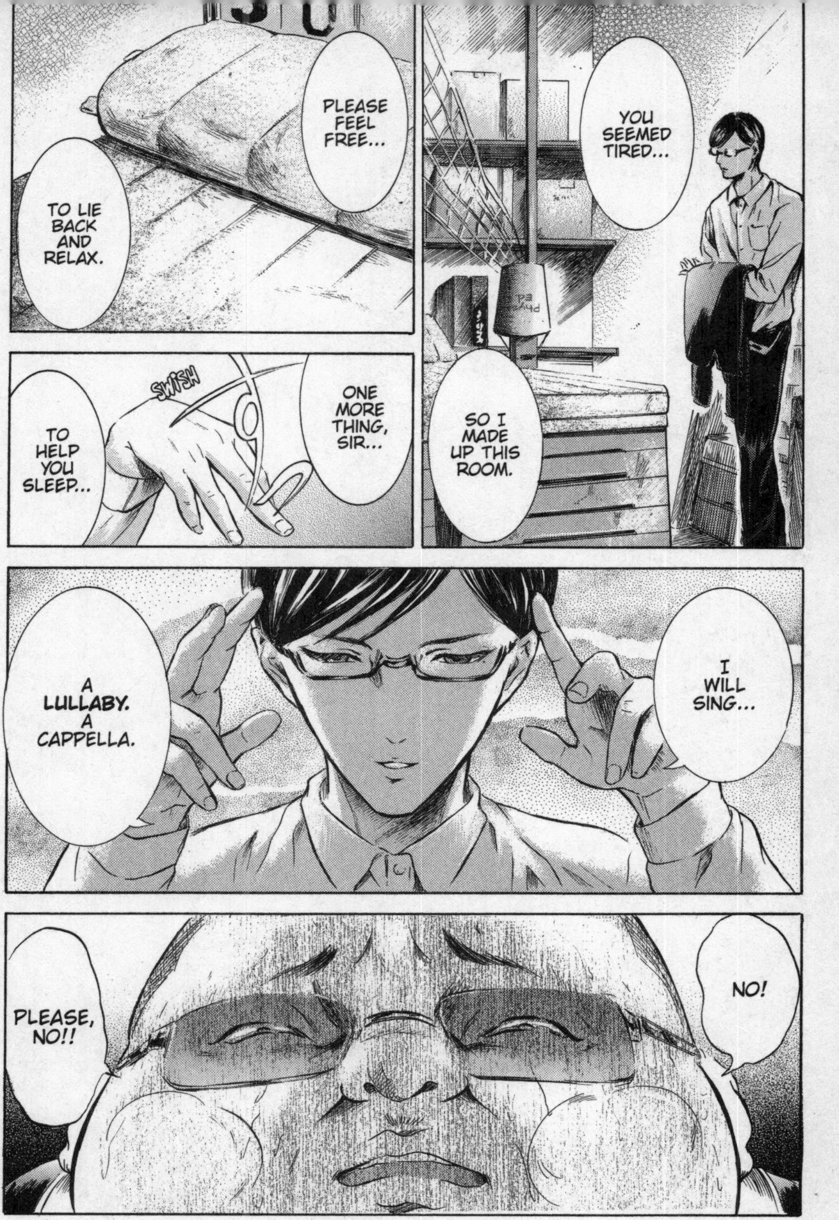
YOU SEEMED TIRED...
SO I MADE UP THIS ROOM.
PLEASE FEEL FREE...
TO LIE BACK AND RELAX.
ONE MORE THING, SIR...
SWISH
TO HELP YOU SLEEP...
I WILL SING...
A **LULLABY.** A CAPPELLA.
NO!
PLEASE, NO!!

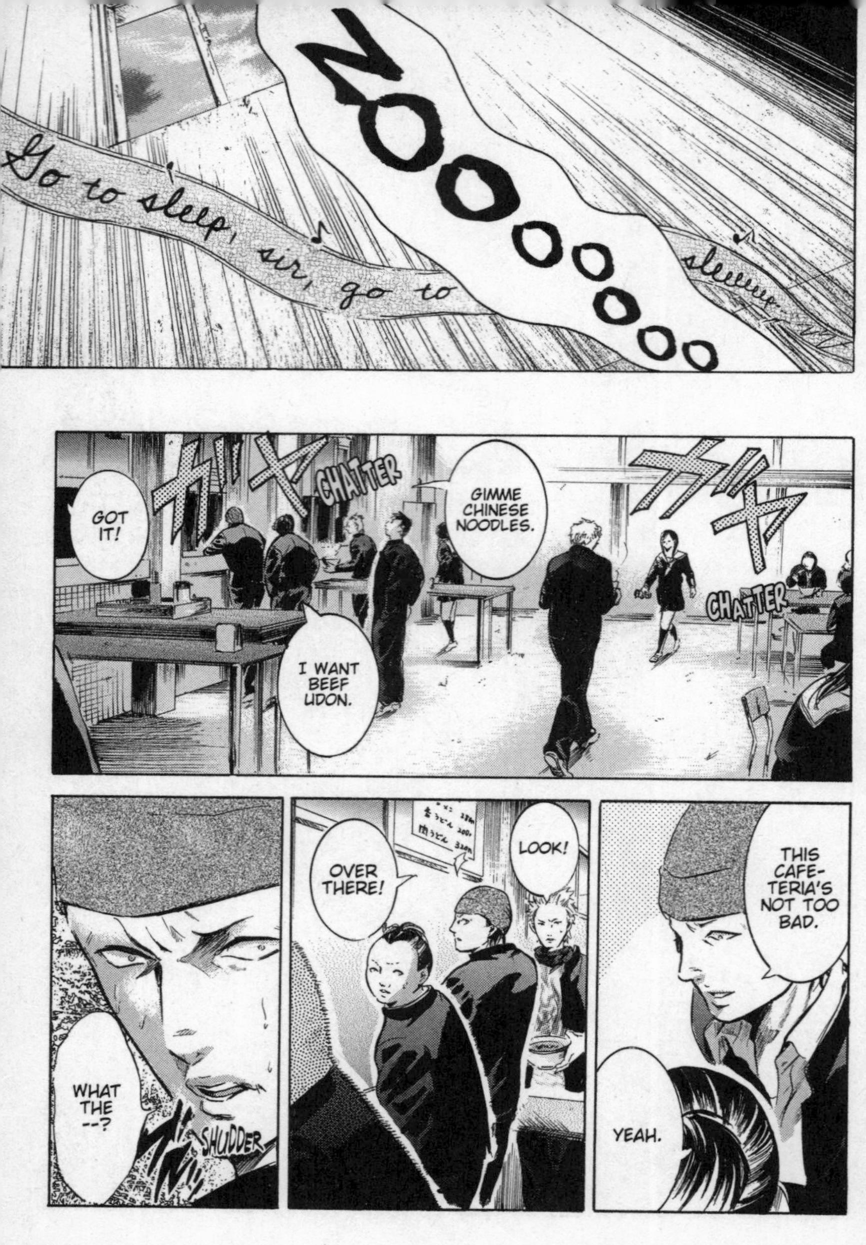
ZOOOOOOO
Go to sleep, sir, go to sleeeep
CHATTER
GIMME CHINESE NOODLES.
I WANT BEEF UDON.
CHATTER
GOT IT!
THIS CAFE-TERIA'S NOT TOO BAD.
YEAH.
LOOK!
OVER THERE!
WHAT THE --?
SHUDDER

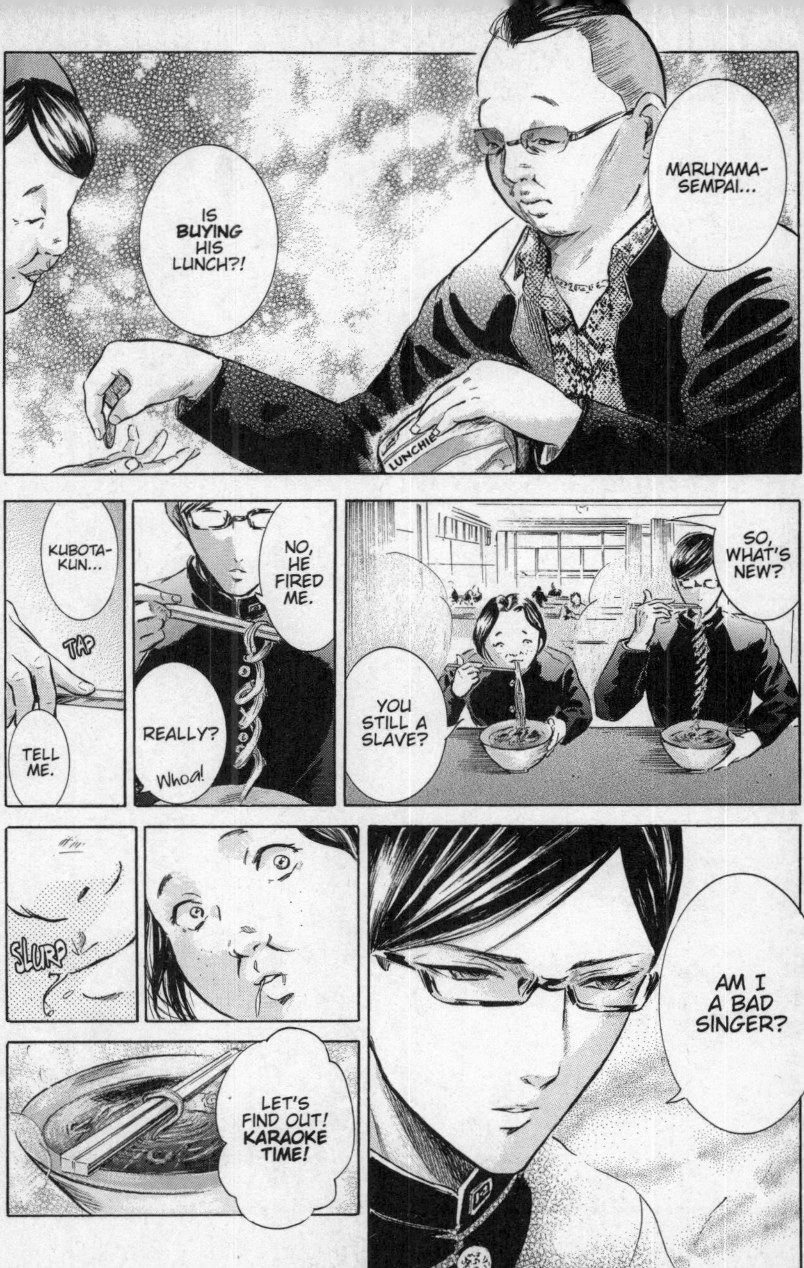
MARUYAMA-SEMPAI...
IS BUYING HIS LUNCH?!
LUNCHIE
SO, WHAT'S NEW?
YOU STILL A SLAVE?
NO, HE FIRED ME.
REALLY?
Whoa!
KUBOTA-KUN...
TAP
TELL ME.
AM I A BAD SINGER?
SLURP
LET'S FIND OUT! KARAOKE TIME!

End of Chapter 5

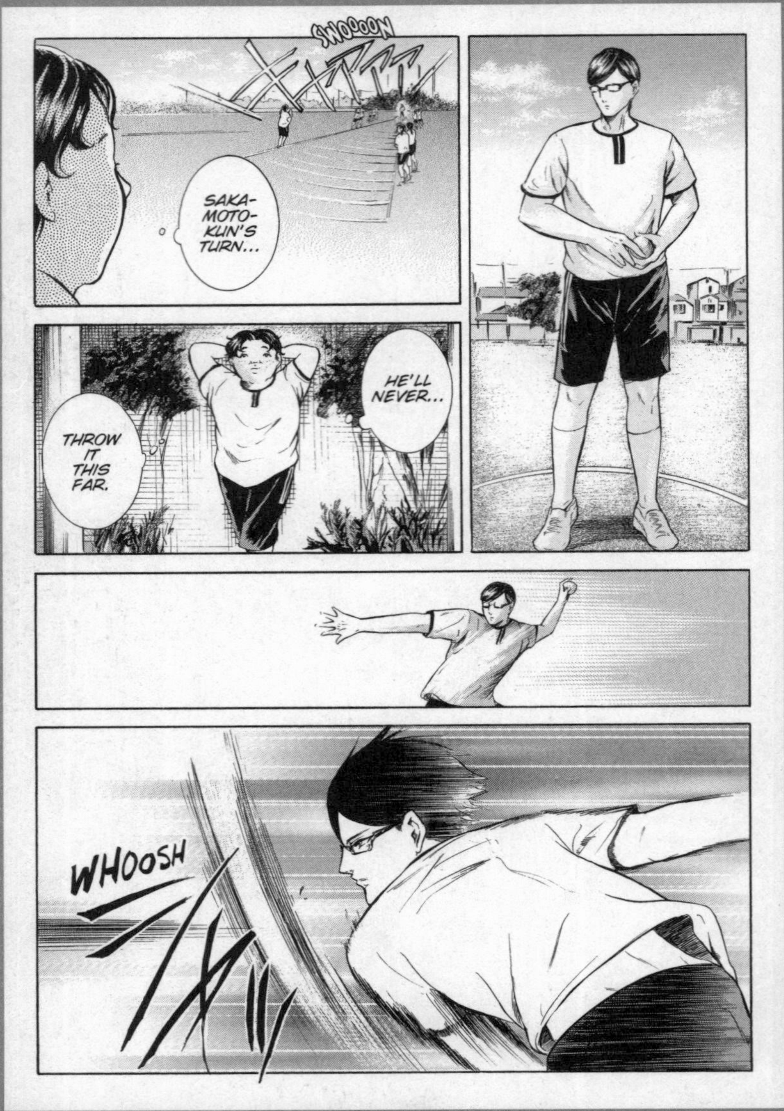
SWOOOON
SAKA-MOTO-KUN'S TURN...
HE'LL NEVER...
THROW IT THIS FAR.
WHOOSH

P.E. Test #5: Softball Throw

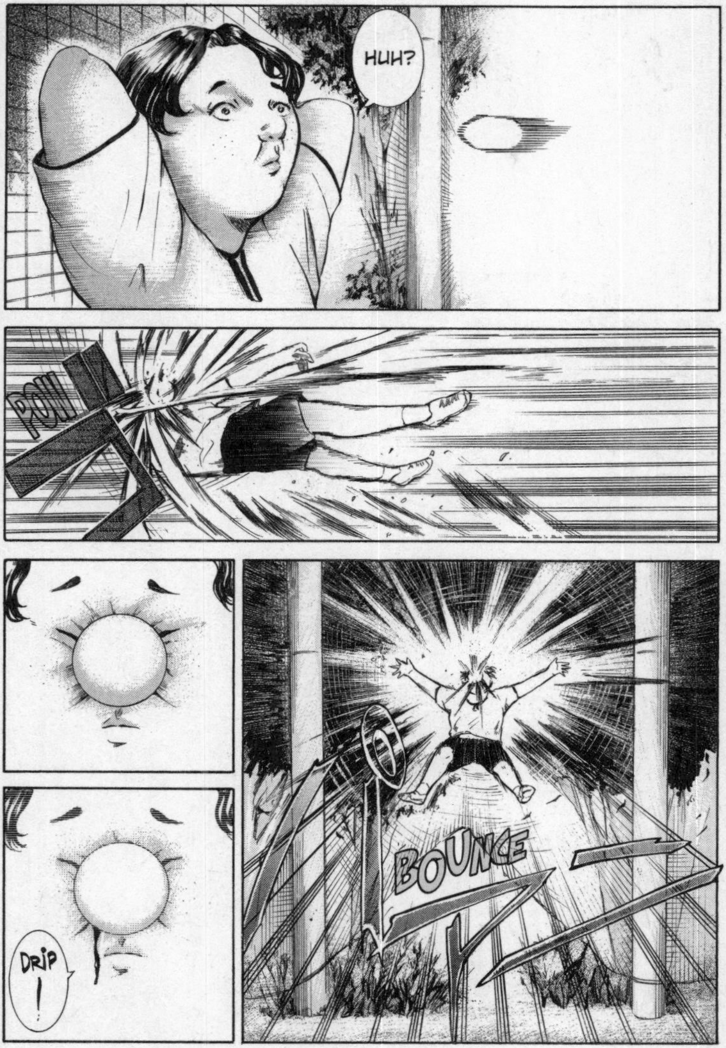
HUH?
POW
BOUNCE
DRIP !

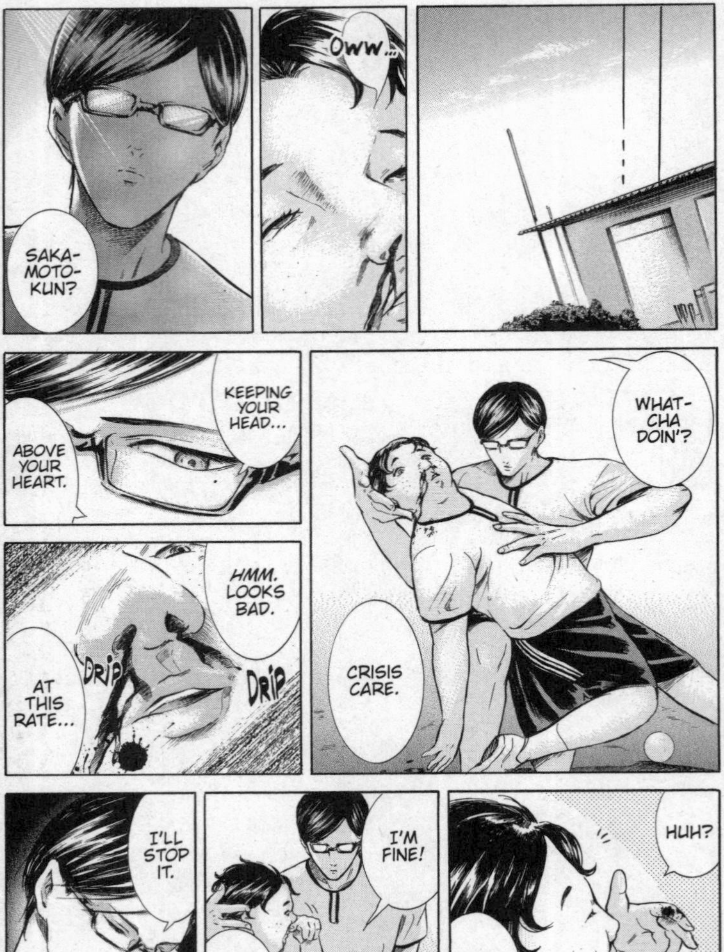
OWW...
SAKA-MOTO-KUN?
WHAT-CHA DOIN'?
CRISIS CARE.
KEEPING YOUR HEAD...
ABOVE YOUR HEART.
HMM. LOOKS BAD.
DRIP
DRIP
AT THIS RATE...
HUH?
IT'S A NOSE-BLEED!
I'M FINE!
JUST NEED TISSUES ...
I'LL STOP IT.
CHOMP

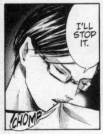

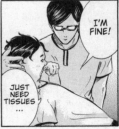

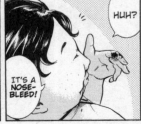

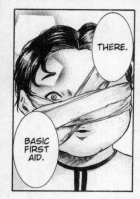

THERE.

BASIC FIRST AID.

RRRIP

SWSW

SWSW

AND NOW...

JUST REST A WHILE.

QUIET, PLEASE!

SHH!

AH, WELL...

SQUEE

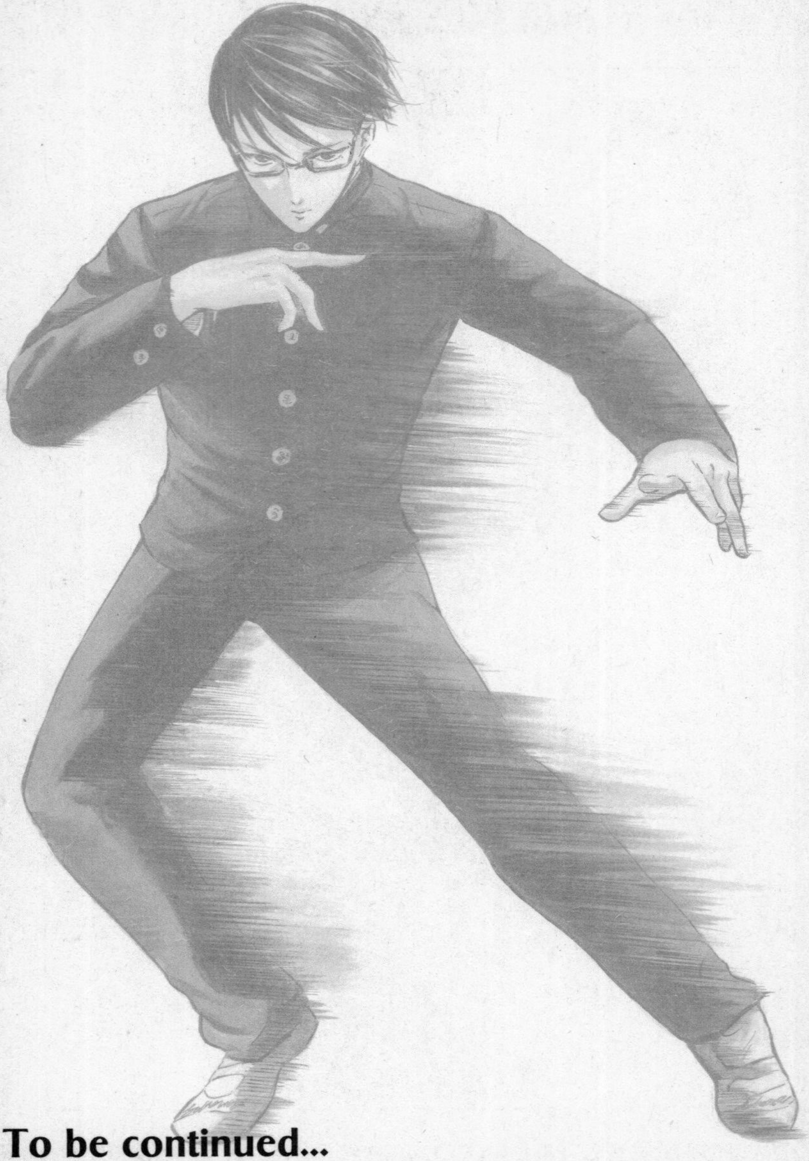

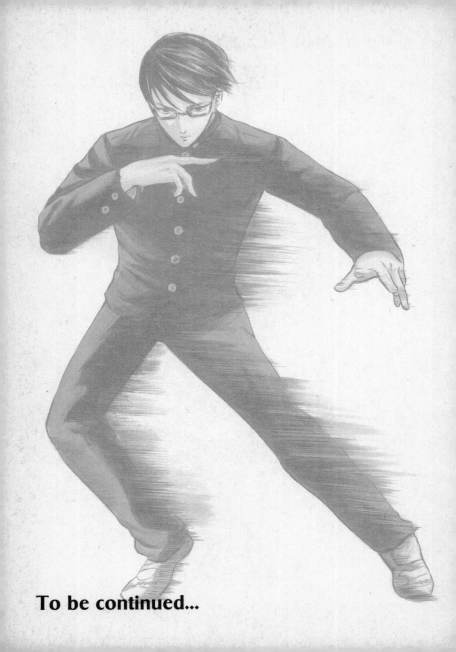

To be continued...

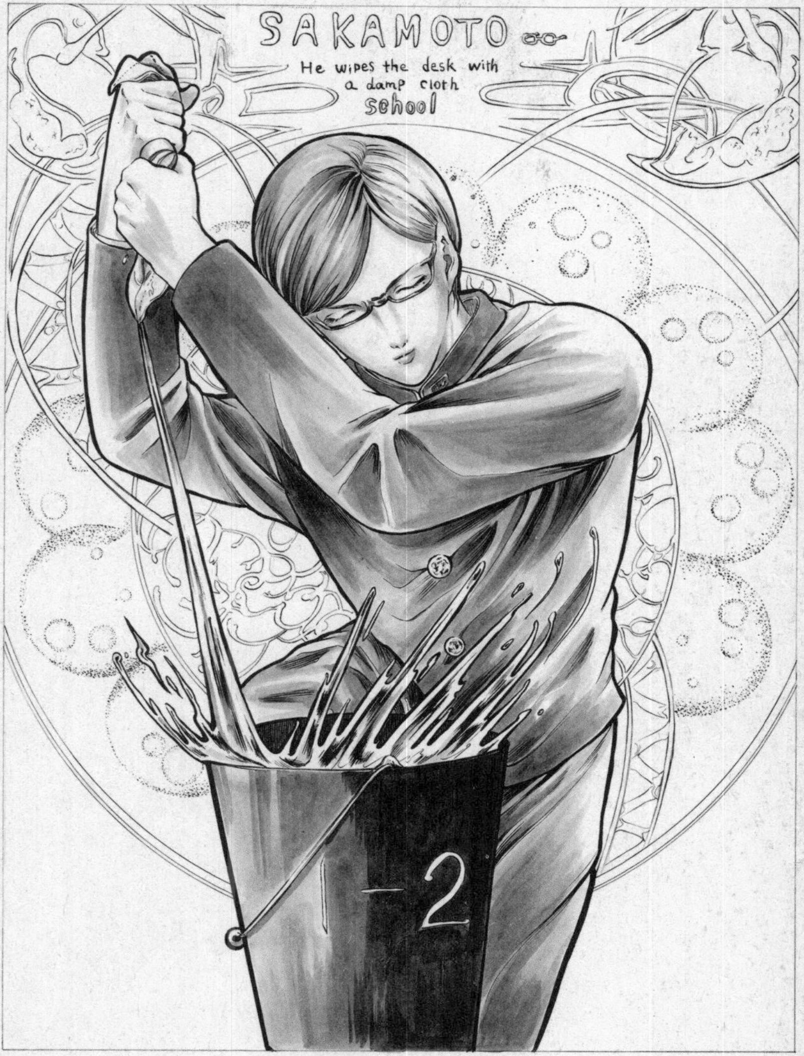
SAKAMOTO
He wipes the desk with
a damp cloth
school
1-2

SPECIAL EXTRA:
"BROAD SHOULDERS"

Haven't You Heard?
I'M SAKAMOTO

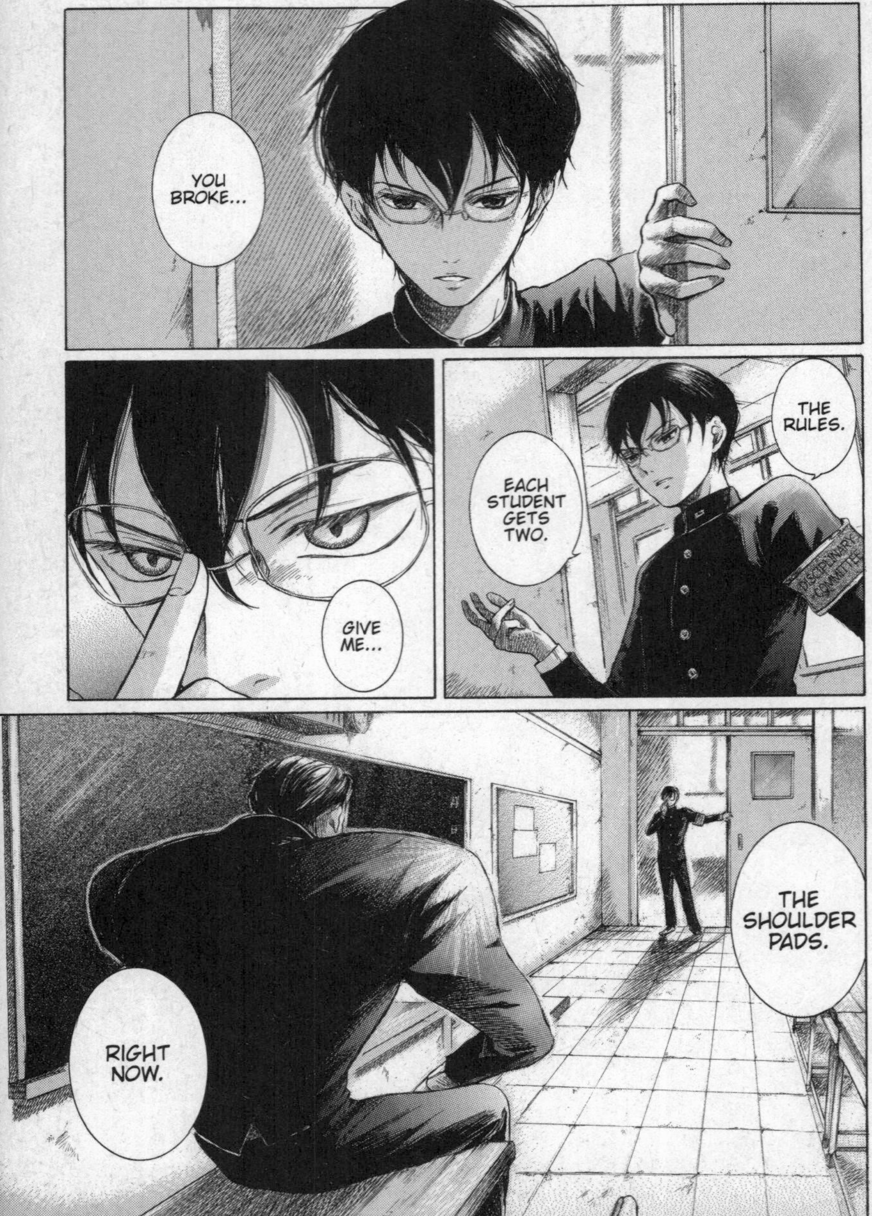
YOU BROKE...
THE RULES.
DISCIPLINARY COMMITTEE
EACH STUDENT GETS TWO.
GIVE ME...
THE SHOULDER PADS.
RIGHT NOW.

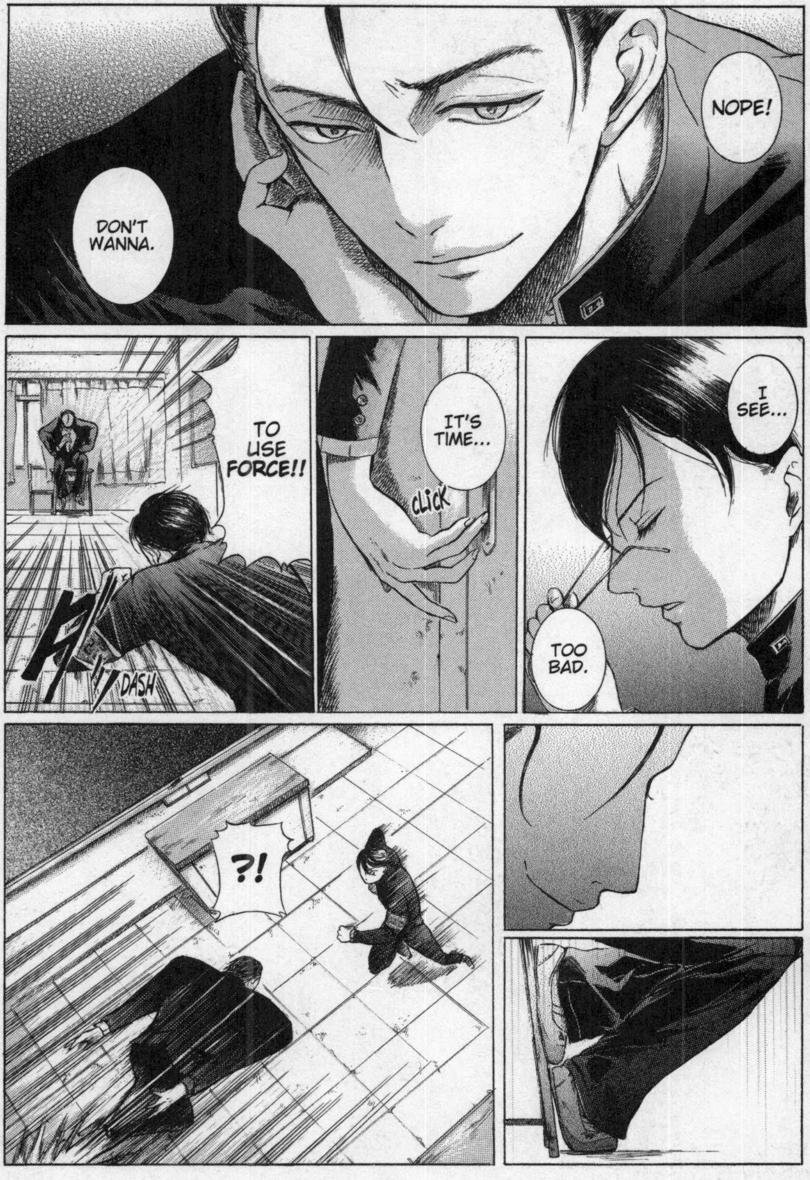
NOPE!
DON'T WANNA.
I SEE...
TOO BAD.
IT'S TIME...
CLICK
TO USE FORCE!!
DASH
?!

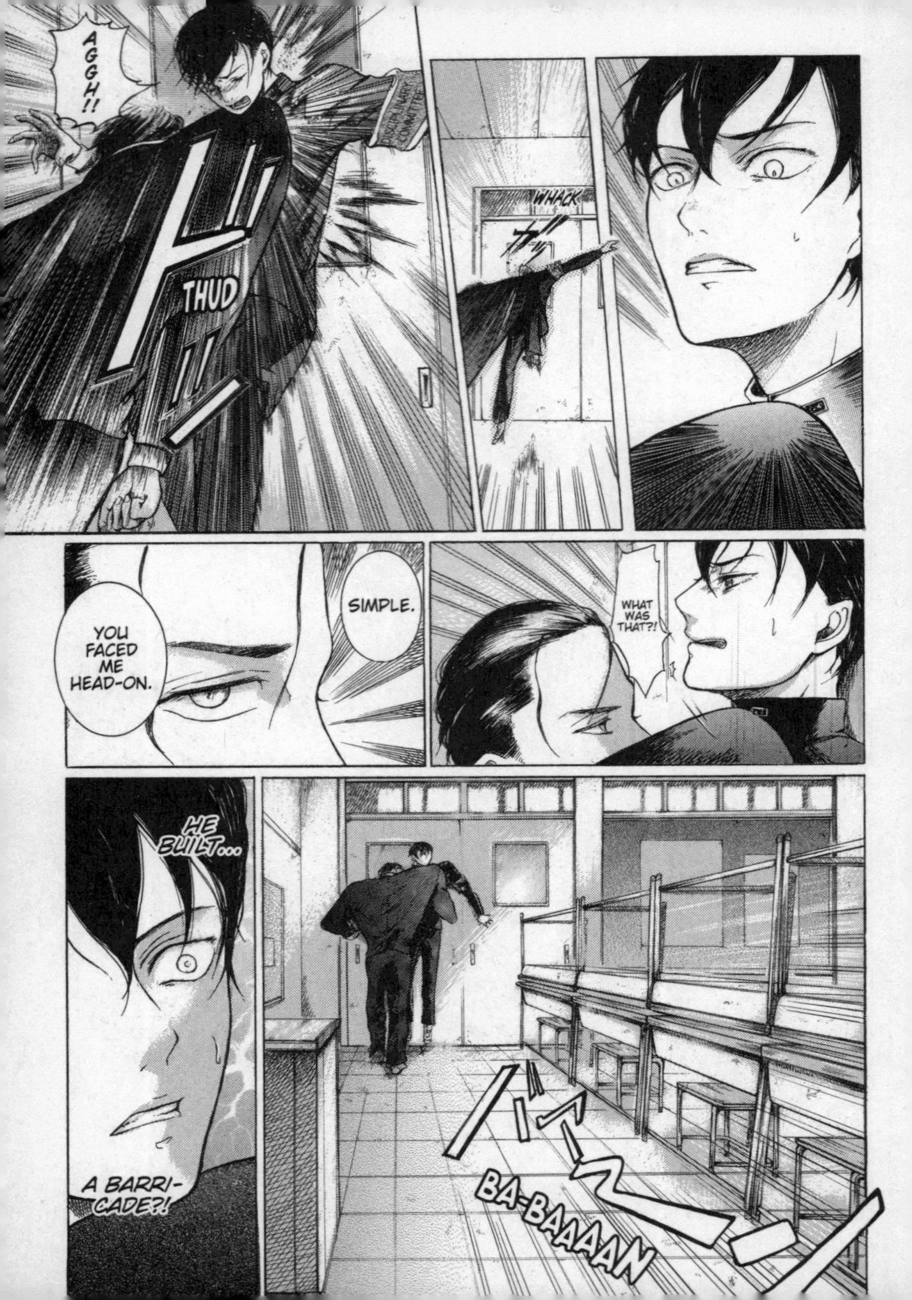
WHACK
AGGH!!
DISCIPLINARY COMMITTEE
THUD
WHAT WAS THAT?!
SIMPLE.
YOU FACED ME HEAD-ON.
BA-BAAAAN
HE BUILT...
A BARRI-CADE?!

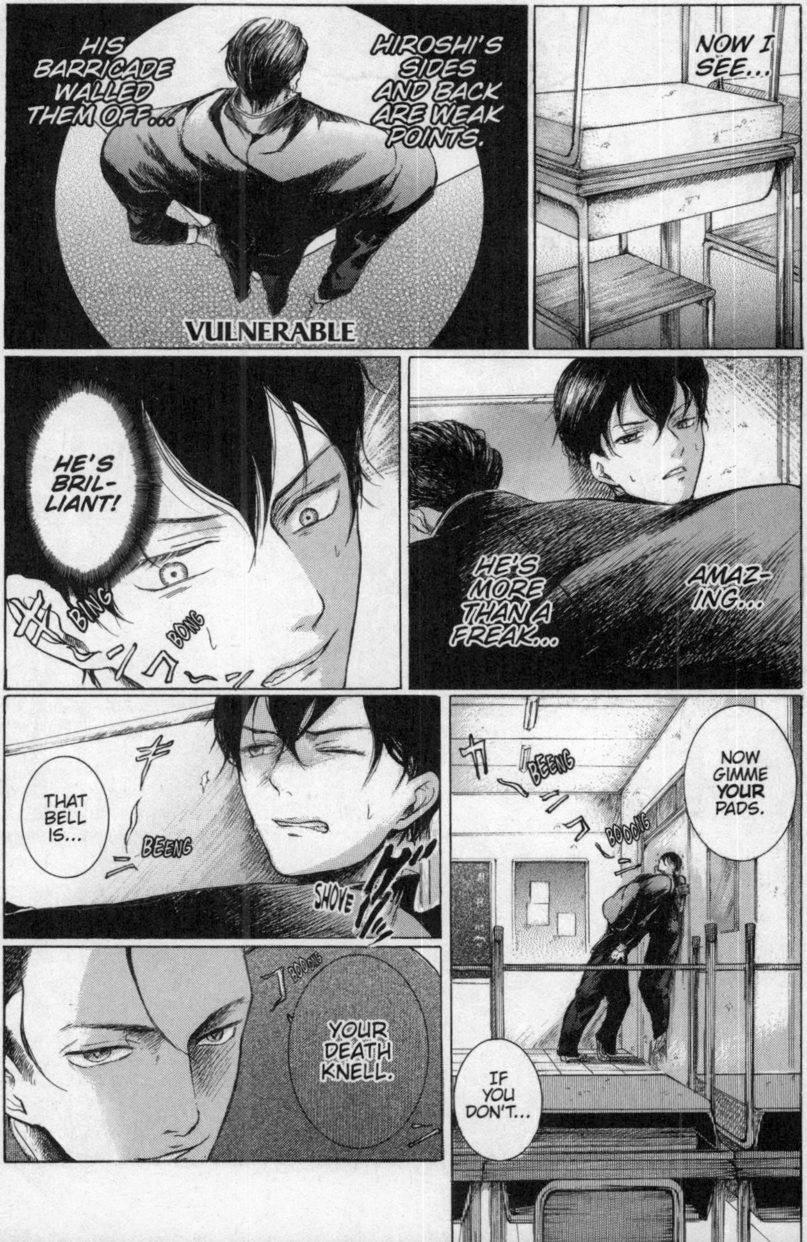
NOW I SEE...
HIROSHI'S SIDES AND BACK ARE WEAK POINTS.
HIS BARRICADE WALLED THEM OFF...
VULNERABLE
HE'S MORE THAN A FREAK...
AMAZ-ING...
HE'S BRIL-LIANT!
BING
BONG
BEENG
BOOONG
NOW GIMME YOUR PADS.
THAT BELL IS...
BEENG
SHOVE
IF YOU DON'T...
BOOONG
YOUR DEATH KNELL.

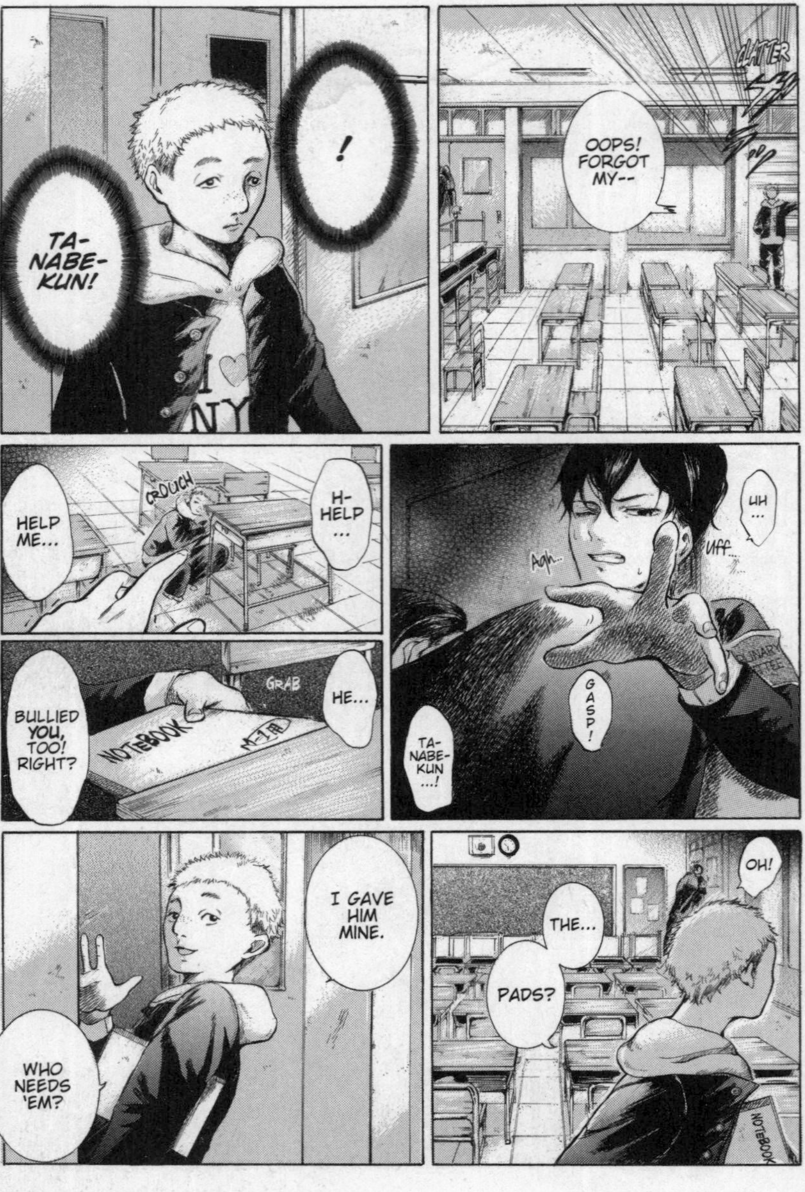
CLATTER
OOPS! FORGOT MY--
!
TA-NABE-KUN!
UH...
Uff...
Agh...
GASP!
TA-NABE-KUN...!
H-HELP...
CROUCH
HELP ME...
HE...
GRAB
BULLIED YOU, TOO! RIGHT?
NOTEBOOK
OH!
THE...
PADS?
NOTEBOOK
I GAVE HIM MINE.
WHO NEEDS 'EM?

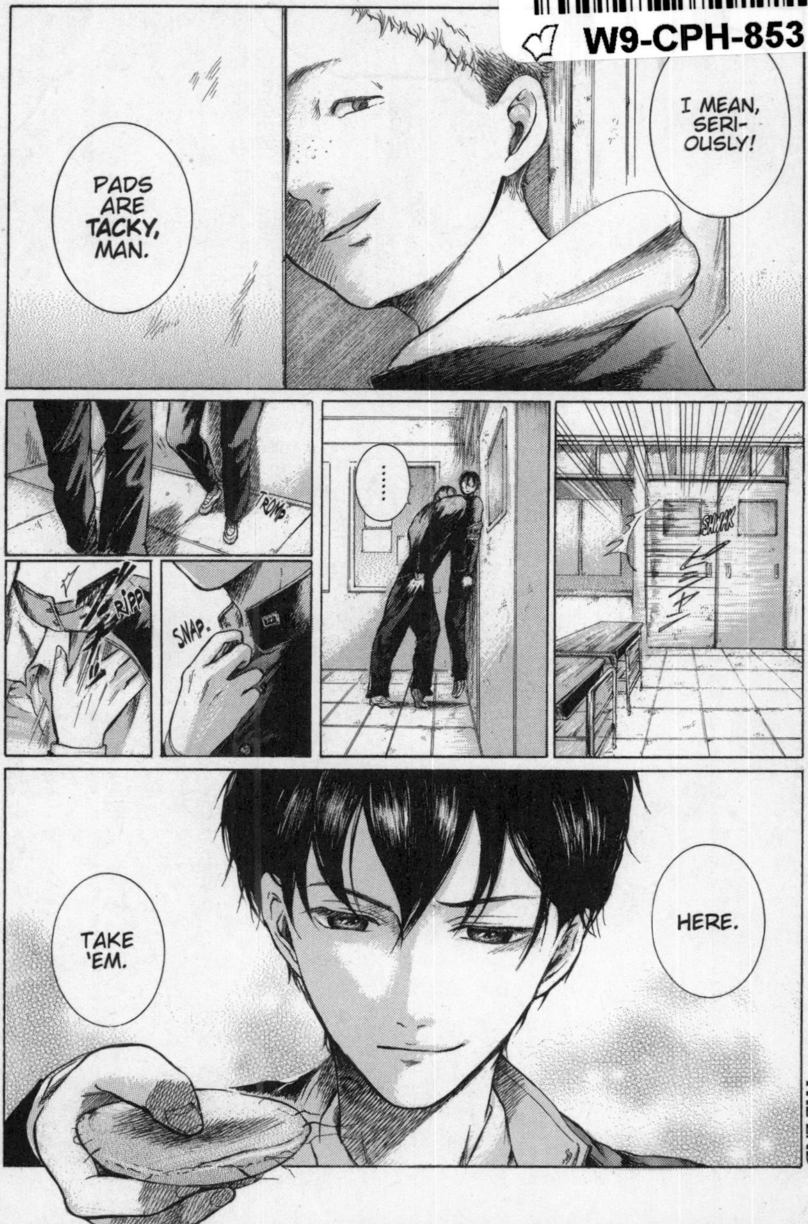
I MEAN, SERI-OUSLY!
PADS ARE TACKY, MAN.
SHWAK
......
TROMP
SNAP.
RIPP
HERE.
TAKE 'EM.

THE END